BAMBER GASCOIGNE

THE TREASURES AND DYNASTIES OF CHINA

With photographs taken in China by
Christina Gascoigne and Derrick Witty

Jonathan Cape
Thirty Bedford Square London

This book was designed and produced by George Rainbird Ltd
Marble Arch House, 44 Edgware Road, London W2
House editor: Penelope Miller
Designer: Margaret Thomas
Cartographer: Tom Stalker Miller

Colour plates printed by Westerham Press Ltd, Westerham, Kent
Text printed and bound by Jarrold and Sons Ltd, Norwich

At no period in the history of the world has the attention of the civilized nations been so fully directed towards China, its early history and modern position, as at the present moment. The single fact that that nation comprises within its limits a population of three hundred and sixty millions of human beings is of itself sufficient to awaken the deepest degree of interest.

Such were the opening words of the catalogue of the Chinese exhibition which, in 1843, drew vast London crowds to pay their money in the ornate Chinese pavilion erected for the occasion at Hyde Park Corner. Inside they found themselves 'transported to a new world . . . China in miniature'. The same show had already broken records in Philadelphia.

It was a time of exceptional interest in China because, as the catalogue pointed out, until recently that country had been 'covered as with a veil'. 'The inner traits of the nation, the minute peculiarities, the fashionable *boudoir*, the literary *coterie*, and the domestic temples of this numerous people, have been hidden from the eyes of European and American curiosity.' Moreover it was less than a year since Britain had made the first effective rent in that veil. The Opium War had initiated the process by which Europe and America would expose to their fumbling embraces this ancient and now secretive empire.

A hundred and thirty years later, China is again emerging from a period of seclusion, this time voluntarily. Once again her years behind the veil have given her a special fascination. Once again a Chinese exhibition is travelling the world, and once again – it is to be hoped – it will be displayed in surroundings 'worthy of the visit of the respectable of all classes'.

In the interval between the two exhibitions the West has become more attuned to certain aspects of Chinese culture. It is no longer only to the specialist that the names of the great dynasties are familiar. The word T'ang by now conjures up for many people those bright and sturdy pottery figures of horses and grooms, or of camels even more exotically shaped than the real thing. Ming seems today almost inseparable from the very best in porcelain, suggesting pleasant images of blue and white vases to be followed, in the next dynasty, by the three evocative families, *rose*, *verte* and *jaune*. Chinese poetry, too, has been in the public domain ever since Arthur Waley first revealed how easy on the mind are those word-pictures of water and moonlight and bibulous scholars. The towering peaks of a painted Chinese landscape, or the few brushstrokes that go to make a bamboo stalk, a flower, a solitary fisherman – these are

7

among the most immediately recognizable of art forms. And then the lacquer, the bronzes, the silks . . .

And yet these images float, for most of us, in something of a vacuum. An educated layman confronted with a Greek vase, with a mural from Pompeii or Lascaux, with a Persian miniature or the features of Tutankhamun, can place each in a fairly specific context; he is less likely to be able to do so with a T'ang horse. People who can date with a reasonable degree of accuracy the lifetimes of Xerxes or Alexander the Great, or even of Jenghiz Khan, Akbar or Atahualpa, may well find it hard to hit on any of the three centuries covered by the T'ang dynasty. And although China's empire lasted incomparably longer than any other, how many non-specialists can name a single Chinese emperor? Kublai Khan will probably be the first to come to mind, and he was not Chinese. No other country has suffered such an imbalance between the fame of its art and the obscurity of its history.

In harness with our own vagueness about China goes a suspicion that the fault is China's own. For is she not, after all – and the word is reserved almost exclusively for the Orient – somewhat inscrutable? Has she not a written language composed of tens of thousands of separate characters, and a spoken one which seems to demand the ear of a musician to separate one subtle inflection from another? Will we ever master those elusive and yet strangely repetitive little monosyllables which make up all Chinese names? (It is no accident that K'ung Fu Tzu, the one man in Chinese history familiar to us all, is recognized only by the Latin version of his name, Confucius.) How can we ever understand the apparently static quality and suffocating politeness of ancient Chinese civilization, or grasp the nature of a society in which scholars, of all people, inherited the earth – an idea almost as improbable elsewhere as the meek doing so.

Differences such as these have led to the conventional image of inscrutable China. But the convention is inaccurate. To read, even in translation, some of the many surviving texts from more than 2000 years ago is to experience that same thrill of recognition that one gets from the cultures of Greece and Rome but from very few others at that distance in time. The attitudes of Confucius and his contemporaries (a century before Socrates) seem incomparably much closer to ourselves than those, for example, of the ancient Egyptians. The image of China as inscrutable derives only from her having been throughout most of her history almost inaccessible behind that distant barricade of mountains, and it was reinforced in the last century by her perplexing refusal to fall instantly in love

with the ways of the West. The road to Xanadu remained a mysterious one because it was so long and difficult – not, in spite of Coleridge's opium dreams, because what one found at the other end was at all improbable.

The aim of this book is to provide a general setting for the beautiful images of China's long history, such as those which appear in the photographs. It is in no sense a survey. No one person or city or event has been allowed an automatic place in the index. I have concentrated instead on whichever incidents or people seem to provide the most vivid picture of each of the eight major dynasties – dynasties whose names are always used to identify Chinese objects, whether a Shang bronze, a T'ang pottery figure or a Ming dish, and which are known to most of us only in that adjectival form.

BETWEEN THE PEKING MAN OF THE ANTHROPOLOGISTS AND THE PEKING
man of today there lies a span of some 400,000 years. The remains of
Sinanthropus pekinensis, a man of limited intelligence but already in
possession of fire and primitive stone implements, were found in 1927 in a
cave about thirty miles southwest of the modern city. In another part of
the same complex of caves were the skeletons of a group of men who lived
some 20,000 years ago. Closer again to our own time, the neolithic period
is represented in the area by profuse remains of stone tools and pottery.
These can be matched in many countries, but they were followed in this
part of China by a bronze age culture unrivalled anywhere in the world
in the technical skill of its vessels and implements. Within only a few more
centuries one reaches, in about 1000 B.C. and still in this same region, the
earliest surviving Chinese literature. Then, still before the birth of Christ,
begins the astonishing series of dynastic histories which would continue
unbroken up to 1911. No other place can offer such detailed evidence of
man's development as this North China plain, cradled, as if in the crook of
an arm, by the great right-angle bend of the Yellow River.

It is a natural centre. In prehistory it was a good habitable compromise
between the bleak steppes to the north and the tropical swamps of southern
China, malarial and full of alarming animals. In more civilized times the
region has almost invariably provided the capital of the empire, and the
reason is not accidental. China consists basically of two large plains, that
of the Yangtze, humid and extremely fertile, and above it that of the Yellow
River, harsher in climate but still suitable for agriculture. To the west
these plains are protected by the mountains of Tibet, to the south by the
jungles of the Indo-Chinese peninsula, and to the east by the sea. Only the
great steppe-lands of the north and northwest leave them unprotected,
and it was against this flank that the Chinese, some 2300 years ago, began
building their Great Wall.

The advantage of a capital city in the north is that while drawing its
food supply and its wealth from the much richer south (the reason for that
other engineering marvel of China, the Grand Canal), it is well placed in
times of peace to trade with the rest of the world along the only land-route
out of China (the northwestern chain of oases which were to become the
Silk Road) and in times of danger is sufficiently close to the Great Wall to
mount an effective defence against the warlike nomads of the steppes.
Even today Peking is still the natural centre of gravity, for where the
nomads once roamed in Manchuria is now an industrial area. At the other
end of recorded history is the Shang dynasty. It too, in about 1500 B.C.,

Chapter 1

SHANG
(c. 1600–c. 1100 B.C.)

Bronze ritual food vessel or ting *of the late Shang period*

had its capital city and indeed its whole kingdom in this same northern plain.

The traditional Chinese view of the world's history begins in the usual manner with legend, before merging almost imperceptibly into fact – much like the Old Testament. In the beginning was an egg, according to one Chinese version, which hatched into a man called P'an Ku. One half of the shell remained above him as the sky, the other was below him as the earth, and every day for 18,000 years P'an Ku grew taller and taller until the two were well separated. Suddenly he collapsed, and the fragmented remains of his body formed the observable details of nature. His limbs were the mountains, his blood the rivers, his breath the wind and his voice the thunder, his two eyes the sun and moon. And the parasites on his body became mankind.

It is a story perfectly attuned to later Chinese philosophy. Nothing could be more in keeping with the humanistic traditions of Confucianism, characterized by ancestor worship and a general distrust of metaphysics, than that the founder of the universe should have been a man (typically the legend refrains from asking who laid the egg). And nothing could suit better the Taoist ideal of communion with nature than that the first man's body should have become the mountains and streams.

According to tradition, most of which was added long after the Shang dynasty itself, the 18,000 years of P'an Ku were followed by the reigns of three emperors, whose names link them too with the process of creation. The first was the Emperor of Heaven, the second of Earth, and the third of Mankind. After them came five more emperors, each credited with the introduction of some specifically useful development in technology or culture. The most revered of them all, for example, the Yellow Emperor, was famous for his laws, his engineering works, his establishment of the sacrificial rituals and his understanding of astronomy and the calendar, while in the meantime his queen was inventing silk.

After this group of eight emperors, still plainly schematic and therefore mythical, there came the first three dynasties. The rulers of the earliest one, the Hsia, still had suspiciously heroic attributes. Its founder, Yü, was a great engineer who for the benefit of his people cut the ravines by which China's rivers make their way through the mountain ranges. ('If it had not been for Yü, we should all have been fishes',[1] went the saying.) The men of the next dynasty, the Shang, were recorded in the traditional stories as behaving in more believable fashion, but no contemporary evidence had survived to back up the tradition. The third dynasty, the

Chou, was entirely historical. Confucius lived roughly in the middle of its span, and it lasted until 256 B.C.

But in this long progression from certain myth to certain fact, where did the fact begin? Naturally, over the centuries, most Chinese scholars had accepted the entire tradition at face value, a degree of faith no stranger than Europe's belief in Genesis or than the labours of Archbishop Ussher to establish the year of the Creation (books can be found, printed as late as the second half of the nineteenth century, which still give his conclusion, 4004 B.C., as the precise date of that first hectic week). But nineteenth-century scepticism took its toll in China as well as Christendom. P'an Ku and the eight emperors were very properly given legendary status. The Hsia followed them into mythology, and soon it was even suggested that the Shang had been invented by later historians to support their own theories of the rise and fall of dynasties. By the first quarter of this century it was argued that the Chou was the first truly historical dynasty.

Then, in the late 1920s, scepticism suffered a setback in one of the most dramatic of modern archaeological discoveries. For years the peasants near the modern city of An-yang, close to the mountains and north of the Yellow River, had been turning up with their ploughs mysterious pieces of bone which had notches cut into them. They were assumed to be the bones of dragons, a popular ingredient in those days in many Chinese medicines, and they were bought as such by a local merchant. Several of the bones had little pictures and marks on them, in addition to the notches. These perhaps seemed slightly unusual on the bones of a genuine dragon, so the merchant scraped them clean before reselling them to medicine men. Dragon bones were known to be particularly beneficial for nervous disorders, in the curing of which these priceless historical documents – for such they were – were no doubt over the years reasonably effective.

In 1899 some of the bones with the writing still intact came into the hands of an antique dealer who recognized their value. He offered them to various collectors, and in 1903 a number of the inscriptions were published by a famous politician who was also a novelist (this highly cultured combination of connoisseur, author and administrator is almost the norm in Chinese history). There was immediate and world-wide interest. Back in An-yang news reached the farmers that their bones were even more valuable than those of dragons. They dug deeper, and in addition to further bones a steady stream of exquisitely fashioned bronzes began to appear on the market. The pillage continued for twenty-five years until, in 1928, official excavation at last began.

An oracle-bone TOP; *and part of a book made up of bamboo strips tied together with threads, 1st century* A.D.

The site turned out to be the capital city used during the last two or three centuries of the Shang dynasty, and the bones were oracle-bones. The Shang rulers had practised scapulimancy (divination by use of shoulder-blades) to help them in their decisions. Many of the bones were the shoulder-blades of oxen, others were flat strips cut from the animals' leg-bones, and in the later years a more sophisticated and expensive surface had come to be used – the bottom layer of a tortoise's shell, smoothed off and polished. Into one of these surfaces the Shang diviners cut a groove and then applied a red-hot bronze point. The way the material cracked gave the answer to the question, usually in the form of a simple yes/no or good/bad alternative. Luckily for modern research, the diviners sometimes later inscribed the questions, using a repertoire of more than 2000 characters, and they even occasionally added details of the result. Then, already showing a proper bureaucratic thoroughness, they filed the bones away. In 1936 the archaeologists came upon a circular pit containing some 17,000 items – a complete and undisturbed archive. The bones were strung together into bundles, and it is the pictogram of one such volume ⧣ that has evolved into the modern character for 'book'.

Several of the diviners tended to include their own names, so their identities have gradually become revealed and have helped to place the bones in some sort of order. Thus the diviner Ti was working in the late thirteenth century B.C., and began perhaps as an apprentice younger than most, because his hand has at first an unusual immaturity but then develops; in the following century Yung and Huang are outstanding for the charm and delicacy of their inscriptions. The personalities of the kings too have gradually emerged. They seem to have differed in their attitudes to the oracles, some making much greater use of them than others. In general the questions were limited to matters of some formal or communal importance, such as the sacrifices, war, hunting or agriculture, but Wu-ting, the most partial of all the rulers to the services of the oracle, was prepared to trouble the priests with such queries as which of his ancestors was causing his present toothache. A good example of the way in which questions and results were recorded comes from this same reign at the hand of the diviner Ku:

Ku made this inquiry, by divination, on the day *mou-wu*;
We are going to hunt at Ch'iu: will there be any capture?

Hunting on this day, we actually captured 1 tiger, 40 deer, 164 foxes, 159 hornless deer.[2]

Some kings seem to have done their own divination, particularly when the question related to the birth of a royal child – emphasizing, perhaps, that this was one area in which they would have no deputy.

The bones brought to modern scholarship two startling revelations. The first was that the traditional facts about the Shang dynasty, known only through the work of a historian writing a thousand years later, were substantially correct. Ssu-ma Ch'ien, China's earliest and most famous individual historian, had written in about 100 B.C. an account of thirty Shang rulers. The existence of nearly all of them has now been proved by the appearance of their names on the oracle-bones. It is not known what Shang records were available to Ssu-ma Ch'ien, and certainly none has survived, but his accuracy on a period that far in the past demonstrates how thorough and early was the Chinese obsession with history. Now that he has been proved right about the Shang dynasty, it seems likely that there is also some historical basis to his account of their predecessors, the Hsia. They may have been a dominant group among the neolithic tribes whose place was later taken by the Shang.

The other surprise was that the characters on the bones proved to be the direct ancestors of the modern Chinese script. Indeed in one sense they were themselves only an intermediate stage, for the bronze vessels from An-yang contain in their inscriptions even older characters which are simply pictures of the thing represented, as in many Egyptian hieroglyphs. The discovery of the missing link on the oracle-bones made clear the development from pictograph to abstract script. The antique sign for 'great' on the bronze vessels is 杰; on the bones it has become 大; and in modern Chinese it is 大 (a matter of three quick strokes which take far less time to write than 'great', though this is certainly not true of the more complicated characters).

Only a small fraction of modern Chinese characters derive in such a direct line from ancient beginnings, but there is a more subtle and significant way in which the writing on the oracle-bones was the source of all that followed. The Shang had already evolved in their script all the principles by which their own vocabulary of 2000 characters was capable of being extended to one of more than 50,000. (Nor was the Shang repertoire, in fact, as small as it might sound. A modern Chinese newspaper uses only some 3000 characters, and even a scholar will not encumber his memory with more than about 6000–8000. Ogden's 'basic English' uses only 850 words.)

There are several ways in which new Chinese characters are formed.

One is by the simple juxtaposition of two physical realities to suggest a third. The character for a man is Y. The character for a door or gate is 門. By placing the man in the doorway 閃, a character is arrived at meaning 'to get out' or 'to get out of the way'. In similar fashion physical objects can be brought together to symbolize an abstraction. A house, showing only the roof, is 宀. If one places beneath it a heart 心, and a cup 皿, the resulting 寗 is taken to represent peace.[3] Another character for peace, often quoted and arrived at on the same principle, is a woman under a roof.

The largest single group is formed on a rather different basis, combining the character for the type of object with another which suggests the sound of the word. Since this is a form of pun and puns are untranslatable, one can only demonstrate by inventing an entirely imaginary character that would fit the English language. If 宀 were house in English, then 宮 would be an acceptable character for a small castle. The reason? When an elephant appears on a chess board it is called a castle, so the elephant would be an acceptable pictograph for that type of castle. Its presence inside the house tells us that we are referring to the type of house which, when spoken, is pronounced 'castle'.

Such are the rich associations buried in the Chinese script, East Asia's most formative single cultural possession, and they were present in principle 3500 years ago. But the operative word is buried. It would be misleading to think of the Chinese being conscious of these pleasant pictorial origins as they read. Seeking them out is the game of the etymologist. How many of us are put in mind of our ancient methods of writing when we used the word pen? Yet a foreigner, pointing out that the word derives from the Latin for feather, *penna*, would seem to give it the same sort of antiquarian charm which one can wrongly attribute to Chinese characters.

The uniqueness of the Chinese script lies elsewhere. There are certain profound differences in the experience of reading Chinese, but they derive from its being the only system of writing ever to have become fully sophisticated without finding the need for an alphabet. An alphabetic system attempts to capture on the page the sound of the spoken name for an object or concept. The Chinese, taking in this respect a short cut, place a symbol for that object or concept directly on the paper. One immediate result of this is that written Chinese transcends all the barriers caused elsewhere by dialect or by the changes in pronunciation over the course of centuries. Educated people from far-flung regions of China have always been able to write to each other with ease even though they might under-

stand hardly a word of each other's spoken language. To each the characters in the text would seem entirely their own, yet they would ring quite different sounds in their ears – just as the symbols 5 or 23 do in the ears of a modern Frenchman, Spaniard or German.

The chaos of English spelling up to the Elizabethan period shows the difficulties of the opposite method, with each writer trying to express on the page his own pronunciation of each word. A Scotsman's spelling at the time was so different from an Englishman's that their communication was hardly easier on paper than in person. As late as the seventeenth century a *Historie of the Kirk* was not above printing *quhilkis* for 'which'.

The Chinese script has the same advantage with historical distance as with geographical. The largest single reform of the characters occurred a little over 2000 years ago. Educated Chinese can read the poetry and literature of any period in those 2000 years with equal ease and in its original form. In the West we are limited to about a quarter of this span. To enjoy anything much before Chaucer requires a specialized training.

The nature of the script and of the language also has a profound effect on Chinese methods of expression. Just as the characters on a page are stable, self-contained symbols, unaltered in shape by other characters around them, so too are the words of classical Chinese. Each is unsusceptible to changes of gender, to considerations of singular or plural, to past, present or future tenses, to agonies of choice between accusative and dative, and most of them can be noun, adverb, adjective or verb at will. Each sits alone in its sentence (to which there is no full stop), influencing its neighbours and being influenced by them only as a result of the order in which they are placed. This is something profoundly different from the tight grammatical fabric of a European sentence. If a European writer is a weaver, a Chinese one is more like a jeweller.

One result of this lack of connection, or of a sentence being made up of a series of separate images, is that a statement of any complexity is much more ambiguous in Chinese than in a European language, a fact which has undoubtedly contributed to the Chinese reputation for being enigmatic. A sentence needs to be interpreted almost like a poem. An American scholar, the translator of many classical Chinese texts, once composed an English paragraph to give some impression of his unpunctuated and largely monosyllabic originals:

Sky spans high   earth bears up   beast herds teem there
winged flocks fly by   four seas close round   ten streams race on

so too kings reign   lords aid   men plow   wives spin
good sires rear sons   good heirs serve sires[4]

The potential for poetry in such a language is obvious, even in a paragraph in no way intended to make that point. The very density of images and monosyllables seems even to suggest a peculiarly modern form of verse, like Gerard Manley Hopkins's sprung rhythm in such lines as 'each tucked string tells, each hung bell's / Bow swung finds tongue to fling out broad its name'. But a Chinese eye, accustomed to making the connections, would not find the paragraph as dense as this.

A Chinese poet is a jeweller in two ways. Not only is he making a selection of bright images, his characters, to set in a line above each other. He is also using all the skill at his command to shape each character as a beautiful object, for such it is essentially capable of being. Thus a poem becomes in itself a form of painting. The same brush is used for both calligraphy and landscape, for writing out an imperial edict, for painting a poem of affection on the wall of a friend's house, or for capturing in a few quick strokes on silk the mountain view from one's country retreat. Skill in the use of this brush was to become over the centuries one of the special attributes of that peculiarly Chinese figure, the scholar who is also an administrator and an artist, and by virtue of all three accomplishments a complete gentleman.

I have allowed the characters of the Chinese script to carry me on this digression forward in time to the later flowerings of Chinese civilization precisely because all these significant details are prefigured at An-yang. Even the brush itself is there. The diviners painted their characters onto the bone or shell in red ink, and then used a blade of bronze or jade, several of which have been found, to carve away the painted areas. The delicacy with which this operation was carried out, the scholarly process of filing away the oracles in the archives, the ability to influence public decisions (with skill, the cracks could probably be guided), and the prominence of their own names in the records, figuring almost as largely as those of their rulers – all these seem to establish the diviners as true ancestors of China's refined bureaucrats.

In the Shang culture unearthed at An-yang sacrifice played a very prominent part. One of the royal tombs contained 45 complete skeletons, a further 34 skulls, and the remains of some 52 birds and animals. But human sacrifice was far from limited to the event of a royal death. The consecration of any large building involved extensive slaughter. A dog or a small child was first of all buried among the foundations. The bases of

the pillars were safeguarded by the burial of a human victim in a kneeling position together with a dog, a sheep and an ox. For the door there were four men in separate pits outside the threshold, again in the kneeling position and each armed with a dagger-axe and sometimes a shield, while on the inside five men were buried face down with their heads towards the centre of the building. Finally, when the structure was complete, several hundred people were sacrificed and buried in front of it, together with five war chariots and all the necessary weapons. These dead figures, armed and in positions of solemn respect, were the spirit guardians of the building. In macabre fashion, the layout revealed in one of these mass burials has helped in the reconstruction of a Shang fighting unit. In the centre were five chariots, each with its crew of three : a driver, an archer and a man with a dagger-axe. In front of them came 25 men, to the right another group of 125, and beyond them again a single man, presumably the commanding officer. It would seem that an entire battalion was sacrificed to guard this particular building.

19

For most sacrifices the victims were prisoners of war, and the Shang rulers organized hunting parties for the specific purpose of rounding up people from the more primitive tribes to the northwest. But it is possible that for important purposes certain valued members of the Shang community itself were sacrificed – perhaps, for example, genuine Shang soldiers in this ghostly battalion. Certainly the principle of sacrifice at a burial was that the dead man should be accompanied by people and objects which were genuinely useful to him. An early Chinese poem tells of how a ruler in the seventh century B.C. left instructions that three of the ablest men in his kingdom should attend him in his tomb as advisers. One of them was Tzu-che Chen-hu:

> *Who followed Duke Mu to the grave?*
> *Tzu-che Chen-hu.*
> *And this Chen-hu*
> *Could withstand a hundred men.*
> *But when he came to the grave,*
> *He looked terrified and trembled.*[5]

On the same basis the Shang ruler had his most treasured objects buried with him. The tombs have yielded up a wealth of carvings in marble and jade, and above all the magnificent bronze vessels by which the dynasty is now most widely known. It is generally admitted that even if one or two later periods elsewhere in the world could equal the technical brilliance of the Shang craftsmen in their casting of bronze, none, including our own age, can better them.

For several years after these objects had first been accurately identified and dated, it seemed as though this level of skill had arrived with almost magical suddenness in China. Bronze was first used in China at least 1000 years later than in the Mediterranean area, and it was once argued that bronze workers with a very high degree of skill must have reached China by the steppes route north of the mountains, later to become the Silk Road. But various much more primitive bronzes, greatly inferior both in alloy and casting techniques, have now been discovered in Shang cities earlier than An-yang. It is still probable that the secret of bronze arrived from the West some time around 2000 B.C., but the perfecting of their unparalleled technique was a purely Chinese achievement.

The range of objects cast by the Shang craftsmen in bronze is considerable (bells, axes, drills and polished mirrors, to name but a few), but by far the most impressive are the vessels for food and wine. Their hollow

shape and decorated surface of deep geometric designs made them extraordinarily hard to cast.

The Shang were helped in this task by their skill in an allied art, that of pottery. Their neolithic ancestors were already accomplished potters, producing large thin-walled urns with sweeping decorative patterns which are always limited to the upper half of the pots (colour, page 26) – suggesting perhaps that they were sunk a little way into the ground to prevent them overturning. By the time of the Shang dynasty the potters had sufficient technique to make elaborate equipment for the casting of bronze. One example is an ingenious crucible with a pointed bottom to stand it in the fire, a thin lip to control the pouring, and between the two a very thick wall to the body of the pot which included a cavity filled with sand. This, serving as insulation, prevented too much loss of heat from the molten metal. It is assumed that a straw bag full of sand was built into the wet pot, and the straw was burned away when the crucible was fired.

Equally skilful were the moulds into which the metal was poured. So perfect are the finished bronzes – so free from air bubbles, their indentations so deep and true – that it was at first assumed they must have been made by the *cire perdue* method, the easiest way of casting, in which a wax replica of the finished object is encased in clay. (When the clay is fired, the wax runs out through holes left for the purpose; the holes are then filled and the metal is poured in; once it has set, the clay can be broken away to reveal the bronze.) But separate sections of clay moulds have been found at An-yang. It is evident that the craftsmen built up the moulds from these sections, held together with tenon and mortise and some form of binding. The advantage of this method would be to make possible a primitive form of mass production, since the moulds can be lifted away from the cool bronze and used again. But no two bronzes have yet been found which were cast from the same mould. There is no way of proving that *cire perdue* was never used, for the technique is largely a self-obliterating one, the clay being broken away to reveal the bronze; and late in the next dynasty certain shapes were cast which could only have been produced by the wax method.[6] But it seems probable that the early Shang craftsmen perfected the most difficult of all casting techniques merely because they knew of no other.

No doubt many of these pots and jugs graced the banquets of princes, but their most sacred use was in the various rituals connected with ancestor worship. The most characteristic of all the Shang bronzes is the *li*

A Shang bronze ritual vessel or li, *c. 1500 B.C.; and a pottery tripod bowl, c. 2000 B.C.*

tripod, a shape unique to northern China. It was based on a pottery cooking vessel used by the neolithic ancestors of the Shang, which in its original form clearly reveals its derivation from breasts or udders. Apart from the satisfying symbolism of this for a source of food, it was also an extremely practical design for cooking on an open fire. The three legs which plunged down into the glowing cinders to hold the pot upright were themselves partially hollow, thus bringing a maximum amount of heat to bear on the stew. The bronze version remained one of several used for cooking the animals sacrificed in the temple of the ancestors. As in all good religions, it was the priests and communicants – in this case the family – who ate the food. The spirits of the ancestors were content with the steam.

The pouring of hot wine – a blackish brew derived from millet – was an important part of the ceremony, and the craftsmen surpassed themselves in their designs for the vessels in which the wine was stored. The cooking pots had a practical purpose which to a certain extent limited their shape, leaving the craftsman his greatest opportunities in the matter of decoration. The outer surfaces, in the best examples, crawl with intricate geometrical patterns, fantastic silhouettes and the masks of composite

dragon-like animals. But containers intended only for the storing of liquid suffered no such limitations. The shape of the inside was unimportant, it could follow whatever lines the craftsman had in mind for the vessel as a whole. As a result the weird configurations of birds, animals and dragons make the various types of wine vessels the most fascinating of all the Shang bronzes (colour, pages 25 and 28).

The royal family was not the only one to worship their ancestors, but the number of other families able to do so was comparatively small – estimated from the oracle-bones as being in the region of 200. Everyone else was excluded at this stage by the simple fact that they had no clan names or surnames, an exclusion which was by its nature self-perpetuating. Without a surname it was unusually difficult to keep track of one's forbears; without accurately identified forbears it was out of the question to have a shrine, however small, at which to worship them; and yet it was the existence of the shrine, with the accompanying rituals and record-keeping, which made it feasible to keep track of the developing family tree. In every society the aristocracy have been those who can trace their ancestors back a long way, for the obvious reason that this is a yardstick of having held positions of power for a long time. The Chinese formalized this simple fact of life. No other community has made such a clear distinction between the haves and have-nots in the matter of lineage. As recently as 1948 a descendant of Confucius in the seventy-seventh generation was still in charge of the sacrifices to his ancestor.[7] Upstart Europe, obsessed though she too has been with genealogies, is no match for this. The oldest traceable European family falls short of the Chinese sage by a good nine centuries.[8]

The very nature of archaeological remains tends to focus attention unduly on the ruling classes, or those with solidly constructed tombs, and on the more durable of the art objects buried with them, such as bronze. But even so certain details of life in the capital city at An-yang can be pieced together.

Its name on the oracle-bones is the Great City Shang, and it straddles the River Huan, a tributary of the Yellow River. It was quite an extensive city. Remains have been found over a distance of some four miles along both banks of the river, which formed the city's main thoroughfare. The site was a well-chosen one, because the level plain on all sides gave maximum scope to the Shang war chariots, while only a few miles to the west the foothills of the mountains provided a source of timber and a good hunting ground. Almost certainly the city was protected by a huge wall

of pounded earth, although the remains of it have not yet been found. The previous and considerably more primitive Shang capital, at Chengchow, had such a wall. Some 4000 yards of it have been discovered, in places still twelve feet high and at all points roughly sixty feet wide at its base. This massive structure was made by erecting a timber frame and then pounding layer after layer of earth inside it until each was compacted. Such walls were sometimes built surprisingly fast. An account survives of the construction of one in the sixth century B.C.:

> The superintendent of the work . . . estimated the amount of labour to be done, and the number of days; adjusted the frames, and provided the baskets and pounding tools and other articles for raising the walls; marked out with his feet the foundations; supplied the provisions; and determined the inspectors. The work was completed in thirty days, exactly in accordance with the previous calculations.[9]

The use of vast numbers of people to accomplish huge projects in record time is a long-standing tradition in China. A recent example dates from 1959, when the Great Hall of the People at Peking, which includes among other things a main hall to seat 10,000 people, was completed after a construction period of ten months.

In the Great City Shang the foundations and lower walls of the more important buildings were made of the same pounded earth, with a wooden structure of pillars and perhaps a thatched roof above them. By contrast the ordinary citizens lived in holes in the ground, but this may not have been quite as underprivileged as it sounds. The soil of the area, being largely composed of loess, can be cut to leave a very solid cavity – indeed throughout history the peasants a little further to the west have lived in fairly elaborate cave-dwellings cut into the loess terraces. No less an authority than Joseph Needham, England's leading sinologist, has vouched from personal experience that the loess caves can make 'very convenient homes, cool in summer and warm in winter'.[10] No doubt the Shang version was less convenient, but each dwelling-pit that has been excavated has a stone in the middle of the floor on which a pillar probably rested to support a roof above. In an area notorious for its raging winds, it may have been no bad thing to be half underground.

Needless to say the majority of the people, as in any pre-industrial community, spent almost every daylight hour of their lives working in the fields where they were joined by those prisoners of war or slaves who had not been used for sacrifice. Bronze being the only metal available, and

Detail of bronze yu *wine vessel, Shang.* OVERLEAF *Painted Pan-shan earthenware vase, pre-Shang* LEFT; *and white pottery tripod jug or* kuei, c. 2000 B.C.

extremely expensive, their tools were still the traditional neolithic ones of stone and wood.

The nobles, again predictably, engaged themselves in war, in hunting and in the practice of ritual – much as in other places and times. For their relaxation they had considerable luxuries. Bronzes were used for domestic purposes. A complete toilet set has been unearthed, all in bronze, consisting of a jug for fetching water, a container for storing it, a ladle for scooping it out, and a basin for washing in, completed even by a large pottery pad with a handle which was apparently used for scouring the skin, like pumice-stone. They were already using round polished sheets of bronze as mirrors – items which in later dynasties were to become some of the very prettiest pieces of household furniture, with spectacularly moulded and inlaid backs. Three pairs of chopsticks were found in one of the burial sites[11] (the introduction of chopsticks, the most specifically Chinese of all utensils, had previously been dated very much later, in about the third century B.C.) and more surprisingly perhaps, jade scoops for cleaning out the ears have been found in unusual numbers. For clothing there was both hemp and silk – evidence of the cultivation of silk has been found even in neolithic times – and as ornaments they had gold and ivory as well as bronze. Money, in transactions too large for barter to be convenient, took the form of cowrie shells, one of the world's most popular units of exchange. Its appeal has often been explained by its vague resemblance to the female sexual organ, but it also has various other qualities even more necessary in one's currency, such as being scarce, durable, easy to carry about, pretty and impossible to forge.

Intellectual life may have been far from sluggish. In those scientific matters which interested them, the Shang scholars achieved very precise results. An example was the calendar, a matter of particular importance in agriculture and essential also to the prestige of the king, for the seasons were regarded as his personal responsibility. The astronomers used a lunar month and grappled with the age-old task of fitting it into solar years – a matter so complicated that even Islam, for example, chose to disregard it, allowing each Muslim month such as Ramadan to drift its way slowly through the year. The Shang astronomers solved the problem by adding seven lunar months during each period of nineteen solar years. The resulting length of their average year was only about eleven minutes different from what we now take to be the exact figure.[12]

Writing, too, can be argued to have been used more widely than just on the oracle-bones, if only on the grounds that the characters develop

Bronze ritual wine bucket in the shape of two owls, back to back; late Shang

more rapidly during the period than would have been required for that one purpose alone. Bamboo strips and silk became in later centuries the traditional Chinese writing materials before the invention of paper. Both are easily perishable, and may well have been already in use in the Great City Shang.

It is hard to estimate the extent of Shang control in central China. Certainly the influence of their culture reached far, for traces of it have been found in the Yangtze valley some 400 miles to the south. On one occasion a Shang army made a march of 106 days to fight in support of a so-called vassal state. What is not known is over how much of this territory they exercised actual control, as a ruling power, or how much their influence was merely a cultural one, that of a more highly developed small state which all the other small states would wish to imitate.

Beyond dispute, though, is the extraordinary influence of the Shang way of life and attitudes over the succeeding centuries of China's history. One further example can emphasize the point. It is thought that Shang towns were square, and their buildings carefully aligned according to the points of the compass, two details which have remained true of Chinese town-planning at all periods and can still be seen in Peking and many other cities today. Moreover the Shang regarded the area outside their own as forming another square, occupied by their vassal states, and saw the remainder of the world as a third and final square, at the very intersection of the diagonals of which was the Great City Shang. This sinocentric view of the world was extended even to the universe, for that was held to consist of three layers, heaven above, earth below, and man in the middle. The entire arrangement was rather like those structures recently devised for playing three-dimensional noughts and crosses, with the Shang people and their city represented by the ball in the very centre. It is a delightful theory if you happen to be the ball, and one to which the Chinese have over the centuries remained faithful. Their name for their own land has always been, and remains today, *Chung-kuo* – the Central Country.

THE SUPERIOR CULTURE OF THE SHANG NATURALLY SPREAD TO THE tribes around, and it was one of these, the Chou, who by the eleventh century had learned enough from their masters to be able to defeat them. The Chou had lived to the west of the Shang, in the valley of the Wei, one of the main tributaries of the Yellow River. Their position was virtually that of a buffer state between civilization and barbarism – a situation which on several occasions in early Chinese history proved ideal for a career of conquest. The Chou were able to learn the arts of diplomacy and sophisticated warfare from their luxurious neighbours down the valley to the east, while the marauding nomads in the mountains on the other three sides both kept them on their mettle and gave them an added impulse to expand into those greener pastures. It has even been suggested that in earlier centuries the Chou had themselves been the barbarians who were from time to time rounded up as flesh and blood for the Shang sacrifices.[1] If so, there was a certain poetic justice in their victory.

There has been much argument as to exactly when this change of dynasty occurred. The date given in the traditional Chinese histories is 1122 B.C. In our own century a modern recalculation brought the year forward to 1027 B.C., a figure which was once widely accepted, but by now at least a dozen different dates, ranging from 1137 to 991, have found their individual champions. The confusion arises from the fact that the Chinese have always dated events by reference to the start of each reign. European countries have used the same method on certain types of document, but the Chinese had no longer-term chronology in which to anchor each separate reign. They were not counting from the birth or flight of any prophet. The ladder of Chinese time consists only of its separate rungs, and the disadvantage is that an error in any one reign means an error in every reign. It is hardly surprising if the early dates are in some disarray. More astonishing, and an indication of the Chinese passion for record-keeping, is that even without a unified chronology the dates of Chinese history from as early as the eighth century B.C. are widely agreed upon.

Equally controversial has been the type of rule which the new dynasty established. The Chou rulers sent out their relations and followers, in fairly small parties, to occupy more and more new territory. Each group built itself a little fortress-city from which to control its region. Such a situation, with an interrelated ruling class dotted about the country in separate castles, has a distinctly feudal look and the argument has been as to how far it can validly be described as such. Certainly the arrangement shared many features with medieval feudalism in Europe. There is evidence

that the peasants had to till a certain proportion of the land specifically for the lord of the district, and the lords were expected to present themselves from time to time at the royal court and to raise an army in defence of their king when required. On the other hand the Chou king, in the early part of the dynasty, seems to have had a central authority based more on military and administrative considerations than on the mere concept of allegiance. He maintained fourteen standing armies and interfered in the internal concerns of the various districts, even on occasion sending out inspectors who had the power to punish or restrain the rulers. This is more like a normal network of military or even civil command, except that the local governors had the one essentially feudal advantage of their position being hereditary.

One feature the system certainly shared with European feudalism was a tendency towards disintegration. Each local commander, once he had subdued the indigenous population, had a personal power base from which he could encroach on his neighbours, themselves also vassals of the Chou king. Whatever central authority there may have been at the start grew steadily weaker, and finally, in 771 B.C., the Chou rulers were driven from their capital in the Wei valley by an alliance of barbarian tribes and some rebel Chou dependencies. They were able to install themselves further east, on another tributary of the Yellow River at Loyang, so that the dynasty survived in name at least, becoming known to history as the Eastern Chou. Their rule lasted for another five centuries, but in form and title alone. During that period the different Chou states, still calling themselves vassals, merged and absorbed each other into ever fewer and more powerful units in the long struggle towards a genuinely unified empire – a conclusion made almost inevitable by the geography of this sealed-off subcontinent. It suited these new states, each far more powerful than the small central kingdom, to maintain the fiction of Chou supremacy until any one of them had finally emerged as victor over all the others. And the Chou kings had one other important function, that of continuing the sacrifices to their ancestors. A family of dispossessed spirits could cause a great deal of trouble, especially if they had been kings and Sons of Heaven, and almost every local ruler regarded himself as descended, in some minor line, from the royal house. So, disregarding the existence of the little Chou state in almost all other matters, great regional potentates still solemnly came to consult the king on matters of lineage and protocol.

The process by which Chou rule had spread, and then fragmented, had one result which was to prove of enormous influence in the history of

Bronze ritual wine-mixer or kuang, *with lid based on sacrificial animal, c. 1000 B.C.*

China. The rulers of all the different states felt themselves the inheritors of one single culture, a jealously guarded possession which both linked them to each other and distinguished them from the people of the different regions under their control. This sense of cultural unity meant that, however great the political or military rivalries, there was a very free interchange of ideas throughout the territory, with scholars moving from court to court – just as a medieval cleric in Europe could be assured of a welcome from fellow-members of the one true church, regardless of national boundaries. The very fact of so many small states, all trying new methods of regulating their affairs, led to an equal profusion of theories and an explosion of intellectual energy (much the same thing, at much the same time, was happening in Greece). The results have influenced Chinese thought ever since. To put the matter at its most absolute, it has been said that 'the classical literature of ancient China consists entirely of the documents of the Chou ruling class'.[2]

One of the earliest of these classics is the *Shih ching* (the *Classic of Poetry* or *Book of Odes*), consisting of some 300 poems dating from between 1100 and 600 B.C. This early collection contains folksongs which already show that peculiarly wistful clarity which reappears in so much later Chinese poetry, such as this brief and increasingly urgent appeal from a girl growing old without a lover:

> *The plums are falling –*
> *There are only seven.*
> *For the gentlemen who court me,*
> *Lucky is the time.*
>
> *The plums are falling –*
> *There are only three.*
> *For the gentlemen who court me,*
> *Now is the time.*
>
> *The plums are falling –*
> *In a basket I've gathered them all.*
> *For the gentlemen who court me,*
> *Speak while there is time.*[3]

But the *Book of Odes* also contains a great many poems of a more occasional nature, celebrating the great moments of ceremony or ritual. The following, for example, describes powerful vassals presenting themselves at court:

They appear before their lord, the King,
Seeking their emblems of distinction.
The dragon banners blaze,
The carriage bells and the banner bells chime,
The metal–ornamented reins tinkle.
The gifts shine with splendour.[4]

To us the *Book of Odes* represents an invaluable insight into life in the early Chou dynasty, as well as a delightful anthology of early poetry. To the people in the later Chou dynasty (and it lasted in all some 800 or 900 years, or roughly from, say, the Norman conquest to today), the *Book of Odes* fulfilled these same two functions and one other, the most important of all. It was an extended dictionary of quotations, a storehouse of familiar images in which a diplomat could find an oblique but unmistakable way of expressing his meaning or a scholar could discover an analogy to lend ancient authority to his newest argument. Much as European authors have fed on the Bible, the writers of the later Chou leaned heavily on the first of the Chinese classics while creating the others.

One of the earliest to make use of the *Book of Odes* was Confucius. Almost nothing is known about his background or early life. Both appear, on the scant evidence available, to have been low-keyed. It seems likely that he was born into an impoverished branch of the minor nobility and that he eked out a living as a petty official, concerned with little more than book-keeping. When he acquired a certain reputation in middle age it was not for the practical achievements which he so longed for, those of administrator and reformer, but for the very same qualities for which posterity has honoured him – as a man of wisdom and, above all, a teacher.

Education at the time was a luxury reserved only for the upper levels of the ruling classes. What we would call an Arts education, which in China meant the study of the *Book of Odes* and various other classics, was available only to those who could afford a private tutor for their sons. Education of a more practical sort, in matters of procedure or public ritual, was passed on by officials as part of their everyday work to the young men entering the administration. Confucius, who was to become famous as the best-educated man of his day, was certainly too poor as a child to have had a tutor. It seems probable that he educated himself during his years as a clerk.

When history first takes notice of him, he already had a band of disciples and was running what is traditionally held to have been China's first school. In it he introduced a radical new principle – that of accepting

any student of sufficient intelligence, regardless of his background or means. The names of about twenty of his disciples are known to us and the majority are from high-born families, so the master's net may not have been cast as wide in practice as in principle. But the concept, that merit should be the only consideration in the selection of either pupils or officials, was a new and important one – and one which China, under the influence of Confucianism, was to establish as a part of official policy long before any other country, even if in practice the state often fell as far short of the ideal as Confucius himself. The notion of a meritocracy, or of social mobility made possible by examination, is a widely held modern theory which was first attempted at least 2000 years ago in China and which derives from the ideas of Confucius another half-millennium before that.

Several of the early disciples were almost the same age as Confucius himself, so it is possible that the school developed from a circle of friends or some sort of informal debating society. Certainly the method of teaching was conversational – like that of Socrates, born within a few years of Confucius's death. But Confucius discussed more down-to-earth topics than Socrates and his gullible young friends. Chinese thought has always tended to avoid the abstract, showing little interest in metaphysics or pure logic, and these early Confucians devoted themselves to such practical questions as what conduct was proper to a true gentleman or the precise nature of good government, and above all how the one could best put the other into effect.

Socrates scorned active political life, having always assumed, as he told his judges, that the holding of any office would inevitably lead to the compromise of his principles. Confucius was equally careful of his principles, but he lived in the opposite hope – that sooner or later a ruler of one of the states would allow him to put those principles into effect. Realizing in his late fifties that he was never going to be given more than an honourable sinecure in his native state of Lu, he set off with a few followers to travel through the neighbouring states in search of high political power. His fame as a man of learning was now widespread, so that everywhere he was received with honour. Surely some ruler would translate this respect into something more concrete? 'If only someone were to make use of me, even for a single year, I could do a great deal; and in three years I could finish off the whole work.'[5] No one did make use of him. A hostile and almost contemporary opinion argues that this was because Confucius was 'impractical, conceited, set a high value on ceremonial and had many peculiarities'.[6] Impractical he probably was, and his liking for plain

Bronze kuei *food vessel, Chou*

truths and blunt criticism, evident throughout his table-talk, may well have seemed like conceit to rulers unaccustomed to this type of dialogue. So, after ten frustrating years, he returned to Lu to devote himself to teaching. He must have realized that this, if any, was the way his ideas might be put into effect, for already his brighter pupils had been winning precisely those positions of power which so eluded their master. The skills which he gave them, when not allied to his own crustiness, appealed to self-interested rulers. One reason was their sheer intellectual capacity. Confucius would teach only the most promising and their minds, quickened by contact with his, had proved invaluable on several occasions of delicate diplomacy, in which the ruler with a Confucian by his side got the better of his less well-equipped neighbour. But also in their favour was their own idea of themselves, inculcated by Confucius, as disinterested officials working both for the ruler and for his people, and through them for the well-being of the state.

The vision which Confucius gave them was one of personal and social harmony, a harmony in which each well-balanced and honourable individual plays his role with dignity and self-respect within the strict hierarchy of the family, just as the family itself does within the nation, or the nation within the wider structure of the cosmos. There is thus a pyramid of respect and obligation, having as its symbol at each level the relationship between father and son. The son owes respect to his father; the father has a right to this respect from his son (a right which at some periods of Chinese history has been codified in law), but he himself stands in the relation of a son to the head of his own community, and he to someone above him, and so on up to the emperor whose official title as the Son of Heaven extends the chain through his own dead ancestors to the divine forces which control nature itself. Only if the proper forms of respect are maintained within society will there be peace and order in the nation, and only if due reverence is shown in the ritual sacrifices to the royal ancestors, capable in their new position of lobbying the gods themselves, will there be harmony among the elements instead of flood or drought. It was not a concept introduced by Confucius, for it had existed far earlier, but he gave it its most powerful expression.

Confucius liked to use two images in particular for this essential concord. He stressed the importance of music, which symbolized inner harmony, and one of his favourite words was *li*, often translated as ritual or the sum of all those conventions by which men in a stable society live peacefully together. This vision of a well-ordered hierarchy mirrored

Bronze monster-mask and ring, of type which could only be cast by cire-perdue *method, c. 450 B.C.*

in the sweet certainties of music is almost precisely that which Shakespeare puts into the mouth of Ulysses in *Troilus and Cressida*:

> *The heavens themselves, the planets, and this centre,*
> *Observe degree, priority, and place,*
> *Insisture, course, proportion, season, form,*
> *Office, and custom, in all line of order. . . .*
>
> *Take but degree away, untune that string,*
> *And hark, what discord follows! each thing meets*
> *In mere oppugnancy: the bounded waters*
> *Should lift their bosoms higher than the shores,*
> *And make a sop of all this solid globe:*
> *Strength should be lord of imbecility,*
> *And the rude son should strike his father dead. . . .*

Such a love of degree can seem, to modern minds, the most naked propaganda for the *status quo*, and Confucius – like Shakespeare when in this vein – has often been described as reactionary. 'Those', he said, 'who in private life behave well towards their parents and elder brothers, in public life seldom show a disposition to resist the authority of their superiors. And as for such men starting a revolution, no instance of it has ever occurred.'[7]

But Confucius was not trying to preserve a state of affairs which existed. He hankered for a utopian society which he, and others of his time, believed once to have existed. It was thought that in the early years of the Chou dynasty there had been a perfect feudal order throughout the country, with the ruling classes devoting themselves selflessly to the welfare of the community and to the service of the Chou king. The decline from this ideal to the present state of affairs was plain. Not only was the Son of Heaven in his little kingdom of Chou entirely powerless, but even the hereditary dukes of the various states had in many cases been supplanted, again in all but name, by the families of their own ministers. Warfare between the states was almost constant. Degree had been taken away and discord had all too evidently followed.

In fact the master was less pedantic and hidebound than he came to seem many centuries later, when his ideas had long been established as the official state religion. It was, in a sense, the Confucians who gave Confucius a bad name. The Confucians 2000 years after his death – or, as the Europeans chose to call them, the mandarins – had acquired an entirely justified reputation as being narrow-minded, over-correct, back-

ward-looking and obsessed with detail. Similarly the two texts most widely known as Confucian give – to a foreigner and in translation – a decidedly flat impression. They are two chapters which were included in a late work, the *Li Chi* or *Book of Rites*, and under the titles *The Great Learning* and *The Doctrine of the Mean* they have been memorized by generations of Chinese schoolchildren. The morality they recommend is impeccable if somewhat obvious (Confucianism is above all the religion of commonsense and decency), and it is expounded with corresponding solemnity. The overall effect is like being lectured by the dullest of the school prefects. Indeed the impression often given of Confucius in the West is that of a good reliable schoolmaster.

This does him less than justice. It is hard to get back to the authentic Confucius, for although the traditional Chinese viewpoint was that he wrote several of the classics and edited most of the others, modern scholarship denies him the authorship of any and even doubts him as an editor. The nearest one can come to him is in the *Analects*, a collection of his sayings gathered together a century or more after his death (possibly by his best known disciple, Mencius), and here the tone is very different.

The question and answer form in which many of the sayings are framed seems to hark back to the original discussions of his circle, though there are signs that the favourite moments had become stock anecdotes among his followers, acquiring in the retelling almost the clarity of folk-sayings, before they were finally recorded:

> Tzu-kung asked Confucius, 'What would you say if all the people of the village like a person?' 'That is not enough,' replied Confucius. 'What would you say if all the people of the village dislike a person?' 'That is not enough,' said Confucius. 'It is better when the good people of the village like him, and the bad of the village dislike him.'[8]

Throughout the *Analects* there is an almost Johnsonian air of the unexpected, a love of paradox and surprise. The master's views can never be quite safely predicted. The very type of man, for example, who later came to be thought of as the typical Confucian, correct and in every conventional way admirable, gets on one occasion a surprisingly low rating:

> A person who is extremely careful of his conduct and speech and always keeps his word – that is a priggish, inferior type of person.[9]

One of the most intriguing glimpses of Confucius among his disciples, some of them eager to adopt wholesale his own stated ideas, others more independent, is the following:

Tselu, Tseng Hsi, Jan Ch'iu and Kunghsi Hua were sitting together one day and Confucius said, 'Do not think that I am a little bit older than you and therefore am assuming airs. You often say among yourselves that people don't know you. Suppose someone should know you, I should like to know how you would appear to that person.' Tselu immediately replied, 'I should like to rule over a country with a thousand carriages, situated between two powerful neighbours, involved in war and suffering from famine. I should like to take charge of such a country and in three years, the nation would become strong and orderly.' Confucius smiled at this remark and said, 'How about you, Ah Ch'iu?' Jan Ch'iu replied, 'Let me have a country sixty or seventy *li* square or perhaps only fifty or sixty *li* square. Put it in my charge, and in three years, the people will have enough to eat, but as for teaching them moral order and music, I shall leave it to the superior man.' [Turning to Kunghsi Hua] Confucius said, 'How about you, Ah Ch'ih?' Kunghsi Hua replied, 'Not that I say I can do it, but I'm willing to learn this. At the ceremonies of religious worship and at the conference of the princes, I should like to wear the ceremonial cap and gown and be a minor official assisting at the ceremony.' 'How about you, Ah Tien?' The latter [Tseng Hsi] was just playing on the *seh*, and with a bang he left the instrument and arose to speak. 'You know my ambition is different from theirs.' 'It doesn't matter,' said Confucius, 'we are just trying to find out what each would like to do.' Then he replied, 'In late spring, when the new spring dress is made, I would like to go with five or six grown-ups and six or seven children to bathe in the River Ch'i, and after the bath go to enjoy the breeze in the Wuyi woods, and then sing on our way home.' Confucius heaved a deep sigh and said, 'You are the man after my own heart.'[10]

Perhaps the most convincing summing up of Confucius's merits was one made by a follower some two centuries after his death, who wrote that he was 'benevolent, wise and free from obsession'.[11] The first two epithets may be platitudes, but the third is not.

Confucius died in 479 B.C., and during the two centuries after his death the struggle for dominion in China became increasingly violent – so much so that the name for this period, in the official dynastic histories, is the Warring States period. A thousand or more garrison towns of the tenth century had grouped themselves into some two hundred increasingly independent little territories. By the fourth century, there had emerged, after bitter struggle, seven powerful states. The contest between them was the final convulsion in the long process by which one area would come to dominate all the rest and establish the first Chinese empire.

As the stakes were steadily raised, and skill in government and diplo-

macy became more important, the services of wandering scholars were in ever-increasing demand. More and more set out on their travels, imitating Confucius's ten-year pilgrimage in search of political employment, and on the whole with far greater success. As one of them was reported to have said, 'if you are successful . . . you become a high official; if you fail you are boiled alive. That is the kind of business it is.'[12]

A favourite story gave an example of how a scholar could benefit his master. Around 300 B.C. the two states of Chao and Ch'in made a treaty along the lines that 'whatever Ch'in desires to do she is to be assisted by Chao; and in whatever Chao desires to do she is to be assisted by Ch'in.' Soon afterwards Ch'in attacked another state, but Chao, instead of assisting its aggressive ally, went to the defence of the third party. Ch'in protested strongly at this apparent infringement of the pact, but the ruler of Chao carried the argument when he was advised by his resident scholar how to reply: 'According to the pact each side guarantees to help the other in whatever either desires to do. I now desire to save the state of Wei, and if you do not help me to do so, I shall charge you with infringement of the pact.'[13] The phrasing of the original treaty looks suspiciously as though it were shaped long after the event, but even as a philosophical tale it suggests well what was hoped for from the scholars.

The particular genius credited with this stroke of diplomacy was Kung-sun Lung, generally classified as a member of the rather minor school of Logicians and this type of advice may have been his special forte. But a ruler could find a scholar of almost any philosophical persuasion to suit his own tastes, for this was the famous period when 'all flowers bloomed and a hundred schools of thought contended'. (It is typical, again, of the continuity of Chinese culture, even after the most apparently complete breaks, that Mao Tse-tung, introducing a cultural thaw in February 1957, should have chosen to announce it with the words 'Let a hundred flowers bloom together, and a hundred schools of thought contend.')

The squabbles between the contending schools were not all conducted in the purest spirit of Confucian courtesy. The school of Mo Tzu, for example, minced no words about the Confucians, writing that they

corrupt men with their elaborate and showy rites and music and deceive parents with lengthy mournings and hypocritical grief. They propound fatalism, ignore poverty, and behave with the greatest arrogance. . . . They behave like beggars, stuff away food like hamsters, stare like he-goats, and walk around like castrated pigs. When superior men laugh at them, they reply angrily, 'What do you fools know about good Confucians?'[14]

Mo Tzu was born within a few years of the death of Confucius, and for two centuries his theories provided the leading rival philosophy. Puritanical, utilitarian, and advocating a frugal and dedicated life, Mo Tzu was particularly outraged by the aestheticism of the Confucians and their willingness to indulge in empty form and ceremony, such as the evident waste of time in spending three years in mourning as a sign of respect to a dead parent. Above all he was against any form of humbug:

> When a parent dies, the Confucians lay out the corpse for a long time before dressing it for burial while they climb up onto the roof, peer down the well, poke in the ratholes, and search in the washbasins, looking for the dead man. If they suppose that they will really find the dead man there, then they must be stupid indeed, while if they know that he is not there but still search for him, then they are guilty of the greatest hypocrisy.[15]

The very zest of the prose in which Mo Tzu's thoughts have been handed down, combined with his concern for the practical problems of poverty, give the writings of his school a surprisingly modern ring when quoted in short extracts (longer passages are less impressive, for argument tends to get lost in litany). The following, for example, seems refreshingly down-to-earth after the more generalized commonsense of Confucius:

> There are three things the people worry about: that when they are hungry they will have no food, when they are cold they will have no clothing, and when they are weary they will have no rest. These are the three great worries of the people. Now let us try sounding the great bells, striking the rolling drums, strumming the zithers, blowing the pipes and waving the shields and axes in the war dance. Does this do anything to provide food and clothing for the people? I hardly think so.[16]

The followers of Mo Tzu also looked back, like Confucius, to a vanished Utopia, but in place of his benevolent hierarchy theirs was joyously egalitarian. Indeed their image of it is remarkably reminiscent of that collectivism from which Marx believed society had sprung and to which, in the higher form of communism, it would return:

> When the Great Tao prevailed, the whole world was one community. Men of talents and virtues were chosen [to lead the people]; their words were sincere and they cultivated harmony. Men treated the parents of others as their own. Competent provision was made for the aged until their death, work for the able-bodied, and education for the young. Kindness and compassion were shown to widows, orphans, childless men and those disabled by disease, so that all were looked after. Each man had his allotted work, and

every woman a home to go to. They disliked to throw valuable things away, but that did not mean that they treasured them up in private storehouses. They liked to exert their strength in labour, but that did not mean that they worked for private advantage. In this way selfish schemings were repressed and found no way to arise. Thieves, robbers and traitors did not show themselves, so the outer doors of the houses remained open and were never shut. This was the period of the Great Togetherness [*Ta Thung*].

But now the Great Tao is disused and eclipsed. The world [the empire] has become a family inheritance. Men love only their own parents and their own children. Valuable things and labour are used only for private advantage. Powerful men, imagining that inheritance of estates has always been the rule, fortify the walls of towns and villages and strengthen them by ditches and moats. 'Rites' and 'righteousness' are the thread upon which they hang the relations between ruler and minister, father and son, elder and younger brother, and husband and wife. In accordance with them they regulate consumption, distribute land and dwellings, raise up men of war and 'know-ledge'; achieving all for their own advantage. Thus selfish schemings are constantly taking their rise, and recourse is had to arms.[17]

Not surprisingly the Mohist phrase *Ta Thung* or the *Great Togetherness* is one which modern Communists in China have enthusiastically borrowed from their classical literature.

Unfortunately the Mohist's practical recommendations were almost as utopian as this picture of the distant past. They argued that if every person and each country would love each other like the members of one family (they had in mind a Chinese family), there would be no more strife. Their method of moving towards this new state of affairs was authoritarian whereas that of Confucius, to strain the modern term slightly, was liberal. They seem to have lived frugal and utterly dedicated lives in small communities over which the leader had powers even of life and death, almost like revolutionary cells within the community. They were advocating rapid change through a programme of total commitment, as opposed to the Confucian hope for gradual improvement through education, the spread of culture and the force of moral example. The more radical approach was understandably attractive at the period of greatest chaos, when the followers of Mo Tzu were at least as much in evidence as the Confucians. Once things became calmer, in the second century B.C., the modest demands of Confucianism were more appealing. The Mohists, with surprising suddenness, seemed to have vanished.

A much more influential philosophy in the long run was Taoism, which was to dominate the mind and soul of China, side by side with

Confucianism, for over 2000 years. Its traditional founder, Lao Tzu, is probably a mythical figure – or if he did exist nothing is known of him, much like that equally mysterious author described by Max Beerbohm as 'those incomparable poets, Homer'. Later Taoist writings report several instances of Lao Tzu meeting the slightly younger Confucius and invariably getting the better of him, but the very short work attributed to Lao Tzu, the *Tao te ching*, appears to be an anthology compiled not earlier than the fourth century B.C. What is beyond doubt is the enormous influence exercised by this little book, not only in China but throughout the world. At least 700 commentaries have been written on it over the centuries in Chinese, and some forty versions made in the English language alone.

Tao te ching means *The Way and its Power*. The way is the way of nature – to put it in a simple form which does less than justice to the deliberate elusiveness of this central Taoist concept – and the power is that of the man who gives up ambition and somehow surrenders his whole being to nature. It is an idea not far from the central theme of Buddhism (although the Taoists had no interest in eliminating sexual desire), and the very rapid success of the Indian religion when it arrived in China soon after the time of Christ was largely due to the Taoists' recognizing and welcoming it as a close relation. A favourite Taoist image was water, for this mysterious and elusive substance seemed to symbolize everything that they most admired. Indispensable to all forms of life, it modestly seeks out for itself the lowest available spot, seeming to wish to merge with the earth.

> The highest good is like that of water. The goodness of water is that it benefits the ten thousand creatures; yet itself does not scramble, but is content with the places that all men disdain. It is this that makes water so near to the Way.[18]

In the same way the *Tao te ching* describes the wise man who has adopted the virtues of water:

> He does not show himself, therefore he is seen everywhere.
> He does not define himself, therefore he is distinct.
> He does not boast of what he will do, therefore he succeeds.
>
> He is not proud of his work, and therefore it endures.
> He does not contend,
> And for that reason no one under heaven can contend with him.[19]

It is an attitude which has had an increasing appeal in recent years in the

West, and is of course the very opposite of the Confucian ideal by which the official, the equivalent of the 'organization man' in modern Western mythology, consciously tries to better himself through education and to rise to a position of power. One of the most cherished Taoist fantasies was that of introducing the pompous Confucian to the peculiar pleasures of humility. Chuang Tzu, the first important Taoist writer whose historical credentials are impeccable, has a pleasant passage in which a Confucian meets Lao Tzu at an inn and is profoundly influenced by him:

> When he [the official] first arrived at the inn, everyone in the place turned out to meet him. The keeper of the inn brought him a mat, the innkeeper's wife brought him towel and comb. His fellow-guests made way for him; the kitchen-men retreated from the stove. But when the time came for him to depart, so changed was he by Lao Tzu's lesson that people were already pushing him off his own mat.[20]

Confucianism and Taoism are both opposite and complementary. They represent town and country, the practical and the spiritual, the rational and the romantic. Educated Chinese throughout the dynasties very sensibly contrived to live by both. It has been well said that the Chinese official became a Taoist when the political situation in the capital made it wise for him to withdraw to the country, where he passed his time in painting and contemplation; and that he returned to the city a Confucian when the climate had changed and he could again expect a place in the government.

Although Confucianism and Taoism were to triumph in the long run, it was yet another radical system of thought that was to be the early winner in this race of the philosophies – the system variously described as Legalism or Realism. Its solution to the lawlessness of the times was a simple one – more and better enforced laws. Where other Chinese philosophies had relied on improving human nature, the Legalists took a cool look at the world and based their creed on the very imperfections of man. A good official might be more desirable than an evil official, this they were willing to concede, but there were never likely to be sufficient good officials to make any difference. Self-interest was the only factor in human life sufficiently constant to base a policy on.

In certain parts of the Legalist texts this extreme rationalism looks refreshingly modern. Han Fei Tzu writes in the third century B.C.:

> The carriage maker making carriages hopes that men will grow rich and eminent; the carpenter fashioning coffins hopes that men will die prematurely.

It is not that the carriage maker is kindhearted and the carpenter a knave. It is only that if men do not become rich and eminent, the carriages will never sell, and if men do not die, there will be no market for coffins. The carpenter has no feeling of hatred towards others; he merely stands to profit by their death.[21]

Carried to its ruthless conclusion, this frank recognition of the self-interest in man becomes less attractive. Greed and fear are identified as the two prime motives of human conduct, and the state must make use of this fact through a rigid system of rewards and penalties. Rewards will be given to those who fulfil precisely their allotted task; those who deviate from what they were ordered to do will be severely punished (and as so often in such systems, to do too much is as bad as to do too little, 'for the discrepancy is not atoned for by the additional work done'[22] – an extreme image of mass conformity). As to the proper balance between encouragement and threat, an early Legalist work, the *Book of Lord Shang*, leaves its readers in no doubt; 'one reward to nine punishments' is its constant refrain. Good government comes to mean nothing other than bringing benefit to the state, or – to personify the abstraction – benefit to the ruler. Among his subjects he requires only two types of people: peasants to provide the wealth of the state, and soldiers to guard it. There is no need of merchants, a parasitic class of whom the Chinese have always professed themselves suspicious, and there is no place for scholars; 'if the court is filled with men discoursing on the former kings and discussing benevolence and righteousness, the government cannot escape disorder.'[23] There is not even any justification for books or teachers, for the existing officials can pass on their knowledge to those below them. Thus a blueprint for a totalitarian state is arrived at, complete even with those neat equations so much loved by dictators: 'Punishment produces force, force produces strength, strength produces awe, awe produces virtue. Virtue has its origin in punishments',[24] proclaims the *Book of Lord Shang*.

Naturally this doctrine had considerable appeal for the rulers, and it was to them that most of the rival schools of philosophy had been addressing themselves. But it is perhaps significant that it was in the most culturally backward of the seven states that Legalism first took hold. Ch'in was a buffer state between the civilization in the northern plain of China and the nomads to the northwest, occupying the very same Wei valley from which the Chou had descended on the Shang and from which the Chou had themselves later been ousted by the same continuing pressure from wilder men on the periphery. Like the Chou, the Ch'in were at

first regarded by the Chinese at the centre as semi-barbarian – a concept which had nothing to do with race, for barbarians could become Chinese merely by adopting Chinese culture. It was in this respect that the Ch'in were backward. They had, for example, continued to indulge in human sacrifice long after the other states had given it up, and even as late as the fourth century B.C. their very existence as a Chinese state was officially disregarded. There were supposedly only Six States. Ch'in, the seventh and already one of the most powerful, took no part in the occasional conferences held by the Six.

In 361 B.C. a statesman by the name of Shang Yang travelled to the state of Ch'in to offer his philosophy of ruthless efficiency and his own services to put it into effect (it is on his ideas that the *Book of Lord Shang* is based). He received a warm welcome from the Ch'in ruler who, in the words of a scholar of the next dynasty, already 'cherished the idea of rolling the empire up like a mat, of lifting up the whole world in his arms and of tying up the four seas in a sack.'[25]

A century later the Ch'in appeared to do almost exactly that. They had been one of the first two states to learn from the nomads the art of fighting on horseback, instead of in the cumbersome Chou chariots, and from the beginning of the third century they inflicted a series of crushing defeats on their more civilized neighbours. In 256 B.C. they overran the tiny and feeble central state of Chou, ending with abrupt lack of courtesy the fiction that the kings of Chou were still the rulers of China. Then, in a sudden hectic decade, Ch'in annexed one by one its six rival states. For the first time, in 221 B.C., China was in effect – as opposed to pious myth – one single empire. 'The world', as a historian a little later put it, 'was finally united.'[26]

Those eight centuries had seen many social changes as well as the political and military ones. A passage from the book of Mo Tzu gives a picture of the various levels of society in their daily life in the fourth century B.C. The main difference from the time of the Shang and the early Chou is that the group immediately below the ruler is presented now not as a warrior-nobility but as a class of officials, though at this stage the majority of them would still owe their position to their birth:

> The rulers and ministers must appear at court early and retire late, hearing lawsuits and attending to affairs of government – this is their duty. The gentlemen must exhaust the strength of their limbs and employ to the fullest the wisdom of their minds, directing bureaus within the government and abroad, collecting taxes on the barriers and markets and on the resources of the hills,

forests, lakes and fish weirs, so that the granaries and treasuries will be full – this is their duty. The farmers must leave home early and return late, sowing seed, planting trees, and gathering large crops of vegetables and grain – this is their duty. Women must rise early and go to bed late, spinning, weaving, producing large quantities of hemp, silk and other fibres, and preparing cloth – this is their duty.[27]

The craftsmen and merchants are notably absent from Mo Tzu's puritanical world, but they too had their duty. Tomb excavations reveal that the ruling classes now lived in considerable style. The carriages used by officials, for example, must have been magnificent sights. Their bronze fittings were immaculately cast and were often inlaid with gold and silver, or decorated with precious stones. A silk canopy or a form of umbrella fluttered overhead. The woodwork was covered in lacquer, a material which had become extremely fashionable by the end of the dynasty and which figures largely in all the excavated tombs (its peculiar properties make it exceptionally durable when buried; in its natural form, as the resin of a tree, it is pliable and easily worked; it hardens not by drying out but by being submerged in water, after which it will even resist corrosion by acid). Jade, too, another substance with something of the quality of eternity, was reaching new heights of craftsmanship. The great expense of importing it from Khotan, far away in Central Asia, and the difficulty of carving it (it is too hard to be scratched even by steel) made it the most highly valued of all ornaments.

In the Shang and early Chou periods China had been technologically backward compared with some other parts of the world. Notwithstanding the great skill acquired by the Shang bronze-casters, bronze itself had arrived late in China (*c*. 2000 B.C.) and the same was to be true of iron (800–600 B.C.), but such excellent use was made of both metals that in certain respects the Chinese began to pull ahead of the West. Iron was both cast and forged, for example, in the late Chou period, whereas in the West it was almost exclusively worked in the forge until the fourteenth century A.D. Similarly, the crossbow was invented in China – with a most delicately cast trigger-mechanism in bronze – some thirteen centuries earlier than its introduction in Europe. In major engineering works, too, the achievements of the period were considerable. Several of the warring states built massive walls as a defence against the barbarians or each other (it was three of these that were joined up by the Ch'in emperor to form the first Great Wall), and there is still functioning today in Szechuan a magnificent irrigation project of the third century B.C., in which a gorge

was cut some forty metres deep in rock, and a river diverted through it to flow in a system of canals and locks over 10,000 square kilometres.

The man who in 221 B.C. established the first empire had succeeded to the throne of Ch'in as a young man in 246. With the experience of a quarter of a century of autocratic rule behind him – and with the help of a chief minister, Li Ssu, who was one of the most able of the Legalists – he set about a drastic reorganization of the Chinese world. The most powerful families from all the states were herded together to his capital (a figure of 120,000 families was recorded), where they were appeased with honorary titles and were encouraged, presumably as an antidote to homesickness, to build in the suburbs exact replicas of the palaces they had left behind. All private weapons were collected and melted down. In place of the traditional structure of a new regime, with territories given on a feudal basis to faithful relations and followers, the full Legalist concept of a state was established, by which both the civil and military administrations were to be run on centralized lines. Out of the various suggestions for his own title put to him by his advisers, the new ruler chose Shih Huang Ti, meaning First Sovereign Emperor. He was confident, with his police state to back him up, that he was to be the first in a line of Sovereign Emperors reaching 'unto one thousand and ten thousand generations'.[28] In the event, it was to stretch to about two and a half.

A section of the Great Wall north of Peking, much altered and restored in later dynasties

The actions for which later Chinese historians most execrated the memory of Shih Huang Ti were the notorious Burning of the Books and the reported killing, a year later, of 460 Confucian scholars. Those of them who had read the Legalist texts should have been forewarned. Other schools of philosophy might conduct their bickering in brilliant flights of abuse or elaborately structured argument. The Legalists were of the type to turn plain words into effective action. Their leading philosopher, Han Fei Tzu, had included scholars along with merchants and artisans under his heading of the Five Vermin, proclaiming that 'in the state of an enlightened ruler there are no books written on bamboo slips; law supplies the only instruction.'[29] In 213 B.C. the order went out that all those in possession of books should destroy them within a month, on pain of branding and forced labour. The object was, as a historian of the next dynasty noted, 'for the purpose of making the people ignorant, and of bringing it about that none within the empire should use the past to discredit the present'.[30] The utilitarian nature of the exercise was underlined by the three classes of books, all supposedly practical, that were exempt – those on medicine, agriculture and divination.

Other practical reforms were put into effect, all in the same pursuit of efficiency (one of the main objections to scholars had been that they were liable to 'cause the ruler to be of two minds'.[31] An attempt was made to standardize the system of weights and measures. A thoroughgoing system of compulsory labour was introduced, by which peasants had to work for a month at a time on public projects (the administration of this scheme, and the census returns required for it, led to the working classes at last being given surnames). And, in one of the most often quoted reforms, the emperor insisted on a uniform width of axle for all carts and carriages. This is invariably explained as being a sensible measure because of the nature of the roads in north China, which are unusually liable to develop deep ruts. But the explanation is hardly adequate. If all carts can travel in the same rut, sooner or later they will come to rest on their axles. Perhaps the intention was to pave just two narrow strips of the main roads, at the appropriate distance apart. But it seems possible that another darker reason was behind the obsession with standardization, and one that contributed to the rapid collapse of the new dynasty.

The emperor was intensely superstitious, and he fell more and more under the influence of various schools of popular magic. One, deriving possibly from the early Chou period but not formalized into a single system of thought until the emperor's own century, held that five ele-

ments controlled the universe, namely earth, wood, metal, fire and water. Like the children's game with paper, stone, and scissors, each of these could subdue one of the others and was itself vulnerable to another. Fire melts metal, water puts out fire, earth soaks up water and so forth. The sequence of conquering is eternally fixed by the nature of the elements, and as the symbol of the Chou dynasty was thought to be fire those who had succeeded in overcoming it must themselves be represented by water. As in any such scheme of superstition, other symbols soon became attached to the original five elements. Thus the colour of water was black, so the emperor insisted on black flags and black clothing. In the same way its number was six. Officials' hats had to measure six inches, chariots have six horses. And, in keeping with this process of standardization too, the length of axles had to be six feet.

If the axle length was one result of the emperor's superstition, it was far from being the most disturbing. Another very popular form of magic, now and for many centuries to follow, was the whole range of alchemy which had attached itself to the more purely mystical philosophy of early Taoism. The Way of the Taoists had been a method of transcending life, of getting in touch with some form of eternity beyond life. Among their humdrum successors this ideal often became lost in the more common quest for eternal life itself, and as in any search for the elixir the charlatans often had the upper hand. Their advice to the emperor was that he would stand more chance of living for ever if neither the evil spirits nor his subjects knew where he was at any one time. This advice no doubt struck a pleasing chord, quite apart from being a sensible precaution against assassination, for it chimed with the Legalist idea that the ruler should live far removed from everyday matters, leaving the running of affairs to his officials. Their necessary fear of him would be increased by this remoteness, and sharpened yet further by his habit of suddenly striking them down from afar if they once put a foot wrong: 'Hide your tracks, conceal your sources, so that your subordinates cannot trace the springs of your actions. . . . The enlightened ruler reposes in non-action above, and below his ministers tremble with fear.'[32]

So the emperor set about the construction of a vast complex of palaces, all linked by covered roads so that no outsider should know in which of them he was to be found. The murder of the 460 scholars was said to be a reprisal for the leaking, on one occasion, of this vital information.

The emperor's actions may suggest a certain lack of mental stability, but he was a sufficiently powerful figure to hold his empire together

during his own lifetime. In spite of three assassination attempts he died, in 210 B.C., from natural causes – or for lack of the elixir. He was as paranoid in death as he had been in life. He was accompanied into his massive tomb not only by a vast number of concubines, but also by the workmen who had constructed it – so that none should know its secret ways, which included crossbows permanently cocked to rain their arrows on any intruder.

After Shih Huang Ti's death his empire crumbled. Only four years of his eternal dynasty remained, during which the chief minister, Li Ssu, engineered the suicide of the heir apparent and placed his own protégé on the throne as Second Emperor. Almost immediately Li Ssu was himself done away with by the chief of the palace eunuchs, and soon the Second Emperor too had been destroyed by someone else proclaiming himself the third. By 206 B.C. the Ch'in empire had been swept away, and China was in the turmoil of a civil war. From it would emerge a dynasty capable of sustaining itself for four centuries, that of the Han.

In those last four years, when in desperation the laws were being made ever more severe, it was said that 'persons who had suffered corporal punishment made up half of those to be seen on the roads, and the men who died daily formed a heap in the market-place.'[33] The scale of five standard punishments was, in ascending order of severity, the branding of the forehead, the cutting off of the nose, the cutting off of the feet, castration and death. This same scale had been in existence before the Ch'in, but they made unprecedentedly wide use of it.

It is significant that the three most distinguished statesmen or authors whose names are linked with the Legalist philosophy themselves all met violent deaths. Shang Yang, who founded the real power of Ch'in by his reforms as chief minister in the fourth century, ended by offending the king and was torn apart by chariots. The other two, Han Fei Tzu and Li Ssu, had in their youth studied together at the feet of the Confucian teacher Hsün Tzu, but this did not prevent Li Ssu manœuvring his fellow student into a position where he felt it wisest to swallow the poison which Li Ssu thoughtfully provided. And Li Ssu himself, after his long reign as adviser to the First Emperor, seems to have died by suffering each of the first four punishments in turn until, without his nose, feet, or genitals, he was finally flogged and then cut in two at the waist. After this his parents, brothers, wife and children were executed, in accordance with the principle which the Legalists had themselves introduced, that a whole family was collectively responsible for the guilt of any one of its members. It

Bronze vessel lid with ornamentation of a bird, early Chou

was largely the violent philosophy of the Legalists which both gave the Ch'in dynasty its beginnings and brought it to its violent end.

Throughout the rest of history Legalism, even in the broadest sense of too much reliance on any codified system of laws, had a bad name in China – though certain emperors calling themselves Confucians would not be averse to applying a few principles more apparently Legalist in tone. But even if the Ch'in dynasty itself had disappeared, the unified empire which it established was to remain at all future times an ideal, and in most periods also an established fact. And it was this small aggressive northwestern state and its short-lived dynasty which was to provide the rest of the world with its name for the entire subcontinent – China.

周

Pottery figure of a woman, an attendant in a Ch'in dynasty tomb, c. 210 B.C.

Chapter 3

HAN

汉

WITH THE ARRIVAL OF THE HAN DYNASTY THE BONES OF HISTORY GET more flesh on them, entirely thanks to one man – Ssu-ma Ch'ien. Born in about 140 B.C. he was descended from a long line of court historians and astrologers. He inherited the position of Grand Historian from his father, and with it, he says, some work in progress – an undertaking which was to run eventually to 130 chapters and well over half a million characters. His sharing of the credit with his father seems to have been a conventional case of filial piety – one of the foremost Confucian virtues – for the work was almost entirely Ssu-ma Ch'ien's own. His book is nothing less than a one-man account of the history of the entire known world.

It was finished in most difficult circumstances. Ssu-ma Ch'ien lived in the reign of a Han emperor, Wu Ti, who was almost as brutally auto-cratic as the first Ch'in emperor a century before. One day Ssu-ma Ch'ien was rash enough to speak in defence of a general who had dis-pleased the emperor. For this error of tact he was sentenced to castration. Under the accepted code of behaviour this amounted to death, for a gentleman was expected to commit suicide rather than submit to such an indignity. Honourable suicide, sometimes even of whole families, figures prominently in the annals of classical China, and it was a code which contributed to the later Japanese ritual of *hara-kiri*. But Ssu-ma Ch'ien decided that it was more important for him to be able to complete his history, even though he should live from now on a shameful existence as 'a remnant of the knife and saw'. He explained his decision in a letter to a friend:

> A man has only one death. That death may be as weighty as Mount T'ai, or it may be as light as a goose feather. It all depends upon the way he uses it. . . .
>
> Yet the brave man does not necessarily die for honour, while even the coward may fulfil his duty. Each takes a different way to exert himself. . . . If even the lowest slave and scullion maid can bear to commit suicide, why should not one like myself be able to do what has to be done? But the reason I have not refused to bear these ills and have continued to live, dwelling in vileness and disgrace without taking my leave, is that I grieve that I have things in my heart which I have not been able to express fully, and I am ashamed to think that after I am gone my writings will not be known to posterity. . . .
>
> I have examined the deeds and events of the past and investigated the principles behind their success and failure, their rise and decay, in one hundred and thirty chapters. I wished to examine into all that concerns heaven and man, to penetrate the changes of the past and present, completing all as the work of one family. But before I had finished my rough manuscript, I met

with this calamity. It is because I regretted that it had not been completed that I submitted to the extreme penalty without rancour. When I have truly completed this work, I shall deposit it in the Famous Mountain archives. If it may be handed down to men who will appreciate it, and penetrate to the villages and great cities, then though I should suffer a thousand mutilations, what regret should I have?[1]

His great work did indeed penetrate to the villages and great cities. It had been a private undertaking, within the family, so the book was unknown until Ssu-ma Ch'ien's grandson began to circulate the manuscript. Its merits were immediately recognized, and about a century after the historian's death his descendant was given the hereditary title Viscount Master of History.

Ssu-ma Ch'ien's solution to the problems of historical narrative was a highly original one. He arranged his material in five separate but complementary sections. The first was the annals of the ruling dynasties, and it was here that he recorded with such accuracy the names of the Shang kings. It is not known what sources he had for this information. A chapter in the book of Mo Tzu had said that the way of knowing the past is through 'what is written on the bamboo and silk that has been handed down to posterity, what is engraved on metal and stone, and what is inscribed on bowls and basins',[2] and Ssu-ma Ch'ien may well have inherited records on bamboo and silk from within his own family of historians.

Other sections of his work include a series of chronological tables and graphs, treatises on separate topics such as the calendar, ritual or economics, histories of the different states, and finally the section that interested him most – biographies of all types of influential people, whether generals, good or bad officials, self-made men among the merchants or even the homosexual favourites who had been able to influence the emperors. Although his method would later be varied, the ambitious scope of Ssu-ma Ch'ien's history was to set a historical standard throughout all the remaining dynasties. Every period from the Han to 1911 was fully documented in the series which became known as the Standard Histories, a complete span of historical record unrivalled in any part of the world. In later centuries there was a government department responsible for keeping a day-to-day account of the present dynasty while writing the official history of the previous one. The last of the series, dealing with the Ch'ing dynasty, was published as recently as 1961 in Taiwan. But there were certain disadvantages in treating history as a branch of bureaucracy. The dynasties of China seem to lack the rounded characters who enliven

the histories of other nations – partly perhaps because of the traditional limitations of a committee in any form of creative work, but also because there was nothing a Chinese bureaucrat so much enjoyed writing about as another Chinese bureaucrat. Never again was Ssu-ma Ch'ien's lively and very personal example to be matched.

His technique in his many short biographies was almost that of a novelist. Not only did he use dialogue to dramatize the inherent clash within a situation (an extreme example is the interchange between the emperor and a rebel on the field of battle: 'Spying Ch'ing Pu in the distance, the emperor shouted to him, "What is your grievance that you revolt against me?" "I want to be emperor, that is all", Ch'ing Pu shouted back'[3]), but he also allowed his separate biographies to picture the same piece of history from different angles, according to the way in which his central character of the moment was affected. The result, when his book draws near to his own lifetime, is a most vivid account of the first century of the Han dynasty, from its beginnings in the widespread rebellion against Ch'in tyranny.

The flash-point came when a group of peasants, selected for a spell of compulsory military service, were made late in reporting for duty by heavy rain and impassable roads. In accordance with the principles of the Ch'in reign of terror, the penalty for this minor infringement was death for at least the two leaders of the party. Recognizing that they had nothing to lose, they decided on rebellion. They were not above a little hocus-pocus to encourage their fellows to join them. One of the two leaders was called Ch'en She, and the message 'Ch'en She shall be a king' was written on a piece of silk and stuffed into the belly of a fish which one of their party had recently caught in a net. The message survived the boiling of the fish, and when it was discovered during the meal had a most excellent effect.

Even if Ssu-ma Ch'ien's account sounds lightly fictionalized, the gist of it is true. The civil war which resulted from Ch'en She's rebellion rapidly swept away the Ch'in dynasty. After several years of turmoil another man of peasant origin, known later as Kao Tsu or Exalted Ancestor, emerged as the dominant survivor and founder of the new Han dynasty.

Kao Tsu 'had a prominent nose and a dragon-like face with beautiful whiskers on his chin and cheeks; on his left thigh he had seventy-two black moles'[4] (a fortunate sign, surprisingly). He was a man of few social graces with, in his early years, little liking for learned men. Indeed the

conventional image for his attitude to scholarship became the one put by Ssu-ma Ch'ien into the mouth of one of his followers: 'Whenever a visitor wearing a Confucian hat comes to see him, he immediately snatches the hat from the visitor's head and pisses in it.'⁵ The colleagues who came to power with him were equally rough. Until now each new dynasty, however barbarian in origin, had been headed by the princely families of the conquering state. Kao Tsu himself had been a minor village official and even for a while a bandit before the civil war, and his immediate circle of followers included several farmers, a dog butcher and an undertaker. But there was no element of class warfare in the attitudes of the new dynasty. Its motive had been a straightforward wish for power. To retain his position Kao Tsu was forced to return in some measure to the older system of feudalism which the centralized Ch'in state had abolished, and he rewarded his relations and his followers with fiefs, much as had the founder of the Chou dynasty some 800 years before. As a result there was half a century of instability, with constant threats from the more powerful vassals. The Han rulers succeeded, however, in asserting their authority and by 154 B.C. the dynasty was secure. By the end of the century they had included within their empire part of Vietnam in the south, part of Korea in the northeast, and in the northwest a long thin tongue of land just above the line of the Himalayas and Tibet which would soon make possible the movement of the precious caravans along the Silk Road. One intrepid Chinese general even led an army as far west as the valley of Ferghana, returning with 3000 of the fine horses for which the district was famous. He was then only 200 miles short of Samarkand which Alexander the Great, after travelling much the same distance from the opposite direction, had captured two centuries before.

Another reason for the instability of the opening decades of the dynasty was the unscrupulous scheming of the first emperor's wife. The Empress Lü was even more rough and dangerous than her husband. Although rather higher born than him, she had shared his village life and had helped him throughout the long struggle to the throne. It was natural that she should have great influence in the new regime. But her position as empress was far from assured. Her struggles to maintain that position provide a fascinating insight into palace life in early imperial China.

This was a society in which a man kept as many women as he could afford. Within the household there was a principal wife, but in royal circles her position could be precarious. The empress was merely the mother of whichever prince was designated heir apparent. If for reasons of

death or disfavour the position of heir to the throne changed hands, so too did that of empress.

At the start of the Han dynasty the eldest son of Lady Lü was announced as the heir, and so she became Empress Lü. But her charms were fading – to judge from her later career they can never have been her strongest point – and soon Kao Tsu wanted to change the succession in favour of the son of his new favourite, Lady Ch'i. For several years he was on the verge of doing so, against the wishes of most of his advisers, while the empress struggled to stave off disaster. During Kao Tsu's lifetime she fought with the conventional methods of palace intrigue, enlisting the support of different factions and persuading learned men to urge her case – they would be summoned to the palace and she would brief them from behind a screen. She achieved her aim. Kao Tsu died in 195 B.C. with the succession unchanged.

After his death the empress had no further need of polite methods. Lady Ch'i's son was poisoned, and any girl within the royal household of whom Kao Tsu had been unusually fond was killed. The fate of Lady Ch'i herself was particularly gruesome. For convenience in removing the night-soil, a privy at this time consisted of a small room set above the pigsty (diagrams of Chinese houses in the 1940s show the pigsty and the toilet still side by side at the back). According to Ssu-ma Ch'ien, the empress cut off Lady Ch'i's hands and feet, gouged out her eyes, burned her ears, gave her a potion which made her dumb, then threw her into the lower part of the privy and brought visitors to see the 'human pig',[6] a phrase which became a part of Chinese literary tradition. Obviously legend has considerably embroidered the facts, but there is no reason to doubt that the empress's revenge was correspondingly brutal. The power of an empress dowager, once her son was safely on the throne, was greater than that of an empress – partly because nothing short of a change of dynasty could now rob her of her position, but also because the respect due in a Chinese family to an aged parent gave her wishes a very special force in the emperor's court.

For seven years the Empress Lü ruled virtually as regent for her weak and sickly son (his character had been one of Lady Ch'i's more statesman-like arguments) and for another eight years, after his death in 188 B.C., she herself openly directed the state, keeping a boy-emperor out of sight in the private apartments of the palace until, at her convenience, she murdered him and replaced him with another even younger. Meanwhile she was granting large feudal territories to members of her own clan of Lü,

frequently after killing the previous hereditary families to make room for them. By the time of her death in 180 B.C. it was clear that the sons of Kao Tsu by his other wives could only retain his empire by defeating the relations of his empress. They did so, annihilating the leaders of her clan, and the emperor's fourth son ascended the throne to inaugurate the period of increasing Han stability.

Fortunately these melodramatic highlights are not the only details of palace life which survive from this period. The word harem is the most convenient one available for a large number of wives or concubines kept in seclusion by one man, but the Chinese harem shows marked differences from the Muslim pattern. There was at this time, for example, far less emphasis on the purity of the women, or even indeed on their virginity. The absolute sanctity of a Muslim harem, together with the veil and all

63

the other elaborate precautions of *purdah*, was designed to preserve the precious purity of the women from even the glance of another man. The Chinese arrangement seems more of a safe place in which to keep one's pretty possessions. Thus, for example, when a Han emperor gave a banquet or picnic in company with his empress or a leading concubine, other men were sometimes present,[7] and a homosexual favourite of Wu Ti was given *carte blanche* to move around in the private apartments of the palace. This was not because he was thought to be as harmless as a eunuch – or if it was, the illusion was soon shattered when one of the girls was found to be pregnant. The empress dowager's outrage was such that she was able to secure the man's death, but in a Muslim palace the freedom granted him would have been unthinkable. This same empress dowager, the mother of Wu Ti, had reached her exalted position by a devious route which would have been emphatically closed to an honourable girl in Islam. She had already been married into an ordinary family when her parents learned from a diviner that the omens promised her a great future. Realizing their mistake, they removed her with considerable difficulty from her new family, who were perfectly satisfied with the girl, and then placed her, lacking even the pretence of virginity, in the household of the heir apparent as one of his concubines. If Ssu-ma Ch'ien is to be believed, she had the wit when first pregnant with the prince's child to have a dream in which the sun entered her breast. The heir apparent was delighted ('This is a sign of great honour,'[8] he told her) but, even so, when he came to the throne, he chose the child of another woman as his heir. Only by dint of long scheming, more skilfully carried out than that of Lady Ch'i, did the future empress dowager have the choice altered in favour of her own infant.

With bureaucratic thoroughness, the steps by which a concubine could climb the ladder of the emperor's affection were all neatly numbered and named. There were fourteen ranks in all, ranging from plain Beauty at the lowest level to Brilliant Companion and Favourite Beauty in the top two ranks. The girls lived in graded halls with names as romantic as their own titles. Brilliant Companions, for example, dwelt in the Sun-bright Residence, while Favourite Beauties, with still one rank above them to attain, lived appropriately enough in the Residence of Increasing Perfection.[9]

Harems were not restricted to the royal family, though no doubt it was only in the palace that they were so efficiently graded. Ssu-ma Ch'ien writes of one high official, a man of magnificent physique, who kept vast

Bronze figure of a galloping horse, with its hoof on a flying swallow, 2nd century A.D.
OVERLEAF *Bronze model of a Han dynasty official in his carriage, with attendant, 2nd century* A.D.

numbers of concubines and lived to be over a hundred, by which time he 'had not a single tooth in his mouth, but lived on milk, employing a young woman as a wet nurse'.[10]

Life was no doubt as steamy and indolent in a Chinese harem as in any other, but it is given in retrospect a special fragrance and delight by the Chinese love of exotic names. A short story written in the Han period, and based on a real event, tells of the love of an emperor for a pair of beautiful sisters, the elder of whom he sees first and makes his empress. Then he hears that the younger is even more beautiful and summons her to his presence;

> Before she met the Emperor she first bathed herself, anointed herself with the Nine Bends of the River Diving-water Perfume, loosened her hair in the so-called New Hair Style, painted her eyebrows thinly in the Distant Mountain Range Style, and applied a little rouge with the powder Nonchalant Approach. She was dressed in a short traditional costume with embroidered skirt, shortened sleeves, and matching stockings that were decorated with plum-blossom patterns.[11]

The empress tried to fight back by sprinkling herself with the Hundred-Ingredients Perfume of the Heavenly Spirits who Descended in the Rain Shower. But, in the way of such stories, simple beauty won through, unscrupulously changing the rules of the game on the way. While the empress was trying to cap her younger sister in the matter of elaborate perfumes, her sister 'bathed merely in nutmeg water and powdered herself with pollen powder'. The emperor was later overheard to comment to a friend that 'while the empress, it is true, exudes an exotic fragrance, nothing can be compared with the natural scent that emanates from Ho-teh's body.'

One further example can complete this picture of the palace women as pampered chattels, as well as introducing another palace group equally important in Chinese history. The second Han empress, born of a good family, had been sent as a girl to be lady-in-waiting to the Empress Lü. One day Empress Lü decided to make a gift to various provincial kings (the higher of the two feudal titles conferred during the Han dynasty, the other of which is usually translated as marquis). Each of the kings was to receive five girls, and one of those selected was the future empress. A eunuch was put in charge of making up the lists of who should go where. She begged him to put her down for the court of Chao, where she would be near her own family;

A painted pottery vase or hu *from the Western Han period*

. . . but the eunuch forgot and by mistake entered her name on the list for the court of Tai. The lists were then presented to the throne and received imperial approval. When the time came to depart she was furious with the eunuch and, weeping bitterly, refused to go. Only after considerable urging was she persuaded to start on her way.[12]

She pleased the King of Tai, bearing him two sons, and it was he who was made emperor after the death of the Empress Lü. Thus, through an accident, the girl became the wife of one emperor and the mother of another. Of course Ssu-ma Ch'ien is dramatizing in his usual way when he introduces the eunuch's forgotten promise and the tears, but he would not have told the story if the central fact had not struck him as true – that a high-born girl could be sent as a gift to a stranger regardless of her wishes and at the whim of a eunuch official.

Every culture based on the harem has used eunuchs, but they achieved even more power in China than elsewhere. The freedom to approach a ruler within the privacy of his own quarters provides an obvious source of influence (the rise of the eunuchs in China has been rather aptly compared with that of the Lord Chamberlain in Britain), and emperors were often inclined to trust eunuchs more than other men for one very good reason – that there was no danger of their siring a rival dynasty. From the point of view of the eunuchs themselves, their very disability, that shared lack which made them an object of scorn, was in some ways also a political strength. A small party, membership of which is both evident and irreversible, united by the rejection of others, undistracted by family ties, by the demands of children, or even, presumably, the lures of the flesh, and blessed with exclusive entrée to every corridor of power – as qualifications for a self-interested pressure group these can hardly be improved upon. The Masons, in comparison with eunuchs, are but babes in the wood.

The natural enemies of the eunuchs were the only other group not born into power but given now a chance of achieving it – the bureaucrats, who during the Han dynasty came to be increasingly synonymous with the Confucians. Scholar-officials who had won their position through ability resented, not surprisingly, those whose only qualification was their disability. Moreover they could argue that this disability was often linked with a criminal record, for although most eunuchs had been sold by their impoverished families as children, some of the most powerful were men who had been castrated in adult life as a punishment.

The high point of the eunuchs' power in the Han dynasty came towards the end and partly led to that end. Between A.D. 168 and 170 they were

powerful enough to conduct a great purge of their Confucian opponents, killing, it was said, thousands of officials. (They, in their turn, were extensively slaughtered in 189.) They were even able, in this last century of the dynasty, to negate one crucial part of their usefulness to the emperor, for they won permission to found families by adoption, thus making their wealth and at least part of their power hereditary. It was a descendant of one such adopted son who gave the *coup de grâce* to the ailing Han dynasty in A.D. 220, setting up one of the three smaller dynasties which between them divided up the empire.

The rise of the Confucians had been a steady one throughout the first two centuries of the Han dynasty. Kao Tsu overcame his aversion to them sufficiently to commission a Confucian work on the principles of good government, which still survives, and he and several of his successors did to a certain extent honour those principles and attempt to rule with reason and benevolence. The actual moment of the scholars' achieving real power is usually placed during the long reign of Wu Ti (the 'Martial Emperor', 141–87 B.C.), the most powerful of all the Han monarchs and the one under whom the empire achieved its greatest expansion. That he should be credited with the patronage of Confucianism is paradoxical, for he was among the least Confucian of emperors, ruling with a barefaced autocracy which in some ways outdid even the hated Legalism – the severity of his measures being based not so much on the abstract demands of a severe code of laws as on his own unpredictable whims.

It is true that many apparent milestones in the establishment of Confucianism fell within Wu Ti's reign – the banning from court of scholars trained in other disciplines (in particular the Legalists), the establishment of the Imperial Academy for the study of the master's supposed works, and the increasing use of examinations to seek out, as Confucius had recommended, the best available new talents. But one incident will suggest Wu Ti's real attitude to these innovations.

In 130 B.C. one of the examination candidates wrote an answer relying heavily on Legalist concepts, emphasizing the importance of an effective system of punishments and rewards. The examiners marked him bottom out of more than a hundred, but the emperor, looking through the papers, disagreed with them and awarded him top place. Within a few years the fortunate candidate was occupying the highest office in the government, and it was he who finally succeeded, where his less congenial predecessors had failed, in persuading the emperor to found an academy which would give training and employment to faithful Confucians.

Thus the emperor contrived to employ many of the ruthlessly efficient methods of Legalism while sweetening them with the name of Confucius, a method notably more subtle than that of the first Ch'in emperor with whom he had much in common. Like him, he was domineering, wilful, hysterically allergic to criticism but capable of injecting huge expansive energies into his followers. Like him, he was child-like in his willingness to believe any wandering magician who would promise him the elixir of eternal life. Like him, he relied heavily on harsh punishments – boiling alive was particularly favoured, on occasion being carried out in the emperor's presence – and to Shih Huang Ti's law of collective responsibility he added the concept that anyone who failed to report a criminal was as guilty as the first offender. What was established in his reign was not so much Confucianism as officialdom; not so much the ideal of fearless advisers guiding a selfless and attentive ruler, as the machinery for a self-perpetuating and potentially stifling bureaucracy; not so much the free play of well-stocked minds, which was what Confucius seems to have understood by scholarship, as a pedantic obsession with detail which was over the centuries to characterize the worst of the mandarins.

The Ch'in edict against the private possession of books had been rescinded in 195 B.C., but by now more had been lost than in that first holocaust of 213. Certain exceptions made at that time prove that the motive was not so much the destruction of learning as the presentation of it for the ruling clique alone. Those scholars most intimately connected with the government had been allowed to keep their books and, more important, a copy of every work had to be placed in the imperial library. The single most disastrous moment for the transmission of Chinese scholarship was the burning of this Ch'in imperial library when one of Kao Tsu's rivals in the civil war sacked and entirely destroyed the capital city.

It was the extreme shortage of surviving documents which gave such passion and excitement to the Han efforts to recover the classical literature of China. Old scholars who could remember long passages by heart were in great demand. There were romantic incidents of bamboo or silk manuscripts being recovered from the walls of houses, where their owners had hastily sealed them away before fleeing from the Ch'in soldiers. Many of these turned out to be forgeries, for an ancient document was a valuable possession. A family of scholars could live for generations by teaching the contents of one rare manuscript and by elaborating their own commentaries upon it. The leading historian of the Later Han

dynasty, for example, would never lend out the copy of Ssu-ma Ch'ien's work which he had inherited. It was his stock-in-trade.

Han scholarship was a turmoil of collation and reconstruction, in which many genuine passages were mingled with some forged for gain and with others written in a pious effort to plug gaps, and it was through this murky filter that the Chinese classics came down to later centuries. Each of these centuries added its own comments and emendations in an inexhaustible process of accretion. Modern attempts to separate the original from the gloss had a few honourable antecedents as far back as the Sung dynasty (960–1279), but only in recent times has much progress been made.

A parallel development, side by side with the growth of Confucian scholarship, was the worship – later to become almost the deification – of Confucius himself. He was given posthumously a title which had existed in his own time, usually translated as duke, and since it was improper that the ancestral shrine of such a great man should be tended by commoners, his descendants were granted the hereditary title of marquis. Ssu-ma Ch'ien himself made a pilgrimage to the place:

> When visiting Lu, I saw the carriages, robes and sacred vessels displayed at the Temple, and watched how the Confucian students studied the historical system at his home, and hung around, unable to tear myself away from the place. There have been many kings, emperors and great men in history, who enjoyed fame and honour while they lived and came to nothing at their death, while Confucius, who was but a common scholar clad in a cotton gown, became the acknowledged Master of scholars for over ten generations. All people in China who discuss the six arts, from the emperors, kings and princes down, regard the Master as the final authority.[13]

In the Later Han dynasty three of the emperors paid his shrine the honour of a personal visit, and in A.D. 59 it was ordered that sacrifices should be made to him in all government schools, thus establishing him officially as the patron saint of the scholar class. The regular ceremonies at his temple remained at this stage a purely family affair, in keeping with the principles of ancestor worship.

The periodical remembrance of an ancestor at his tomb was in effect a repetition of his funeral, and the basic form of the two ceremonies was the same. A young member of the family – a grandson of the deceased if the death was recent – was dressed up to impersonate the ancestor, wearing whatever was the highest rank of clothes he had been entitled to. It was to this child that the wine was offered, together with the cooked meat of the sacrificed animals. He tasted them and pronounced himself, on behalf

of the spirit, to be satisfied, after which the guests – other members of the family – could consume the rest of the food secure in the knowledge that their ancestor would continue to exert himself on their behalf. Ancestor worship was now indulged in by the official classes as well as the hereditary nobility, but they seem to have been eager to pull up the drawbridge behind them. 'He who eats by the labour of his hands', noted Hsün Tzu sternly, a few decades before the Han dynasty, 'is not permitted to set up an ancestral temple.'[14]

The early manuals spell out the details of the ritual with characteristic thoroughness:

> The assistants bring in pickled mallows and snails, the snail stew being on the north side,[15]

or

> The Grand Soup is set to the north of the pickled stew.[16]

The cooking was equally carefully regulated:

> When the meat is cooked, the left shoulder, upper and lower foreleg, thigh, lower hindleg, spine, ribs, divided lung, three pieces of pork for offering taken from over the breastbone, and one lung for offering, are placed in the top tripod; nine fish, pike and carp, are placed in the middle tripod; in the lowest is placed the game, the left half of the carcass only without the rump.[17]

The ceremony itself was like a more elaborate version of the European procedure with a loving cup, each person tasting the food or drink, bowing to another, and passing it on. Again, every tiniest detail is specified:

> A cook hands to the second guest a ladle with an engraved handle, and a stand which he has received from the west of the tripods, and the guest, grasping the left edge of the stand in his left hand, and holding the stand straight out from himself, takes the handle of the ladle with his right, palm inwards, and lays the ladle along the stand. He then goes and stands, facing east, to receive what is to be placed in it, at the west of the tripod of mutton.[18]

Once the spirit of the ancestor was satisfied, the occasion turned into a normal and relaxed family supper party. A poem about such an occasion, dating from before the time of Confucius, ends as follows:

> *The musicians go in and play,*
> *That after-blessings may be secured.*
> *Your viands are passed round;*

No one is discontented, all are happy;
They are drunk, they are sated.
Small and great all bow their heads;
'The Spirits', they say, 'enjoyed their drink and food
And will give our lord a long life.
He will be very favoured and blessed,
And because nothing was left undone,
By son's sons and grandson's grandsons
Shall his line for ever be continued.'[19]

The books of ritual also discussed what type of objects should be placed with the dead man in his tomb. The Shang nobles had believed that nothing but the best would do, so they had buried expensive bronze vessels for the spirit's household and ritual needs, real carriages for his transport, and – the ultimate in this uncompromising realism – living people for his servants. The Chou rulers gave up the human sacrifices, but continued to bury valuable objects. The *Li Chi* or *Book of Rites*, compiled during the Han dynasty, argues against this literal-minded extravagance on the ground that it shows a confusion between two different types of reality. It would be more appropriate, it says, that symbolic objects, mere representations of the real thing, should be specially made, and made in such a way that they are clearly not intended for use in the everyday sense. Pots should be left crude and unfinished, musical pipes should have no hole through which they can be played. It is in keeping with this new attitude that pottery figures of entertainers and attendants or bronze models of horse and chariot (colour, pages 66–7 and 87) now take the place of their living counterparts in the Shang burials. This substitution had begun in the Chou dynasty, and it would continue throughout most of Chinese history. Nearly all the famous T'ang pottery figures of horses, camels, grooms and servants were made specifically to accompany great men in their tombs.

The Han nobles were not willing to follow the scholars entirely on this matter. They added the pottery figures, but without excluding the objects of real value – to the great benefit of modern archaeology. There have been several astounding discoveries in the past few years in China, of which the most spectacular were two tombs cut deep into a hillside near Mancheng. One belonged to a brother of Wu Ti, and the other to his principal wife. Each tomb consisted of several interconnecting chambers, with even a room for bathing, and they contained in all nearly 3000 objects – bronze, gold, jade, silver, pottery, silk and lacquerware. Each

entire treasure house had been sealed with a solid iron wall, made by pouring molten metal between two layers of bricks.

The most magnificent of the contents were the two jade suits – by now already famous throughout the world. Each was composed of more than 2000 separate squares of jade, every one of them with four holes drilled in the corners to attach it with gold wire to its neighbours. The work involved was colossal, given the extraordinary hardness of jade, and in terms of their purpose these expensive garments were a complete failure. It was considered that jade contained a magical property of preserving bodies. In fact its very hardness and weight seem to have had precisely the opposite effect. In various other tombs bodies have been found which, although treated far more simply, have survived in an almost mummified state. Of Liu Sheng and his wife Tou Wan there remained, within their beautiful suits, nothing but dust.

There could hardly have been a more fortunate tomb to uncover from the point of view of demonstrating the Communist thesis, for no less an authority than Ssu-ma Ch'ien reveals that Liu Sheng, who had been given by his father the kingdom of Chung-shan, was as irresponsible as he was extravagant. Not only was he inordinately fond of wine and women. His theories of rule were blatantly opportunist:

> He was always criticizing his older brother, the king of Chao, saying, 'Although my brother is a king, he spends all his time doing the work of his own clerks and officials. A true king should pass his days listening to music and delighting

himself with beautiful sights and sounds.' The king of Chao replied with criticisms of his own, declaring, 'The king of Chung-shan fritters away his days in sensual gratification instead of assisting the Son of Heaven to bring order to the common people. How can someone like that be called a bastion of the throne?[20]

As a Chinese pamphlet puts it, describing the treasures immured with the king, 'the discovery of the two tombs reveals the feudal rulers' crimes of cruelly exploiting the people during their lifetime and dreaming of continuing to do so in another world.'

The treasures of Liu Sheng and his queen had been protected from robbers not by their walls of iron but by the invisibility of their tombs once the scars in the natural hillside had been long sealed and overgrown. The majority of their royal relations were buried underground with a great pile of pounded earth above them to dignify the spot. We should certainly not now have the treasure of Tutankhamun if he had been honoured with a pyramid. A poem written less than a century after the end of the Han dynasty tells of the fate of those eye-catching mounds in the period of chaos that followed:

> *At Pei-mang how they rise to Heaven,*
> *Those high mounds, four or five in the fields!*
> *What men lie buried under these tombs?*
> *All of them were Lords of the Han world.*
> *Kung and Wen gaze across at each other;*

The jade funeral suit of Tou Wan, wife of Liu Sheng, late 2nd century B.C.

The Yüan mound is all grown over with weeds.
When the dynasty was falling, tumult and disorder arose.
Thieves and robbers roamed like wild beasts.
Of earth they have crumbled more than one handful,
They have gone into vaults and opened the secret doors.
Jewelled scabbards lie twisted and defaced;
The stones that were set in them, thieves have carried away,
The ancestral temples are hummocks in the ground;
The walls that went round them are all levelled flat.
Over everything the tangled thorns are growing;
A herd-boy pushes through them up the path.
Down in the thorns rabbits have made their burrows;
The weeds and thistles will never be cleared away.
Over the tombs the ploughshare will be driven
And peasants will have their fields and orchards there.
They that were once lords of ten thousand chariots
Are now become the dust of the hills and ridges.[21]

Even so (such is the profusion of archaeological sites in China) other Han tombs in addition to those of Liu Sheng and his queen have survived to be opened in the past few years. It was one of these in Kansu, from the later part of the dynasty, which yielded the beautiful bronze horse (colour, page 65) – a creature of such airy speed, and so well suited to galloping in another world, that the artist has portrayed it with its hoof pressing down on a flying swallow.

One peculiarity of burials of the Han period is the pottery models of houses which were so often included in the tombs. From the most mundane structures, such as the privy over the pigsty, to neat little dwellings (colour, page 86) or towering painted edifices, they offer the best available indication of the architectural ideas of the time. Tombs have also produced the earliest surviving documents written on strips of bamboo and tied together with silken cords. They date from just before and during the Han dynasty, and are invariably inventories of the treasures contained in the tombs – written out with typical thoroughness, and intended presumably for the assistance of opposite numbers in the spiritual bureaucracy.

The range of objects found in these tombs, and the fact that Chinese silk was now on sale in the markets of Rome, demonstrate how greatly trade had by now developed. The reason is partly connected with that age-old problem, the threat from the nomadic tribes to the north and

northwest. During the early years of the Han dynasty one tribe in particular, the Hsiung-nu had emerged as the chief danger. They have often been identified with those other fierce nomads, the Huns, who some five centuries later would suddenly appear from the east to become the scourge of Europe. Certainly the Huns' devastating technique of warfare, as terrifying to the Goths as to the civilized Romans, was precisely that used with such effect by the Hsiung-nu against the Chinese – brilliant riding skills, combined with the use of a compound bow short enough to

Painted pottery model of a tower-house, Han

fire in any direction from horseback, even straight backwards over the animal's rump. Too little is known about where the Huns arrived from to identify them positively with the Hsiung-nu. But the latter were decidedly Hunnish.

For the first few decades of the Han dynasty the emperors attempted to buy peace from their troublesome neighbours with massive gifts of food and silk, and even occasionally with the hand in marriage of a princess from the royal household. For a girl used to a sheltered life

inside a Chinese palace, it must have seemed a terrible fate to wander on the steppes, sharing a felt tent with her wild chieftain and drinking the hated kumiss – a concoction of fermented mare's milk, nectar to the nomads but the ultimate symbol of barbarity in the minds of the Chinese, traditionally suspicious of even the mildest of dairy products. One of the most poignant of all Han poems is said to have been written by one such princess, who was sent in about 107 B.C. as a gift to a chieftain of a tribe living beyond the Hsiung-nu, with whom Wu Ti hoped for an alliance:

> *My people have married me*
> *In a far corner of Earth;*
> *Sent me away to a strange land,*
> *To the king of the Wu-sun.*
> *A tent is my house,*
> *Of felt are my walls;*
> *Raw flesh my food*
> *With mare's milk to drink.*
> *Always thinking of my own country,*
> *My heart sad within.*
> *Would I were a yellow stork*
> *And could fly to my old home!*[22]

By that time the policy of conciliating the Hsiung-nu had plainly failed, and Wu Ti was taking a more aggressive line. The expansion of the empire and its trade during his long reign was intimately connected with these undertakings. It is too simple to say that the opening of the Silk Road was a result of the campaigns to push back the Hsiung-nu, for a small amount of trade must for centuries have been coming along the narrow corridor between the mountains of Tibet and the Gobi desert. But undoubtedly the search for allies further afield expanded to an unprecedented degree the horizon of the Chinese and their attitude to foreign trade.

The most spectacular of these Chinese missions was also the earliest. In 138 B.C. Wu Ti, hearing that there were powerful tribes to the west of the Hsiung-nu in a state of almost constant warfare with them, sent an envoy on the dangerous mission of attempting to make contact. The man chosen was Chang Ch'ien, with whom Ssu-ma Ch'ien must certainly have been at least acquainted. He was, he says, 'a man of great strength, determination and generosity; he trusted others and in turn was liked by the barbarians.'[23] His party numbered about 100, of which the

most important member – the Passepartout to this early Phileas Fogg – was a former slave who had been born among the Hsiung-nu before being captured and put to work in a Chinese family. It must have seemed an alarmingly small and vulnerable little expedition that passed through Jade Gate, the frontier post at the western end of the Great Wall, beyond which the security of China gave way to the vast and inhospitable areas over which roamed the Hsiung-nu.

Nothing more was heard of them for thirteen years, and then the envoy suddenly reappeared. His retinue of 100 had long since dispersed. He was now alone, except for the faithful slave and a woman whom the Hsiung-nu had given him in marriage. His story created enormous interest. The Hsiung-nu had captured him as he attempted to cross their territory, and had detained him at their leader's court for the first ten of his thirteen years, during which he continued to insist on his dignity and status as an envoy of the Chinese emperor. He seems to have been well treated, and had a son by the wife with whom he was generously provided. At last, when his movements were less closely watched, he managed to slip away and continue his mission. He passed through Ferghana and eventually reached the northern part of Afghanistan, an area known to classicists as Bactria, into which the Hsiung-nu had recently pushed the most powerful of their western enemies. Chang Ch'ien may hardly have realized it, but his presence in this area was to be the first recognizable link between the two extremes of ancient civilization, China and the Mediterranean. The Bactrians, tucked away to the north of the Hindu Kush, had been an outpost of Greek culture ever since Alexander had passed so rapidly by, two centuries before. Their script, their coinage, their sculpture, their architecture, all were Greek.

The very decade of Chang Ch'ien's visit was one of crucial transition, with the nomadic horde known as the Yüeh-chih retreating westwards from the Hsiung-nu and pressing down upon these distant Greek colonials. So far the barbarians were content with tribute. Within a few years they would occupy the territory and put an end to the Greek rule.

This meeting-point of east and west seems more significant to us than it did to Chang Ch'ien. His own predominating emotion now that he had finally got so far was one of disappointment. The leader of the Yüeh-chih 'considered the Han too far away to bother with and had no particular intention of avenging his father's death by attacking the Hsiung-nu'.[24]

Chang-Ch'ien had once more to brave the territory of the Hsiung-nu,

to bring back to China the news that his embassy had failed in its main purpose, and once again they captured him. This time he managed to escape after only a year. The new information that he was able to produce about distant places and peoples more than compensated, in the opinion of the Chinese court, for the lack of any specific alliance. The emperor was so delighted that Chang Ch'ien was given high office and his assistant, the faithful slave, was even ennobled with the title 'Lord Who Carries Out His Mission'. One further result, notes Ssu-ma Ch'ien, was that in the years to come 'all the barbarians of the distant west craned their necks to the east and longed to catch a glimpse of China.'[25]

The single most startling piece of news was that in northern Afghanistan Chang Ch'ien had seen bamboo and cloth from the southwestern provinces of China. When he asked where these goods had been acquired, he was told that merchants found them in the markets of a large kingdom called Shen-tu to the southeast of Afghanistan. 'The region is said to be hot and damp. The inhabitants ride elephants when they go into battle. The kingdom is situated on a great river.'[26]

Chang Ch'ien then offered the emperor a piece of simple mathematical analysis. We know, he said, that Afghanistan is 4000 miles southwest of China; we now hear that the kingdom of Shen-tu is several thousand miles southeast of Afghanistan and has goods which are produced in China; 'it seems to me that it must not be very far away from China.' His geometry was excellent, even if his distances were somewhat inflated (a common enough fault among returning travellers). India is, as Chang Ch'ien calculated, quite close to China. The emperor sent an expedition to the southwest of Szechuan to try and find a route through. They were frustrated by the terrain and by the extreme ferocity of the tribes, but Chang Ch'ien's guess proved correct. It was discovered that certain merchants did occasionally make their way through to a kingdom in the west whose people rode elephants.

The first caravan to travel along the line of oases right through to Persia, without the goods changing hands on the way, left China in 106 B.C. From that time onwards the development of trade on the Silk Road was rapid. By the middle of the century before Christ the Romans had conquered Palestine, the natural end of the caravan route, and soon a special silk market was established in the Vicus Tuscus in Rome. During the childhood of Christ the Chinese instituted a policy of confiscating all privately held gold in exchange for bronze or copper (it has recently been calculated that by A.D. 23 the state had a hoard of some five million

ounces of gold). Soon the emperor Tiberius, whose reign if he had but known it included the Crucifixion, found it necessary to prohibit the wearing of silk, giving as the specific reason that there was too much of a drain on the empire's reserves of gold. So rapid, after the opening of the Silk Road, had been the establishment of an international economy.

China on the whole was less interested in the products of the West. The image of trade which crops up again and again in the pages of Ssu-ma Ch'ien is of distant places brimming with goods from China rather than the reverse. Horses and jade, the two imports by which the Chinese set most store, came from nearer regions – jade indeed from precisely those places along the Silk Road which the Chinese were now busy protecting from the nomads and gradually bringing within the empire itself. Ssu-ma Ch'ien includes these as internal products in the succulent account he gives of the present and virtually self-sufficient riches of the empire:

> The region west of the mountains is rich in timber, paper mulberry, hemp, oxtails for banner tassels, jade and other precious stones. That east of the mountains abounds in fish, salt, lacquer, silk, singers, and beautiful women. The area south of the Yangtze produces camphor wood, catalpa, ginger, cinnamon, gold, tin, lead ore, cinnabar, rhinoceros horns, tortoise shell, pearls of various shapes, and elephant tusks and hides, while that north of Lung-men and Chieh-shih is rich in horses, cattle, sheep, felt, furs, tendons, and horns. Mountains from which copper and iron can be extracted are found scattered here and there over thousands of miles of the empire, like chessmen on a board. In general, these are the products of the empire. All of them are commodities coveted by the people of China, who according to their various customs use them for their bedding, clothing, food, and drink, fashioning from them the goods needed to supply the living and bury the dead.[27]

In spite of the age-old Chinese hostility to merchants, as a species of parasite on the primary producers of wealth, Ssu-ma Ch'ien does describe the existence of a thriving and very varied community of traders, specializing in anything from slaves to pickles, and he ends his account of them, apparently without irony, with the comment: 'There are various other occupations which bring in less than twenty per cent profit, but they are not what I would call sources of wealth.' He has earlier made a statement about work and wealth which seems timeless in its application: 'When men have no wealth at all, they live by their brawn; when they have a little, they struggle to get ahead by their brains; and when they already have plenty of money, they look for an opportunity for a good investment. This in general is the way things work.'[28]

The capital city at the centre of all this expansionism was in that same rugged northwestern valley from which the Chou had once descended upon the Shang, and from which the first Ch'in emperor had emerged to subdue most of the subcontinent. The founder of the Han dynasty had himself come from the plains, but the long established advantages of this valley decided him to make his capital 'within the passes', as the phrase had it. The city itself, called Ch'ang-an, was almost exactly on the site of the previous Ch'in and Chou capitals.

It was aligned due north and south and was almost certainly constructed throughout on the geometric plan which was to remain typical of so many Chinese cities. Within the tall outer walls, the streets ran straight and parallel. The rectangles left between these streets, like blocks in an American city, were themselves surrounded by walls, each making a separate ward. In Ch'ang-an there were said to be 160 of these wards, and it is possible that here, as in many later cities, separate wards were often reserved for a particular trade or calling. Even the highest officials were expected to dismount from their carriages at the gateway into a ward. Thus the city consisted, in a manner very attractive to modern ideas of town-planning, of broad thoroughfares running between the wards and of little more than footpaths inside them. A less desirable aspect of the arrangement, but one which undoubtedly commended it to Chinese rulers, was that it greatly simplified the control of the population. In many periods of history nobody was allowed to visit outside his own ward after dark, and the curfew was enforced simply by closing the ward gates.

As in every other Chinese capital, the entrance to the royal palace was from the south so that the subject faced north as he approached his ruler. To face southwards denoted superiority, and only the emperor in any formal gathering looked in this direction. There were two exceptions. As a mark of respect, the emperor was expected to meet his teacher or any man famous for learning on an east-west axis (not for nothing were the scholars in charge of the ritual), and for obvious reasons he yielded in the sacrificial rites to the child who was impersonating the spirit of his ancestor.

The exact alignment of the city and of every major building within it not only reflected the importance of the points of the compass in all Chinese ceremonies; it must also in large measure have been what made those ceremonies possible. In a Chinese palace, north or south meant nothing more elaborate than facing towards or away from the door. Even in an ordinary house, in a rectilinear city, the same was usually

Detail of the jade burial suit of the queen Tou Wan. OVERLEAF *Han pottery tomb models of a house*
LEFT *and of a servant or merchant cleaning a fish*

true. So the constant mention of north, south, east or west in even the tiniest details of ritual was less confusing than it might sound. A European householder would be at a total loss if instructed to place the stew north of the pickles in his living-room. His counterpart in imperial China, and even perhaps in the geometric cities of modern America, would fail to see the problem.

The concern with north and south tied in with yet another Chinese system of thought, a form of dualism which had developed during the Chou dynasty and which was expressed in the two complementary principles of *yin* and *yang*. These were not harshly irreconcilable, like the good and evil of the Manicheans. They were more alternatives than opposites, and the alternation between them was the rhythm of nature. *Yang* was male, and *yin* female. By an extension which seems to derive as much from first-choice-to-the-men as from any more fundamental symbolism, *yang* was also light, heat, activity, life, cleanliness, the sun, day, delight, China and civilization; *yin* was left with darkness, cold, passivity, death, dirt, the moon, the night, melancholy, foreign people and barbarism. It may be argued that this division does spring naturally from the original meaning of the words *yang* and *yin*, which related to the sunny side and the dark side of a hill, but if so the feminist may inquire why the sunny side was allotted to the men. In fact the Chinese were not the only offenders. Far away in Greece, at much the same time, the Pythagoreans had devised a similar scale in which right, good, motion, light, square and straight were on the side of the gentlemen, leaving left, bad, rest, darkness, oblong and curved for the ladies.

The great strength of the Chinese system of *yin* and *yang* is that it can embrace all. Everything has its necessary place. The decline of the sun towards the triumph of *yin* at night is as much a proper part of the cycle as its rise to the apogee of *yang* at noon. The inroads made by the *yin* barbarians at certain periods are as natural as the expansion of the *yang* empire at others. Even the Confucian official, who normally represents the principle of *yang* in his city life of self-assertion, can validly replenish himself occasionally with the *yin* of Taoist inactivity in the countryside.

The traditional Chinese view of history consists of dynasties which rise and fall and according to a regular pattern. The Mandate of Heaven is given at the start of a dynasty to a worthy ruler, but not all his successors may be equally admirable. Sooner or later they will betray Heaven's trust and will fail to deal justly with the people. In the disturbances that

Gilded bronze figure of a leopard, inlaid with silver and garnets, found in the tomb of Tou Wan

follow, Heaven withdraws its Mandate from that dynasty and presents it to the founder of the next. The cycle begins again.

It is the most pragmatic of theories. The popular uprisings which characterized the declining years of each dynasty were seen as precisely that indication of bad government which had decided Heaven to withdraw its Mandate; the man who emerged victorious from the upheavals was clearly the one to whom Heaven had now presented it. It is a concept which dignifies that very familiar state of affairs in which the successful hero is a rebel, the unsuccessful one a traitor. It is also more sophisticated than Europe's Right of Kings in that it makes good government a condition of lawful inheritance.

Naturally this theory greatly appealed to each new dynasty, and the civil servants immediately set about writing the history of the previous one as a steady decline from admirable beginnings to a final wretch whose faults cried out for deposition – a procedure similar to that used by Tudor historians in their account of Richard III. The defects in such an approach are obvious, but nevertheless the simple pattern of strength declining into decadence does contain certain inescapable elements of truth.

A new dynasty begins with a clean slate. It has few commitments, and its prestige or strength is sufficient for it to gather more than adequate funds for its immediate needs. With the passage of time the imperial family grows larger and greedier, the official classes become used to luxury and, being themselves the bureaucrats, tend to shift the tax burdens from their own shoulders onto someone else's (in later dynasties the mandarin class was officially exempt from tax). Ever-increasing demands fall, ultimately, on the one group of people without influence, the peasants. When the system has deteriorated so far as to be intolerable, the peasants finally rise in rebellion.

The reign of Wu Ti was a pivotal point in this process. He became emperor sixty-four years after his great-grandfather had founded the Han dynasty. His grandiose building schemes at Ch'ang-an and his policies of military expansion required far more funds than ever before, and his relentless efforts to raise them were in the short term successful. He reintroduced the Ch'in state monopoly on salt and coinage, and bought up grain when there was a glut and sold it in a scarcity (a scheme which was often made to sound like welfare, but in most cases the marked difference between the buying and selling prices left no doubt that it was a way of raising funds). Both these measures would become standard in Chinese history. Slightly less usual was Wu Ti's practice of selling high

ranks or government posts, and of remitting the punishments of the rich on payment of a large indemnity. There is a hint in Ssu-ma Ch'ien that if he had been able to pay he might have avoided his castration.

Wu Ti at one point forced his nobles to buy what was in effect an early and entirely worthless bond. A herd of white deer in the imperial park were slaughtered, and their hides were cut into squares a foot wide and embroidered with many-coloured silks. It was then announced that these squares were now currency, being valued at 400,000 cash each. (Throughout history the cash has been a unit of currency in the Far East, but our familiar word derives, oddly enough, from other sources.) Wu Ti encouraged the nobles to subscribe to his scheme with the most remarkable piece of imperial effrontery. When dignitaries and officials appeared at court to present their jade insignia, these were no longer accepted unless resting on one of these scraps of skin.

The very expansion and prosperity of Wu Ti's reign were to lead to later troubles, when the ruling classes had become used to a level of luxury which the community was unable to sustain and there was no one with the ruthless flair of Wu Ti himself to extract the necessary funds from the rich. With the gradual collapse of central authority, the throne was seized in A.D. 8 by the nephew of a former empress, Wang Mang, who announced that he was founding the Hsin or 'New' dynasty. He adopted extreme measures, including even a form of land-nationalization, in an attempt to curb the power of the rich landowning families, but he lacked the strength to put them into effect. In the struggles which followed his overthrow, in A.D. 23, a junior branch of the imperial family recovered the throne and set up what is known as the Later or Eastern Han dynasty. They moved their capital from Ch'ang-an in the mountainous Wei valley down into the plains at Loyang, just south of the Yellow River. It was not only the move itself which mirrored the change from the Western Chou to the Eastern Chou eight centuries before. Even the sites of both cities were the same.

One of the factors contributing to Wang Mang's downfall had been a massive peasant uprising in A.D. 18. It was led by members of a secret Taoist society who became known, because of a distinguishing mark they adopted, as the Red Eyebrows. They succeeded in shattering his administration, but they were unable to pick up the pieces. In the end they merely enabled members of the former imperial family to re-establish the Han dynasty.

These elements were to recur again and again in Chinese history. In

the declining years of the Eastern Han two peasant rebellions broke out, both in A.D. 184. Again they were led by Taoist faith-healers, and one of the groups had the colourful name of the Yellow Turbans. But once more they weakened the dynasty only to allow other members of the ruling classes to step in over their heads and replace it. This time, with ultimate irony, those who benefited were the very generals who had acquired their power through commanding the large armies mobilized to put down the peasants. In A.D. 221 three of them carved up the Han empire and instituted a brief period known as the Three Kingdoms.

Nevertheless the effective rule of the Han emperors lasted longer than that of any other dynasty – the only one to span a greater period on paper is the Chou, whose real power was shorter and their domain far less extensive. The Han made a viable reality of that concept which the Ch'in emperor had merely superimposed like a blueprint – the ideal of a unified China. It was not only the habit of gilding the distant past that later made this period seem something of a golden age. And the Chinese would often choose, in succeeding centuries, to express their sense of national identity in the phrase 'sons of Han'.

汉

ONE DISADVANTAGE TO FOLLOWING THE CHINESE METHOD OF DYNA-
sties is that it appears to leave large gaps. The last chapter ended in A.D.
220 and this one begins, on the face of it, four centuries later.

The reason is not only that in a general book one has to concentrate
on the major dynasties. It goes deeper. Every part of the period between
Han and T'ang is scrupulously labelled in the Standard Histories – the
subdivisions amount to some ten dynasties and nineteen kingdoms – but
later authors have shied away from such a jumble, preferring to concentrate on the unified and more glorious dynasties to either side. Thus a
vicious circle is set up. The difficult and confused period, receiving less
attention, comes to seem even murkier than it need. A parallel in Europe
is what neo-classical scholars used to call the Dark Ages, a phrase with
which they both dismissed and partly created that apparently yawning
hiatus between the collapse of Rome and the rediscovery of its culture
in the Renaissance. Those rich medieval centuries (for the phrase originally
included them too) long remained dark precisely because of the reluctance
of the scholars to shed light upon them. To a certain extent – at any rate
in Western histories of China – the gap between the great days of Han and
T'ang, sometimes referred to as the Period of Disunion, has suffered in the
same way.

There was one gradual development during this period which was to
have a lasting effect on Chinese civilization, for it was now that Buddhism
became fully established. Tradition maintained that an emperor of the
Han dynasty had a dream in about A.D. 65, in which he saw a divine being,
gold in colour, flying about in front of the palace. One of his ministers
was able to explain that there was a famous sage in India who had learned
how to fly, had a golden body, and was called the Buddha, and that this
must therefore be he. So the emperor sent envoys to find out more and
they returned with the *Sutra in Forty-Two Sections*, the first Buddhist
scripture to reach China.

The fiction that the emperor himself had summoned the Indian religion
into China was dreamed up by later Buddhists to dignify their own
presence, but the date is close to the first mention of Buddhism in Chinese
records. It had arrived along the Silk Road from Central Asia. Many of the
travelling merchants would themselves have been Buddhist at this time,
and monasteries were set up in the oases along the caravan route. Gradually, accompanying the merchants, the monks came east and stayed.

They received a warm welcome from the Taoists, for the two religions
seemed at first sight to have much in common. Both had priests and

Stone sculpture of an apsara *from Lung-men, c. 500*

monasteries and something of the structure of an organized religion, elements entirely lacking in Confucianism. Both were interested in spells and charms, for the northern form of Buddhism which reached China was a religion less pure and ascetic than that which had gone south to Ceylon. Both laid great emphasis on breathing exercises, and one of the first Buddhist texts to be translated into Chinese was a *sutra* containing the methods of Buddhist yoga. And both advocated a withdrawal from everyday affairs, although here one crucial difference must have been rapidly apparent. The Taoists withdrew from the bustle of life in the hope of prolonging, perhaps indefinitely, their spell on earth. The Buddhists did so for precisely the opposite reason – to achieve such a state of enlightenment that they would be spared the pain of being reborn.

The very similarities between the two religions led to a convenient fiction which greatly eased the acceptance of Buddhism. It was soon decided that Lao Tzu, the supposed founder of Taoism, must himself have travelled to the west to convert the barbarians, who had given him the name of the Buddha. Buddhism was therefore only returning to China. This enabled the Taoists to borrow from the Indian religion, without loss of face, whatever elements they wished, and the early Buddhists were no doubt willing to assent to such a convenient story. It was only in later centuries, when the great success and wealth of the Buddhists roused the jealousy of the Taoists, that the theory was neatly reversed into one of hostility. Since Buddhism was nothing more than an adulterated and foreign version of Taoism, it was argued, what possible need was there of it? This was to become one of several common complaints justifying the persecution of the Buddhists.

The vitality of the new religion had been astonishing. Wherever Buddhism has spread, its devotees have liked to carve great statues in the natural rock or to paint the walls of caves. In China they surpassed themselves. At one site alone near Loyang (only one of several in northern China) there are sculptures, varying in height from a few inches to thirty-five feet, which are so numerous that two attempts to count them came up with widely differing answers. A local magistrate in 1916 found 97,306 separate figures at Lung-men but a more recent study concluded that the total should be nearer to 142,289.[1]

One of the most remarkable surviving complexes of ancient Chinese culture is also primarily Buddhist. The first resting-place on the Silk Road within the security of China itself was Tun-huang, at the very western extremity of the Great Wall. It was a natural centre of Buddhism,

Ladies Playing Double Sixes, attributed to Chou Fang, c. 800 (detail)

since this was the route by which the religion had entered China, and over the centuries a large number of caves were carved out of the loess terraces to make temples, or lodgings for monks and travellers. They were profusely decorated, and as in any Buddhist community there was much sculpture too – made out of baked mud, for the rock here was too soft to carve. The dryness of the climate has led to many of the murals surviving in excellent condition, to provide a complete gallery of Chinese Buddhist painting from the fourth to the tenth centuries.

The accident of the climate contributed to another even more astonishing stroke of luck – the preservation at Tun-huang of an entire library of thousands of manuscripts and many paintings on silk, which had been sealed up some time after 1056 to save its treasures from marauding Tibetans (the library even contained selections from the Old Testament in Hebrew, a measure of how international was the traffic on the Silk Road). A large number of these documents are now in the British Museum, and their progress there provides a disturbing glimpse of Western archaeology at its most buccaneering. The discovery of the library is usually credited to Sir Aurel Stein, one of the most celebrated archaeologists of his day. The actual story of how it was found is rather different.

In about 1899 a Taoist monk, by the name of Wang Tao-shih, began clearing one of the caves at Tun-huang which had been entirely blocked by falls of stone and drifting sand. It was a work of piety, and he set off on long expeditions with his begging bowl to bring back sufficient funds for himself and a few labourers to continue the work. When the cave was clear and they were restoring its murals, a crack in the plaster revealed a surface of brick where there should have been nothing but the rock face. Inside was the great library of scrolls, stacked high to the roof. News of the find was reported to provincial headquarters, and eventually an order came back – said to be from the Governor of Kansu himself – appointing Wang the curator of the manuscripts and telling him to seal them up again until it was decided what should be done with them. That was how the situation remained until, in 1907, Sir Aurel arrived on the scene. The rest of the story can be told in his own words, for it is clear that even in his mind the adventure was from the start a calculated and most exciting act of piracy.

His first meeting with Wang was none too promising. 'He looked a very curious figure, extremely shy and nervous, with a face bearing an occasional furtive expression of cunning which was far from encouraging.' Even so, one good piece of news was established in this first conversation:

Painting on silk of the Bodhisattva Kuan-yin, brought by Stein from Tun-huang

One of the cave-temples at Tun-huang, and the Taoist priest Wang Tao-shih (photographs by Stein)

no official inventory of the library had been sent to the provincial governor's office. The next day Stein's Chinese assistant, Chiang, was able to persuade the monk to take down the brick wall and to bring out a few of the bundles for Stein to inspect. That night, and every subsequent one, Chiang arrived back at Stein's tent with a selection of manuscripts hidden in his long sleeves, for 'what our diplomatic convention styled "closer examination"'. Having glimpsed the possible extent of his haul, Stein was haunted now by the dread that the 'shifty priest, swayed by his worldly fears and spiritual scruples, would be moved in a sudden fit of alarm or distrust to close down his shell before I had been able to extract any of the pearls'. He left all discussion of money to Chiang, who was authorized to go up to 5000 rupees – a sum which Stein considered ample for Wang 'to retire to his native province and a life of peace, if Tun-huang should become too hot for him'. In the event Chiang sealed the bargain for only 500 rupees, and Stein wrote later: 'When I now survey the wealth of archaeological materials that I carried away for this sum, the bargain may well seem great beyond credence.' By the end of Stein's visit, the quantity of material being removed from the cave each night was far too

great even for Chiang's admittedly voluminous sleeves. Three of Stein's most trusted servants were now making midnight trips under the cover of a river bank to convey large sackfuls of the manuscripts. There remained the problem of their final removal, but with considerable forethought Stein had brought with him a great many empty crates. There was no reason why his luggage should appear, on departure, any different from what it had on arrival. He was particularly eager that all this professionalism should reassure poor Wang, who had been showing increasing signs of nervousness. The story can only end with Stein's own words, as he prepares to make his getaway:

> The forethought and care bestowed on such necessary safeguards did not remain unrequited. I had the satisfaction of seeing that the shy Tao-shih, honest in his own way, now breathed freely again.[2]

Naturally the Chinese have regarded this as the most blatant of thefts. Stein had not even Elgin's excuse that the treasures were deteriorating, although he occasionally makes noises to this effect. Perhaps the best British line of defence is that Stein saved these 7000 precious rolls from being taken to France, for the following year a French scholar arrived to cart away another 3000 for the Bibliothèque Nationale.

Tun-huang was already a thriving centre during the Period of Disunion, and the man who united China again after that time of chaos, establishing the Sui dynasty, was himself an enthusiastic patron of Buddhism. He took as his title Wen Ti, the Cultured Emperor, and devoted great energy to spreading the religion, erecting stupas throughout the land (it was the Buddhist stupa that gradually developed into the Chinese pagoda), sending out parties of monks to exhibit sacred relics, and even referring to himself in an edict as the Disciple of the Buddha. It has been suggested that his zeal was partly a political device to consolidate his rule;[3] if so, it was a measure of how widely Buddhism had now spread throughout the Chinese people, but the emperor's long-term plans were frustrated. The son who succeeded him (Yang Ti, the Emblazoned Emperor) had more grandiose schemes. He impressed a vast labour force to build extensive palaces at both Ch'ang-an and Loyang, and to construct what was to prove the dynasty's most enduring monument – the first Grand Canal, joining up the network of existing waterways so that barges could travel from the Yangtze to the Yellow River and then on up the Wei to the western capital at Ch'ang-an.

Emperor Wu of the Northern Chou dynasty, from Yen Li-Pen's scroll of Thirteen Emperors (detail)

There was an excellent economic justification for this great project. The wheat and millet crop of the Yellow River plain was now of secondary importance to the great harvest of rice that was being reaped in the lush paddy fields watered by the Yangtze; a large proportion of taxes were still paid in grain, and it was essential to be able to bring the wealth of the south to the centre of power in the north. But to judge by the early histories, the chief motive of Yang Ti was as much to do with self-glorification as with economics. His canal allowed him a spectacular new form of royal progress. He commissioned specially elaborate barges, referred to as dragon-boats, in which he and his retinue moved at stately pace along the canal with the help of thousands of palace servants dressed in brocade and pulling on green ropes. It was said that the procession was at times over sixty miles long.

As with the equally short-lived Ch'in dynasty, the burden of compulsory labour made necessary by these projects was more than the nation could tolerate. The official history – hostile in tone, naturally, for Yang Ti was the last of his line – claims that the workers numbered in the millions, and that more than 40 per cent of those building the palaces at Loyang died under the strain. The carts carrying away the dead 'were always within view of each other on the road'.[4] The phrase is remarkably similar to the description of the last days of the Ch'in, when 'the men who died daily formed a heap in the market-place.'[5]

On the groundwork laid by the Ch'in, the Han dynasty had been able to build its own more stable edifice. The pattern was to repeat itself. In 613 rebellion broke out, and in 616 Yang Ti fled southwards down his own Grand Canal in a newly completed fleet of those spectacular barges (the original ones had been destroyed in the troubles). Two years later he was assassinated by his own troops. In the north one of his high officials had seized the western capital at Ch'ang-an, and was soon strong enough to found a new and far more glorious dynasty.

The T'ang dynasty is both a climax and a new beginning in the history of China. In many ways its greatest artistic achievements are a culmination of all that had gone before. The exquisite metalwork of the period, such as the chased golden bowls and filigree ornaments (colour, pages 107 and 120) or the beautifully modelled backs of bronze mirrors, can be seen as the final sophistication of those sturdy vessels cast with such skill 2000 years before by the Shang craftsmen. The most familiar of all T'ang objects – the large vivacious figures of horses and camels, grooms, merchants, dancers or demons (colour, pages 108–9 and 119) – were for

the most part made for instant burial in a tradition going back to the less flamboyant figures in the Han tombs. Early Chinese painting is exceedingly scarce, but the evidence suggests that the most highly valued subjects had always been portraits and scenes of human activity. These too seem to reach a peak in the few paintings that survive from the T'ang period. The portraits, of which a series of Thirteen Emperors now in Boston are the most famous example, have an almost monumental quality without any loss of realism.

As a final entry in this list of accomplishments, the T'ang dynasty brings to perfection that element which seems so characteristic of Chinese poetry – a tone of striking simplicity, of images that are effortlessly clear – which had been visible even in many of the poems in the *Book of Odes*, from the centuries before Confucius. It is only one of many equally important elements in the poetry of China, for her poets have been as fascinated as any by problems of form and the subtle uses of allusion, but it is the quality which has always survived best in translation.

The most widely known poet of all, Li Po, was born in 701, some eighty years after the start of the dynasty. He represents all that is most romantic in Chinese poetry and in the Chinese attitude to life. He never sat the examinations, but at the age of nineteen left home to live with a Taoist recluse. It was Taoism which was to shape his life and his work. Most of his years, apart from a brief and unhappy spell at court, were spent wandering the country. His poems dwell on moonlight, rivers, mountains, trees, flowers, the pleasure of friendship, the sorrow of parting, and the absolute necessity of alcohol. No one else can evoke with such economy the haunting images that he achieves in his shortest poems:

> *She, a Tung-yang girl, stands barefoot on the bank,*
> *He, a boatman of Kuei-chi, is in his boat.*
> *The moon has not set.*
> *They look at each other – broken-hearted.*[6]

His explanation of his own way of life was as follows:

> *Why do I live among the green mountains?*
> *I laugh and answer not, my soul is serene:*
> *It dwells in another heaven and earth belonging to no man.*
> *The peach trees are in flower, and the water flows on....*[7]

Throughout his work there is talk of the solace and liberation of wine, but one of the most delightful images of the poet in his cups is given by his slightly younger contemporary, Tu Fu:

A hundred poems Li Po wrote after a cask of wine.
He was asleep at a tavern in Ch'ang-an
When the Emperor called; he would not board the imperial barge,
But said, 'Your humble servant is a god of wine.'[8]

The later years of the T'ang dynasty saw a new kind of poetry, using less literary language and a more everyday realism in its images. It was introduced by Po Chü-i, who deplored verse that was a mere 'sporting with wind and moon, and toying with flowers and grass'. He insisted that poetry must be understandable by an 'old country woman', and out of his own vast output he considered important only those poems which attacked a social or political injustice. This is the style of Chinese poetry which has so much influenced many modern Western writers (in particular Brecht, who translated some of Arthur Waley's versions into German and included one of them in *The Good Woman of Szechuan*). In the following poem Po Chü-i protests – in that particular manner of his which achieves its force only through the vividness of the scene – against the abuses perpetrated by the palace armies under the command of powerful eunuchs:

In the morning I climbed the Tzu-ko Peak,
In the evening I lodged in the village under the hill.
The Elder of the village was pleased that I had come
And in my honour opened a jar of wine.
We raised our cups, but before we began to drink
Some rough soldiers pushed in at the gate,
Dressed in brown, carrying knife and axe,
Ten or more, hustling into the room.
They helped themselves to the wine we were going to drink,
They snatched away the food we were going to eat.
My host made way and stood at the back of the room
With his hands in his sleeves, as though they were honoured guests.
In the yard was a tree that the old man had planted
Thirty years ago with his own hand.
They said it must go, and he did not dare refuse;
They took their axes, they felled it at the root.
They said they had come to collect wood for building
And were workers attached to the Army of the Holy Plan.
'You'd better be careful; the less you say the better;
Our Eunuch General stands in high favour.'[9]

A fascinating glimpse into the life of the times is provided by the twin

careers of Po Chü-i and of his greatest friend, Yüan Chen, a man descended from the royal house of a northern 'barbarian' tribe, and at least as fiery as his pedigree might suggest. Both men were scholars, both of them distinguished poets and high government officials, and both owed their positions solely to their success in the examinations. Their friendship has been described by Arthur Waley as 'perhaps the most famous in Chinese history'.[10]

It was at an examination, appropriately enough, that they first met in 802. Both had already passed the Provincial and Metropolitan examinations (Yüan Chen at the precocious age of fourteen, the earliest at which one was allowed to enter), but these merely gave the successful candidate the status of a scholar and a gentleman. They did not guarantee employment. So the two young men were now at Ch'ang-an – this remarkable city in the Wei valley, which had been the first capital of the Chou, the Ch'in, the Han, the Sui and now was again of the T'ang – to sit a third and even more exclusive examination which amounted to a request for a job. Certain preliminary conditions had to be complied with. Five officials at the capital must be found to vouch for each candidate. He must agree to be grouped with four others, who would be mutually responsible for each other's good conduct. And – a survival of the age-old distrust of the potential middle-classes – he must be able to show that his father was not a merchant or artisan.

Both Po and Yüan passed. (This use of their first names is not an undue familiarity, like referring to Shakespeare as William. With typical commonsense the Chinese have always put the surname first, an arrangement which other countries too have to adopt whenever a list needs to be drawn up or an official document prepared. Thus Mao is the Chairman's family name, and Tse-tung his personal name.)

Together with several other successful candidates, the two new friends were given a remarkably pleasant job in the palace library, where they were only expected to turn up twice a month. It seems to have been a way of placing talented young men on the pay roll while waiting to find them more arduous employment. Po Chü-i moved from a Taoist monastery, where he had been lodging, into a pavilion which he now rented in the grounds of a large house. Here he relaxed into a life of civilized ease, swapping poems with his friends, visiting the studios of painters, or strolling by the Serpentine, a large ornamental lake nearby. As he said, in a poem addressed to Yüan Chen and to other young men of his new acquaintance:

A salary of 16,000 cash
And monthly rice that is always more than enough,
An end to all concern about food and clothes
And very little in the way of business ties –
All this has at last made me young
And each new day is a day of happy ease. . . .[11]

The young men working in such leisurely fashion at the library formed a circle of friends, but between Po and Yüan a special relationship was developing. The departure of Yüan for a while to the eastern capital at Loyang makes Po decidedly wistful, as he walks alone in the park and composes a poem entitled *By the Serpentine, thinking of Yüan Chen*:

Companionless since spring came I have taken few walks;
From every pleasure, without you, more than half is gone.
Today, above all, in the Apricot Garden, I found it hard to bear;
Everyone in the world seemed out for a walk – everyone except you.[12]

In many other societies this slightly precious quality would be assumed to imply a homosexual friendship – of the misty and *fin-de-siècle* sort, rather than the more robust Elizabethan variety – but it seems in China to have been a fairly conventional mood between friends without necessarily implying a physical relationship.

By 806 the two friends were making preparations to sit yet another examination – their fourth, and the most crucial of all for their future careers, since the questions this time would be on matters of contemporary politics rather than the classics and success might at last lead to an important government post. So as to be able to study without distraction, Po and Yüan retired to the same Taoist monastery where Po had stayed during the previous examination. Their choice of lodging did not imply that they considered themselves Taoists. Indeed the religion to which both of them inclined was Buddhism, and their distinguished record in the examinations proved them to be highly proficient Confucians. All educated Chinese felt free to draw whatever they pleased from each of these three main sources.

It was generally assumed that in this final test, the Palace Examination, where the subject of the essay was traditionally set by the emperor himself, it was wise to avoid any criticism of the present state of affairs. But Yüan, more ambitious and more reckless than Po, decided that the climate was changing. After procuring with some difficulty the answers from a previous examination, he calculated that the best chance of a high mark this

Gold pedestal bowl with repoussé design of petals, and tracing of deer, birds and flowers, c. 750.
OVERLEAF *Pottery tomb figures of a guardian trampling on a demon* LEFT *and of a groom, c. 720*

year would be a challenging critique of the government. He claims that Po agreed with him. The other candidates thought him mad.

The subject which was set seemed a dangerous one for Yüan's policy. In the middle of the previous century, in 755, one of the generals commanding a northern frontier had led a rebellion. His name was An Lu-shan. He was so successful that within a short time he had captured both the western and eastern capitals, Ch'ang-an and Loyang, and the emperor had fled. But within two years An Lu-shan was killed by his own son. The T'ang dynasty was able to re-establish itself, although its authority, particularly in the more remote districts, was never to be fully recovered. Now, half a century later, the emperor inquired of his examination candidates what had caused this decline of the dynasty and what they advised him to do about it.

Po Chü-i did indeed, as Yüan expected of him, make certain criticisms in his answer, pointing to heavy taxation as the immediate cause of unrest and to failures of the government as the ultimate cause of heavy taxation, but he kept his terms general and his thesis was of the type that could be supported by any Confucian text book. Yüan sailed very much closer to the wind, but had the wit to concentrate on a specific defect in the system which, though extremely important, could hardly be seen as the fault of the emperor himself. His argument was that the weakness in government derived from the wrong people being selected. The reason, he said, was that the examinations laid too much emphasis on the classics and on literary ability, and thereby gave an advantage to the sons of other such literary gentlemen. The competition should be more genuinely open to all, and important office should go to those who showed skill in dealing with practical problems. It was an answer bearing only a tenuous link to the question, and Yüan may well have gone into the examination intending to give it whatever was asked. It also seemed certain to give offence to those literary gentlemen who had been chosen this year as examiners. Perhaps Yüan hoped to catch the eye of the emperor himself. Perhaps indeed he did catch it, for his gamble paid off. Yüan passed top, and Po second.

Po was given a post in the provinces, but Yüan, as if being taken at his word, was put straight into a palace department responsible for subjecting imperial policy to criticism. If the emperor had liked Yüan's plain speaking on the peripheral topic of the examinations, he soon had more than he can have bargained for and in areas rather more painful. Almost immediately Yüan drew up a ten-point plan for reviving the

A celadon phoenix-head jug of the T'ang dynasty

dynasty. Several of the items dealt with administrative procedure, but the emperor was also informed that he should accept fewer presents, spend less time in hunting, and reduce the size of his harem. Yüan was summoned into the imperial presence to explain this document, and soon appears to have found himself in gaol. He was released within a few weeks and was transferred to a minor post at the eastern capital.

Within a few days of this reversal his mother died, an event which kept him out of political trouble for a while since the Confucian ritual specified between two and three years of mourning for either parent. A civil servant continued to be paid during this long absence, and for many, however sorrowful they might feel, such a break in routine must have had its pleasant compensations. The average man could expect two such periods during his working life – in modern terms a very considerable fringe bene- fit. Naturally, though, an official could not exactly behave as if he were on holiday, and to make love even to his wife within the first year was re- garded as out of the question.

Meanwhile Po Chü-i was making steady if less spectacular progress. In 807, at the age of thirty-five, he became a Doctor of the Hanlin academy, a body responsible for drafting edicts in the name of the emperor (even this appointment had involved the writing of five test compositions – exami- nations were a way of life). He was now sufficiently distinguished to be ordered to have his portrait painted. It was to hang in the Hall of Assembled Worthies.

Once Yüan was out of mourning he was given, perhaps unwisely, another job specifically concerned with looking for faults in others. The censorship system played an increasingly important part in Chinese history, with officials appointed to look over other officials' shoulders, and a stream of adverse reports now flowed from Yüan's brush. Again he soon over-reached himself, when he tried to unseat on his own initiative the mayor of the eastern capital. It was Yüan, rather than the mayor, who was summoned back to Ch'ang-an. On the way he became involved in a brawl with a palace eunuch over the last available stable at a govern- ment rest-house. He arrived in great distress at the capital, where Po's mother put his clothes in order and plied him with medicine. Within days he was on his way into the Chinese equivalent of exile, an unimportant post in a small and distant place.

For the next five years the friendship was continued by mail – still a rather unpredictable business at this period. Official documents travelled with couriers, who might on occasion be persuaded to carry private pack-

ages as well, but most letters to out-of-the-way places progressed on a principle akin to hitch-hiking. The sender gave the letter to someone going in the rough direction of its destination, who in his turn found someone to take it on the next stage, and so on for as long as was necessary. The process sometimes took as much as a year.

Poetry was both the subject and the chief content of most of the letters between Po and Yüan. As in Elizabethan England, to be able to turn a neat verse was more than a branch of art; it was also a game and a necessary accomplishment for anyone pretending to culture (almost 50,000 T'ang poems by some 2300 poets survive). A favourite pastime at wine parties was a form of poetic consequences in which, for example, each person might have to follow a rhyme-scheme established by the player before him. Yüan, from his distant outpost, sent Po some verses in which the rhymes were deliberately made as ticklish as possible, and Po had to match them. The ability to improvise seemed almost the most important part of poetic distinction. In the previous century, news of a child prodigy had reached the court and the infant was summoned to appear before the Empress Wu, the only woman in China's long history ever to rule in her own right. When the prodigy, a little girl of seven, was shown into the presence of this formidable lady, she was ordered to improvise a poem on the theme of bidding farewell to her brothers. The result seems highly creditable:

> *In the pavilion of separation, the leaves suddenly blew away.*
> *On the road of farewell, the clouds lifted all of a sudden.*
> *Ah! How I regret that men are not like the wild geese*
> *Who go on their way together.*[13]

It was in this tradition that Po and Yüan celebrated their next brief meeting, in 815. They rode with some friends to a picnic south of Ch'ang-an, and all the way back capped each other's improvisations in a brilliant rivalry. The other members of the party, Po later claimed, 'had nowhere to put their mouths' – an all too familiar feeling in such company.

Poetry now spread surprisingly far, both in terms of geography and through the classes of society. When Yüan arrived in 817 at another distant place of exile (he seems to have established himself as someone too prickly to keep anywhere near the centre) he discovered written on a dusty wall a poem which he recognized as being by Po. He copied it out and sent it to his friend. It was one which Po had written fifteen years before, just after passing his first examination, as a present for a courtesan. Po himself liked to tell, in later life, the story that such a girl had put up her

price because her accomplishments included reciting the whole of one of his longer narrative poems, and it was said that manuscripts by him and Yüan could be used to pay the bill in tea-houses.

The movements of officials were strictly controlled. Like modern diplomats they went wherever they were sent, and if serving at court they were not allowed to stray further than nine miles from Ch'ang-an without imperial permission. After those first carefree years in the palace library, Po and Yüan saw very little of each other for the rest of their lives. In 819 they were both given new postings at the same time, and by a miracle their boats passed on the river. Yüan turned his boat and accompanied Po for a while upstream, but when he seemed to have gone too far out of his way they reversed again and Po sailed down. Thus they dallied for several tantalizing days, the high spot of which was a moonlit picnic in a strange chasm with a waterfall, where they carved a poem on the rocks. Finally – after no doubt presenting each other, many times over, with the conventional farewell gift of a poem – they went their separate ways.

Two years later they were together again in Ch'ang-an, but now at last – under a new emperor – Yüan had the high office which he so much longed for, and had little time for dalliance. He even became a chief minister but was soon, as usual, by-passing all the normal channels in order to put his plans into effect more speedily. It was not long before he was again removed, this time to become a provincial governor.

In 823 they met for three days. Po, who almost consciously avoided the dangers of the very highest posts, was now most comfortably installed as governor of Hangchow, one of China's most beautiful cities with its scenery of hills and lakes. Yüan was passing nearby and paid his friend a brief visit. Huge crowds lined the streets to gaze at them. Their friendship, says Waley, 'was already a sort of national institution'.

They met only once more, in 829. 'We drank together', wrote Po, 'and when we parted, with tears in his eyes, he gave me two poems.' One of them read:

> *Do not scold me for still being here! I know I have stayed too long;*
> *I have tried hard to say good-bye, but words will not come.*
> *Let me stay, for few are left of our grey-headed band;*
> *Tomorrow you may not get the chance of a meeting such as this.*[14]

Two years later Yüan died. Po was asked by his family to write the inscription for his tomb, and in gratitude they gave him Yüan's silver

saddle and jade belt, insignia appropriate to his official rank. He presented them, in Yüan's name, to a Buddhist monastery.

Po outlived his younger friend by fifteen years. This last period of his life was spent in great comfort and dignity, living now at the eastern capital, Loyang, and holding a well-paid sinecure as Junior Tutor in the non-existent Household of the Crown Prince. When he travelled, he was carried in a most comfortable litter and accompanied by his own cup-bearers and musicians;

> *With me are servants skilled in pipe and string;*
> *On horseback follow bearers of ladle and cup.*
> *Now and again, with the spring wind in my face,*
> *I bid them stop and pour me out a drink.*[15]

His garden was full of treasures that he had brought from his various postings, white lotuses and a dragon-headed punt from Soochow, a small flock of cranes and a curiously shaped piece of rock from Hangchow. He kept a group of ten dancers and musicians to entertain him, and he would sometimes send them to play on one of the islands in his little lake. He had singing girls too, for now it was not only the great nobles who kept a small harem in the back rooms of the house. Willow Branch was his favourite, though even she could hardly compare with what he remembered of Peach Leaf, long ago. When other elderly friends dropped in on him, the wine-jar was soon making the rounds and the scrolls of poetry were lifted out of their boxes. Then Willow Branch would sing or the musicians would strike up some of his favourite music, such as the tunes from a Taoist ballet which he had once seen performed at the palace and which was called, from the dancers' costumes, *Rainbow Skirts and Feather Jackets*. Sometimes he would even take up the lute himself, and play them *Autumn Thoughts*.

The official retiring age was seventy – in actual fact sixty-nine or sixty-eight in our counting, for a child was said to be one on the day of its birth and then two on the subsequent New Year's Day, when everyone in China became a year older. So a baby born late in the year could be two when it was only a few weeks old, and a lucky man might retire when he was only just sixty-eight. The conditions of retirement seem to have been extraordinarily generous. Po was entitled to a hundred days of automatic sick-leave on full pay, and then to half his final salary for the rest of his life. And this was, after all, the ninth century. He had every intention of enjoying his retirement:

Even so, certain luxuries did now seem excessive. Poor Willow Branch was most regretfully dismissed.

Po was also concerned with thoughts of his future fame. In 835 he presented his complete works, brought fully up to date in sixty scrolls, to the Eastern Forest Monastery with the request that they should never be lent to visitors or allowed outside the gate. Later he presented complete sets to two other Buddhist libraries, and in his last year or so added this final computation at the end of his own copy:

> The whole collection of my works in seventy-five chapters contains 3840 pieces, great and small, in prose and verse. One copy is in the library of the Eastern Forest Monastery on the Lu Shan, another is in the library of the Nan-ch'an Monastery at Soochow, another is in the Tower of the Depository of Monastic Rules in the courtyard of the Begging-bowl Pagoda at the Sheng-shan Monastery in Lo-yang; another is in the charge of my nephew Tortoise and another in that of my daughter's son, T'an Ko-t'ung, each of whom is to keep it in his house and hand it down to his descendants. . . . Other works currently attributed to me but absent from the *Collected Works* are not authentic.[17]

His choice of Buddhist monasteries as places of safe-keeping proved an unfortunate one. Government hostility towards the Buddhists had been building up for several years, and it erupted in 845 in a massive desecration of monasteries and dispersal of their precious works of art. Po Chü-i lived just long enough to witness the destruction, and he must have viewed it with horror. He died, at the age of seventy-four, in 846. Even so, his careful editing paid off. His poems have survived in precisely the form he intended.

The initial link between Buddhism and Taoism had gradually become strained, when the guest religion became more rich and powerful than its host. There had been various clashes in the small dynasties during the Period of Disunion. In 446 the Taoists had combined with the Confucians to persuade Emperor Wu of the Northern Wei dynasty to issue an order that Buddhist temples, images and manuscripts should be destroyed and the monks executed. In the following century the tide flowed the other way when another Emperor Wu, founder of the Liang dynasty in the south, became a fervent Buddhist and in 517 ordered the destruction of all Taoist temples. In 574 an emperor of the Northern Chou dynasty (every

Stone head of a bodhisattva *(a disciple of Buddha approaching enlightenment), 6th century*

ruler of a small dynasty now called himself emperor) instituted a persecution of the Buddhists but at the same time, to the considerable surprise of his advisers, prohibited the use of Taoist temples. This emperor, too, was called Wu. Finally, in 845, came the most massive of all the attacks on Buddhism, instigated by Taoists and Confucianists together. More than 4000 monasteries were, it was said, destroyed, and ten times as many temples and shrines. Over a quarter of a million monks and nuns were forced to return to lay life, and vast areas of fertile land seized for the state. It seems almost inevitable, after such a series, that their persecutor was yet another Emperor Wu.

Before looking at how the persecution appeared to one articulate monk caught up in it, it is worth digressing a little to comment on this entirely coincidental run of emperors, all from different dynasties and all named Wu – for this difficulty with names is undoubtedly one of the reasons why so few rulers of China stand out as individual characters in Western histories (another, perhaps, is that they do not appear to very lively effect even in the Chinese histories, for the bureaucrat-historians were not specifically interested in the quirks of their ruler's character). Wu is a clan name in China, but it also means 'martial'. Thus China's only reigning empress was the Empress Wu because that was the clan into which she had been born; but the powerful ruler of the Han dynasty, who in the second century B.C. so vastly extended the frontiers of his empire, chose as a title suitable to his ambitions Wu Ti, or the Martial Emperor. There is nothing odd in itself about this proliferation of rulers called Wu, or anyway nothing that Europe, with no less than eighteen Louis, can call odd. The only difficulty is that the Chinese rejected the simple but undeniably ugly solution of numbering their rulers. The amazing appearance of Louis XVIII on the page is something to which we have grown accustomed, but if we came across it for the first time in another culture it would strike us as barbarously unimaginative. Typically bureaucratic, we might even be tempted to say, especially if the false dignity of the Roman numerals were removed. The Chinese, more than any other people, have appreciated the pleasures of names, and their way of separating rulers is to elaborate rather than to number them. Thus the proper title of the Emperor Wu of the second century B.C. is Han Wu Ti, the Han Martial Emperor also known on other occasions as Hsiao Wu Ti, the Filial Martial Emperor. On the same basis the Wu who persecuted the Buddhists in 845 should officially be T'ang Wu Tsung, the T'ang Martial Ancestor. This is perfectly satisfactory, except for the purely parochial reason that

Pottery figure of a Central Asian horseman, from the tomb of a princess, dated 706

the more elaborate name is even more confusing to the non-specialist Western reader.

One of the most articulate of early visitors to China was Ennin, a monk who arrived in 838 to witness what was probably the heyday of Chinese Buddhism, and who was still in the country at the time of the great persecution of 845. He was part of an embassy from Japan to the Chinese court. Their landing was hardly dignified, for they were washed ashore after being shipwrecked on the shoals off the mouth of the Yangtze, but it was entirely in keeping with the present state of Japanese seamanship. Soon the party was engaged in a more pleasant form of boating, making their way slowly up the Grand Canal. The monk noted in his diary some details of this bustling thoroughfare, with villages, inns and tea-houses along the bank, groves of bamboos, large flocks of white ducks and geese, and plenty of traffic. The only irritation was the mosquitoes 'which hurt like needle pricks'. The Japanese moved peacefully along in forty boats, tied side by side in twos or threes and strung out behind each other on tow-ropes. The entire flotilla, amazingly, was pulled by two water-buffaloes. The emperor who had first moved along these waters in solemn procession, two centuries before, was still remembered. 'The dug canal', notes Ennin, 'is over twenty feet wide and is straight, without bends. It was dug by Yang Ti of the Sui dynasty.'[18]

Ennin had come 'in search of the law' – he wanted to seek out Buddhist texts which he would take back to Japan. He was determined therefore to stay in China longer than the rest of the embassy. At first this seemed likely to prove impossible, with all the difficulties put in his way by officials in the coastal areas, but once safely inland he found himself surprisingly free to wander where he would and almost everywhere he received a warm welcome. Hardly a day passed without his coming to a monastery where he could be lodged and entertained. All over the country there seemed to be officials who took a keen interest in the religion and were delighted to chat with a monk of Ennin's learning and distinction.

In 840 Ennin made a pilgrimage to the terraces of Wu-t'ai, in the mountains northeast of Ch'ang-an. The sacred spot was a group of five rounded peaks, easily visible from each other, which Ennin described as 'looking like overturned bowls'. On top of each a terrace had been built, with pools, pagodas and temples, and Ennin wandered happily with countless other pilgrims through the wooded ravines which rang with the sound of waterfalls and were dotted at this season of the year with alpine flowers. Only the Chinese, among Buddhists, have this very sympathetic

Gold filigree hair ornament TOP, *and a gilded cup decorated with peonies, c. 750*

obsession with mountains and mountain scenery, an attitude which they borrowed from the Taoists.

The area was full of places where the pilgrims could lodge and at one of them Ennin found, among the relics, a memento of one of his predecessors. A Japanese monk called Reisen had made this journey some twenty or thirty years before, and had presented the Monastery of the Golden Balcony with an unusual keepsake – an image of the Buddha painted on a strip of skin from his own arm. It was enshrined in a gilded bronze model of a pagoda, at which offerings were made, and the pagoda was specially opened for Ennin to inspect the fragile icon, four inches long and three wide.

While he was at Wu-t'ai an envoy arrived from the emperor with lavish gifts to celebrate the imperial birthday. There were donations of large quantities of clothing, food and incense, and there was a round of banquets for the monks. It must have seemed to Ennin a fine indication of the official approval under which Buddhism so evidently prospered. Three weeks later he set out to make the journey, several hundred miles southwest, to the imperial capital.

In fact the birthday being celebrated at Wu-t'ai was already that of Emperor Wu. It was his first year on the throne, and this generosity and patronage was nothing more than the automatic continuation of a long-standing custom. At the same occasion on the following year Ennin, now in Ch'ang-an, was already noting in his diary a change of attitude towards the Buddhists. They were invited as usual to the birthday feast, but a marked preference was shown for the Taoists. During the following months the emperor ordered that the Buddhist monasteries should be purged of any monks or nuns who practised magic, broke their vows of chastity, or committed various other offences. This was not in itself unreasonable, but it was to be the thin end of a very destructive wedge.

By 844 Ennin reports that the emperor was so much under the influence of the Taoists that he was doing whatever they suggested in the age-old pursuit of immortality. He built for them a massive Terrace of the Immortals in the palace grounds, from which they promised to ascend and 'roam about the nine heavens and, with blessings for the masses and long life for the Emperor, long preserve the pleasures of immortality'.[19] As to the emperor's personal immortality, he was advised to take a drug compounded of 'ten pounds of plum skins, ten pounds of peach fuzz, ten pounds of the membranes of living chickens, ten pounds of tortoise hairs, and ten pounds of rabbit horns'.[20] Ennin may well have taken delight in

making the list even more ridiculous than it was in reality, and he reports with pleasure that in spite of the merchants being beaten it proved impossible to procure these ingredients in the market.

It was not in fact necessary to blame the emperor's hostility to Buddhism on the evil and eccentric influence of the Taoists. There were, from the Chinese point of view, several other reasons to view the foreign religion with considerable suspicion. In economic terms it was offensive that so much wealth and land should have been accumulated in the monasteries as gifts from the devout while the monks themselves were non-

A Temple in the Mountains *(attrib. Li Ch'eng), and a real temple in the mountains of Shansi*

123

productive, being exempted from any labour duties or military requirements and even paying no taxes. Moreover the monks seemed to consider themselves, as holy men, somehow outside or above the reach of mundane government administration – an attitude deriving from Buddhism's origins in India, where even the poorest brahman priest is of a higher caste than the resplendent maharajah, but one not likely to cut much ice in bureaucratic China. Perhaps worst of all, the monks committed on principle one of the primary offences of the Confucian canon. They were unfilial – not only in shaving their heads, which was a failure to respect and take care of their fathers' greatest gift to them, their own bodies, but also in remaining celibate. The paradox that it is unfilial not to have children may seem hard to accept, but it is perfectly logical when viewed through Confucian spectacles. Only through one's son, and his sons' sons, is it possible to fulfil one of the main obligations to one's father – that of continuing the worship at his ancestral shrine. There was also one rather less philosophical reason for Confucian hostility. The eunuchs were traditionally inclined to Buddhism, and there is evidence that the persecution of 845 was closely connected with the long-standing enmity between these two groups.

A friend of Po Chü-i's, by the name of Han Yü, had put very forcefully some of the main arguments against Buddhism in a memorial to the throne some twenty-five years before, in 819. His particular crusade was to reintroduce a pure form of rational Confucianism, unsullied by the superstitions of either Buddhism or Taoism – a cause in which he was before his time, for it was to become fashionable only during the next dynasty, the Sung, under the name of Neo-Confucianism. On this particular occasion he was protesting against an annual event in which a finger-bone, supposedly one of Buddha's, was paraded through the streets among festive throngs of people before being taken into the palace to be welcomed and honoured by the emperor. This emperor happened to be genuinely well disposed towards Buddhism, and Han Yü soon found himself in exile, but his document became a classic. Part of it reads:

> Buddha was a man of the barbarians who did not speak the language of China and wore clothes of a different fashion. His sayings did not concern the ways of our ancient kings, nor did his manner of dress conform to their laws. He understood neither the duties that bind sovereign and subject, nor the affections of father and son. If he were still alive today and came to our court by order of his ruler, Your Majesty might condescend to receive him, but it would amount to no more than one audience in the Hsüan-cheng Hall, a banquet by

the Office for Receiving Guests, the presentation of a suit of clothes, and he would then be escorted to the borders of the nation, dismissed, and not allowed to deceive the masses. How then, when he has been long dead, could his rotten bones, the foul and unlucky remains of his body, be rightly admitted to the palace?[21]

A quarter of a century later the Emperor Wu had no need of such eloquent promptings, and from 844 the prohibitions followed in quick succession. At first all the smaller temples and shrines were ordered to be destroyed, and any monks or nuns not officially registered as such were to be defrocked. Next all monks and nuns under the age of forty were forced to return to ordinary life (finding no work and having no longer a respectable reason to beg, Ennin records later in his diary, many of them turned instead to petty crime). Soon the age was raised to fifty, and then anyone over fifty with even the smallest error in his documentation was to be defrocked. Finally, in 845, it was decreed that all Buddhist establishments should be destroyed except for one in every major prefecture, and four in each of the two capitals. The precious metals from all the images were destined for the state treasury. 'They have peeled off the gold from the Buddhas and smashed the bronze and iron Buddhas and measured their weight', noted Ennin, adding, 'What a pity! What limit was there to the bronze, iron and gold Buddhas of the land?'[22] That was indeed part of the trouble.

Foreign monks were to be deported. For Ennin this mingled good news with the bad, or as he put it 'there was both sorrow and joy'. Over the last four years he had made more than a hundred written applications to the authorities to be allowed to go home, with no success, but even so this was a miserable way to get his wishes. Many messages of sympathy and goodwill arrived from lay friends. There was a great bustle to get his precious manuscripts packed up and to round off his affairs before departure. He put on lay clothes for the first time in many years; someone brought him a felt hat to hide his shaven head. Even quite high officials sent him presents. Two rolls of silk, a large quantity of tea, and two strings of cash, each of a thousand coins, arrived from the Senior Secretary of the Regional Military Office. But the Censor Li outdid them all. He arrived in person, and his farewell gifts included ten rolls of damask, two sandalwood boxes with images, a bottle of incense, a scroll of the *Diamond Sutra* written in silver characters (which Ennin later presented to the Japanese emperor at home in Kyoto), two felt hats, a pair of soft slippers, and another two strings of cash. The Censor insisted on accompanying

Ennin out of Ch'ang-an, and spent the whole night talking with him in a village store where they made their first halt. Finally he had to say his farewell:

> You now have encountered this difficulty with the ruler, and are going back to your homeland. Your disciple believes that it is not likely that he will see you again in this life, but certainly in the future in the paradises of the various Buddhas I shall again be your disciple, as I am today. When you attain Buddhahood, please do not forget your disciple.[23]

He asked for Ennin's discarded robe and scarf, that he might keep them at home and burn incense before them.

And so it was, to a lesser degree, all along the route. Admittedly the bureaucrats, when confronted in their official capacity with the little party of foreign monks, did not dare to let them dawdle but hurried them on their way to the coast, and Ennin regretfully decided that it was only prudent to hide his precious holy manuscripts and travel on without them. But privately there was an extraordinary amount of help given from all sides.

Ennin's last great stroke of luck was that he had not yet managed to find a ship when, in 846, the emperor suddenly died (very possibly as a result of those Taoist elixirs which he had been taking in the hope of achieving the precise opposite – two of the favourite Taoist ingredients were mercury and arsenic). The next emperor reversed the policy of persecution, re-establishing many of the monasteries and executing a dozen of the Taoist advisers who had most influenced his predecessor. Ennin was able to recover his manuscripts, the original reason for his pilgrimage, and with them he at last sailed home again, in 847, to enjoy a further sixteen years of life as a revered patriarch of Japanese Buddhism.

In China the religion never quite recovered its former glory, yet it was far from finished. The response of lay people to Ennin in such troubled times had shown that Buddhism was too popular ever to be suppressed by decree. It remained an intrinsic part of Chinese life and thought, although just one among many strands. Even in Communist China there is an official Buddhist Association, which in the 1960s was said to represent 100 million lay people and 500,000 monks. A sociologist, studying a village in southwest China during the early 1940s, found among the ancestral tablets in the little family shrines (which by then even the poorest households contained) a friendly mixture of images of Confucius, of Lao Tzu, of Buddha and of Sun Yat-sen, the father of the republic.

China's method, at any rate until recently, has always been to retain whatever happens to suit it in each rival theory.

It is a measure of how much times had changed in the declining years of the T'ang dynasty that the foreign origin of Buddhism should have become an effective argument against it. In the first century of T'ang rule China had been more internationally minded than at any other time in her history, except perhaps for a spell during the early part of our own century. Ch'ang-an, with nearly two million inhabitants in the district and perhaps a million within the city walls, was the largest metropolis anywhere in the world. Foreign merchants and embassies flocked to it, both by land and sea, and their outlandish garments are portrayed with interest and possibly amusement in many of the T'ang pottery figurines. The Sassanid rulers of Persia sought refuge here after losing their throne in about 650. In the other direction, T'ang pottery has been found as far afield as Egypt.

But the year 751 brought a rude shock. T'ang armies had pressed even further into Central Asia than the Han, but now they were decisively defeated at the Talas River, east of Tashkent, by a new force more relentless than any of the wild local nomads. Their conquerors were the Arabs, carrying Islam far afield. Their progress had been astonishing. It was they who had ousted the Sassanids from Persia within less than twenty years of the death of the Prophet. In the other direction they entered Spain in 711 and soon penetrated as far into France as Poitiers, a mere 180 miles from Paris. Now, only a few years after defeating the Chinese on land in the northwest, they almost immediately reappeared by sea in the southeast. In 758 they arrived in sufficient strength to burn and loot Canton. In the seven years between these two disasters had come the rebellion of the young general An Lu-shan, himself of 'barbarian' origin, who temporarily drove the T'ang dynasty from both its capitals. It was not surprising that after a series of shocks China should somewhat draw in its horns.

The rebellion of An Lu-shan, coming precisely in the middle of the T'ang dynasty, in a sense broke its spine – just as the seizing of power by Wang Mang had that of the Han. In each case the dynasty was successfully re-established, but the second half never quite recovered the full glory of the first. It was in its initial flush of strength, during the seventh and early eighth centuries, that the T'ang dynasty had provided the climax – artistic, economic and military – to so many of the most important developments of early Chinese history.

There was one further and rather minor aspect of Chinese culture in which the T'ang dynasty also saw the climax – if the choice of word is not too unfortunate. Sex manuals had long been known in China. Eight were listed in the bibliography of the Han imperial library, with titles such as *Sex Handbook of Master Jung-ching* or *Recipes for Nursing Potency, by the Yellow Emperor and the Three Kings.* None of these survive, but there do still remain some written in the Sui dynasty, the brief predecessor of the T'ang, and such manuals seem to have reached their peak of popularity during the T'ang. They were illustrated with pictures of the various possibilities, and it was apparently quite usual for parents of the bride to slip a copy into the girl's trousseau (a custom which continued in Japan right up to the nineteenth century). The couple would keep it beside them in the bed, which was a spacious affair with wicker walls as well as curtains – almost more like a small cabin. It accommodated among its normal fittings a stand with toilet articles, a mirror, a frame on which to hang one's clothes, and sometimes even a bronze censer for 'scenting the quilts'. So there was ample room for study as well as practice.

The recommended positions, as in any such text book, ranged from the obvious to the impossible, but they were dignified in these Chinese versions by that age-old love of inventing delightful names. Thus the bride was instructed in the mechanics of the Kingfisher Union, Fluttering Butterflies, Phoenix Sporting in the Cinnabar Crevice, or Hounds of the Ninth Day of Autumn. Even the event itself was most poetically described. The husband was advised to vary his rhythm: 'A slow thrust should resemble the movement of a carp caught on the hook; a quick thrust should resemble the flight of birds against the wind.'[24]

There was only one aspect which might give a bride in many other societies cause for complaint. Many of these manuals were closely linked to the practices of Taoism, in which sex often played a central part, and this meant that much of the advice was concerned with the means for prolonging life. It was believed that sexual intercourse could reinforce a man's vitality – his *yang* being recharged by close contact with the woman's *yin* – but it was important to avoid, as far as possible, the loss of semen. The solution was rigorous self-control at the final moment of passion, when the wise lover 'closes his eyes and concentrates his thoughts, presses his tongue against the roof of his mouth, bends his back and stretches his neck, opens his nostrils wide and squares his shoulders, closes his mouth and sucks in his breath.' This would seem to leave the lady rather unattended, but even if fulfilled to the very letter this particular

A bed from an early copy of Ku K'ai–chih's scroll painting, The Admonitions

exercise was only guaranteed to prove effective seven times out of ten. The lover who was taking no chances must have been even less amusing. When threatened by his climax, he must 'quickly and firmly press with fore and middle finger of the left hand the spot between scrotum and anus, simultaneously inhaling deeply and gnashing his teeth scores of times.'[25] Maybe a wise bride kept the book from her husband.

Chapter 5

FEW TOPICS ARE MORE HOTLY DEBATED AMONG HISTORIANS OF China than how best to define the periods of her long history. Some maintain that the feudal period came to an end with the establishment of centralized rule by the first Ch'in emperor in 221 B.C.; some argue that it continued for almost another millenium until the T'ang; others believe that even before the Ch'in the word has no meaningful application to the conditions within China. In the same way the chaotic centuries between the Han and T'ang dynasties are on occasion called the Dark Ages, presumably on the understanding that the Han was the classical period. Elsewhere they can be found referred to as the Middle Ages, thus giving the T'ang the status of the Renaissance. Others award the Sung this treasured title, and then ask why it did not lead to the development of Galilean science, the rise of capitalism and the industrial revolution.

The trouble is that all these terms derive from periods in European history. It is a case of trying to fit out a very large client from a wardrobe of someone else's clothes. An extreme example, in reverse, might be a Chinese historian who observed the fascination of the English with Thomas à Becket – that 'upstart clerk', assassinated by the king to reduce the power of his faction – and who then fixed on this event as a turning-point in the rise of the English mandarins.

Even modern Chinese historians use a system of periods deriving from a Western model. Marx believed that society progresses through certain inevitable stages of economic development between man's original life in tribal communes and the ultimate achievement of a classless society. In his *Critique of Political Economy* he defined these stages as being characterized by 'the Asiatic, the ancient, the feudal, and the modern bourgeois modes of production'. These had already occurred. In the future lay Socialism, during which the state would ultimately wither away for the final achievement of true Communism.

Mao Tse-tung, adapting this theory to fit the Chinese experience, wrote in a text book in 1939:

> Developing along the same lines as many other nations of the world, the Chinese nation (chiefly the Hans) first went through some tens of thousands of years of life in classless primitive communes. Up to now approximately 4000 years have passed since the collapse of the primitive communes and the transition to class society, first slave society and then feudalism. . . .
>
> It was not until the middle of the nineteenth century that great internal changes took place in China as a result of the penetration of foreign capitalism. As China's feudal society developed its commodity economy and so carried

within itself the embryo of capitalism, China would of herself have developed slowly into a capitalist society even if there had been no influence of foreign capitalism. The penetration of foreign capitalism accelerated this development.[1]

Following this analysis, modern Chinese historians describe China as a slave society from 2000 B.C. to 475 B.C. (a date which in the traditional Chinese view of history signified the beginning of the Warring States period), and as a feudal society from then until 1840, when the British forced their way and their ways into China through the Opium War. The increasingly capitalist period, a prerequisite of Socialism in the Marxist view, is taken as running from then until the beginnings of Socialism in 1949.

This scheme differs in many respects from that generally accepted in the West (the economic importance of slaves for example, so evident in Greece and Rome, would be widely disputed in the Chinese context), but to describe the vast span from 475 B.C. to A.D. 1840 as a single period does emphasize one very real fact about the nature of Chinese history. Europe has lurched its way through a series of great convulsions and has emerged from each profoundly altered. China has lapsed at times into just as great chaos – in the gaps between those dynasties made famous by their stability – and it has emerged each time far from unchanged. But the change invariably seems a natural development, of very much the gradual type that might have been expected even without the upheaval. The long period identified in this way by Chinese historians begins, appropriately, just after the death of Confucius. His ideas were the binding agent in the development of traditional Chinese society, and it was to the early classics that later statesmen would invariably turn to find authority for their innovations.

In this gradual evolution, the late T'ang and early Sung is the nearest that one can come to a turning-point. It was now that the unique feature of a non-hereditary ruling class, based on bureaucracy and the examinations, at last established itself and set the pattern for the final thousand years of imperial history. It is in recognition of this most unusual aspect of their own culture that modern Chinese historians often modify Marx's definition of feudal society with the phrase 'bureaucratic feudalism'.

The ascendancy of the scholars over the hereditary nobility had begun with the reintroduction of the examinations under the Sui and T'ang emperors, but throughout the T'ang period there were many loop-

holes in the system – particularly that known as 'protection', by which powerful men were allowed to by-pass the examinations and slip their sons, or sometimes people quite unrelated to them, straight into important posts. Even under the Sung this was not entirely abolished, but now the great majority of the higher posts were reserved for those who had distinguished themselves in the examinations – or who were, in the official jargon, 'regularly submitted names'. It was said that in the first century of the Sung dynasty no one without a doctorate in letters became either a Censor or a Policy Critic, the only two departments in which, short of ministerial level, it was possible to influence important decisions. The scholars had at last come into their Chinese inheritance. From the Sung dynasty onwards they gave China an internal stability unparalleled in history (to their own considerable advantage, it goes without saying), even if at certain later periods it seemed more closely to resemble atrophy.

The founder of the Sung dynasty deliberately fostered the idea of a civil service based on talent alone. The T'ang dynasty had drifted in its last years towards economic and administrative collapse, before being finally exhausted by great popular uprisings in the north. As on other similar occasions, the only people to benefit had been the generals employed to quell the rebellion. A succession of five regional commanders seized the throne in turn during the unstable half-century known as the Five Dynasties. The sixth to do so was the founder of the Sung. He secured his dynasty by ensuring that there would not be a seventh in this series of ambitious generals. He deliberately broke the power of others like himself by bringing the best regiments to the centre under his own command and by replacing them in the border districts with inferior troops – a policy which strengthened his dynasty in the short term but ultimately harmed it – and he set about reducing the danger from the hereditary nobles by laying much greater emphasis on the examinations. His brother, who succeeded him on the throne, summed up the search for talent in a most evocative phrase: 'We are concerned that bosoms clothed in coarse fabrics may carry qualities of jade, and the fact remain unknown.'[2]

The examinations must have been nerve-racking affairs. The candidates had to rise in the middle of the night to present themselves at dawn. They brought food to last them through their ordeal, cold rice and cakes being regarded as normal. There was no question of being late, for during the examination the doors were barred – and in later dynasties even fastened with a seal. Each person sat in his own little kiosk, separated from

contact with anyone else not only by three walls but even by a sloping roof above his head. Examination halls containing row upon row of these tiny cells could still be seen in the late nineteenth century, and were the marvel of Western tourists.

The precautions taken against any sort of cheating or unfair advantage were extremely thorough, and were part of a long-standing Chinese tradition. In the Han dynasty there had been a most ingenious method to prevent candidates selecting a question which they had specially prepared. Each man had to shoot an arrow at the available questions, and must answer whichever he happened to transfix – a particularly appropriate device, since Confucius had encouraged archery as a subject fit for a gentleman. During the T'ang, pieces of blank paper were pasted over the candidate's name before the papers were marked, and the Sung emperors carried this precaution still further. To avoid anyone's handwriting being recognized, a special Bureau of Examination Copyists was established to transcribe all the answers. Even the examiners were subject to the same degree of control. Much like a papal enclave, they were locked up together – sometimes for a matter of weeks – and were forbidden to communicate with the outside world until the final grading of the papers had been agreed. They too were in a sense on trial, for their own merit would be judged by the later careers of those whom they passed with high marks. For this reason a strong link grew up between an examiner and his most successful candidates. It was in his own interest to further their careers. Whenever he later found himself in a position of power he could expect a sheaf of congratulatory poems from his top candidates, reminding him of their undying admiration and present addresses.

One factor which took something of the tension out of the examinations was that one could with honour return an indefinite number of times. There were cases of people passing at the fifteenth attempt, candidates in their seventies were not unknown, and grandfathers and grandsons had on occasion sat the papers together. For success was not solely the entrée to a career; it also bestowed a different status in society. Even in everyday terms it meant, like distinction at a school, that one could wear subtly different clothes. The unambitious, if born into wealth, might well retire after passing the examination to look after the family estate, and to lead a life of culture, ease and privilege which was not unlike the eighteenth-century English concept of the proper existence for a gentleman.

No society, even today, has ever achieved genuinely equal opportu-

nity, for the advantages and disadvantages of background are almost impossible to eliminate. But the Sung did far more along these lines than might seem probable (and did so, to put the matter in perspective, some decades before the time of the Norman conquest). Detailed figures survive for two years of examination results. The successful candidates were from widely differing economic backgrounds, and more than half of them came from families which during the previous three generations had no connection at all with the official classes. It was extraordinary also to what degree high political office was now linked with intellectual excellence. In the early Sung period all the best writers of either prose or poetry, with at the very most three exceptions, held senior posts in the administration. This close connection between artists and government is an idea hard to grasp in the West. There were, for example, in Hangchow two large embankments in the lake which were named after leading poets – Po Chü-i of the T'ang dynasty and Su Tung-p'o of the Sung. This seems familiar enough, for we too have enjoyed naming streets or buildings after poets. A parallel, bringing the situation forward several centuries, might be a Milton Dyke and a Pope Causeway. But there is one crucial difference. The embankments were named after the two Chinese poets because they had been personally responsible for constructing or improving them while holding office in the city.

Su Tung-p'o can be taken as typical of the best elements of the Sung dynasty, much as Po Chü-i was of the T'ang. He was an outstanding example of the Sung scholar-official, a fully rounded gentleman proficient in all the arts, an effortless amateur equally famous for his intellectual, artistic and moral distinction. He has a place in the very highest rank of literature for his prose as well as his poetry. He was admired both as a painter and as a theorist in art, and his calligraphy was considered so outstanding that even during his lifetime examples of it were inscribed in stone. He was extremely convivial, notably partial to wine, and sufficiently interested in food to devise a new way of cooking pork which has passed into Chinese cuisine. Above all, when in office, he was fearless in speaking his opinion.

In 1070, at the age of thirty-two, Su was employed in the palace in the Department of History, a job in which he had no brief to criticize imperial policy. But this was the period when Wang An-shih, the most powerful minister of the entire dynasty, was introducing some much-needed economic reforms. Su opposed the high-handed manner in which Wang was pushing his measures through, dismissing any Censor who did

not agree with him. He therefore submitted, in the course of a year, three memorials to the emperor, the second of which ran to some 9000 words. They were far from muffled in style. He mentioned the disturbing and persistent rumours that the punishment of mutilation was about to be reintroduced to quell popular unrest:

> Even Your Majesty and the few ministers close to you have heard of these rumours. You have disregarded them by saying: 'Why should I worry about these rumours when there is no basis to them?' While it is true that such rumours may not all be correct yet they must have sprung up for good reasons. A man must be greedy before he is accused of being a thief, and a man must be loose in his morals before he is accused of immorality with women. . . .[3]

Dangerously colourful words, one might think, to use to an emperor. But Su was left free to write a third memorandum the following month. He was then moved to a provincial posting, but it was to the delightful city of Hangchow and there is some evidence that the emperor, taking the criticism like a true Confucian, had shielded Su from the wrath of Wang An-shih and his faction.

On later occasions Su was more effectively banished – to remote districts, where he held some insignificant office with almost no salary. Here, in spite of his own comparative poverty, he continued to fulfil the proper role of a scholar living in retirement. He lobbied local officials to redress cases of injustice, and spent his days ploughing his ten acres. In the evenings he would entertain local friends to soirées of poetry, painting and chess – with plentiful wine, home-brewed if nothing else was available.

All educated Chinese felt the pull towards a quiet life among the beauties of the countryside. It was the Taoist respite from Confucian responsibilities, the consolation which made tolerable, even at times almost desirable, the loss of office. Because of the obvious link with Taoism, it was only natural sooner or later to make some effort to find that tantalizing elixir. Su Tung-p'o sought it on several occasions, although, in keeping with the new rationalism of the age, he sought it in a less literal way than most. He seemed to be hoping not for a magic moment of chemistry in the crucible but for a transformation within himself, to be achieved by various forms of abstinence and mental control. On one occasion he remembered in his journal how Po Chü-i had set about it long ago on more conventional lines, constructing a special furnace at his country cottage. Po had tried to fuse sulphur and mercury

in accordance with a recipe of the second century A.D. He failed – perhaps fortunately, since the idea was to eat the mixture – but his light-hearted description of the experiment is most endearing:

> *My platform of clay was accurately squared,*
> *The compass showed that my tripod was perfectly round.*
> *At the very first motion of the furnace-bellows*
> *A red glow augured that all was well.*
> *I purified my heart and sat in solitary awe;*
> *In the middle of the night I stole a furtive glance.*
> *The two ingredients were in affable embrace;*
> *Their attitude was most unexpected,*
> *They were locked together in the posture of man and wife,*
> *Intertwined as dragons, coil on coil.*
> *The bell sounded from the Chien-chi Kuan,*
> *Dawn was breaking on the Peak of Purple Mist.*
> *It seems that the dust was not yet washed from my heart;*
> *The stages of the firing had gone all astray.*
> *A pinch of the elixir would have meant eternal life;*
> *A hair-breadth wrong, and all my labours lost!*[4]

Confucians were able to adapt their reasonable selves, within limits, to the demands of the spirit world. The official state religion, which the cult of Confucius came near to rivalling at times, was the worship of certain nature deities, such as Heaven and Earth, in ceremonies where the emperor identified himself with the cycle of the seasons and the growth of the crops. It was the Confucians who officiated at these rites, and so it was a part of their normal duties to take account of the spirit world. In practice it often seemed as though the spirits were expected to conform to the standards of Confucian bureaucracy, and popular tales told of a duplicate civil service down below, where spirit officials had careers to make and would hope for promotion if they controlled affairs on earth efficiently. Both Po Chü-i and Su Tung-p'o had at various times to negotiate with the spirits. As befitted his more aggressive dynasty, it was Po who took the markedly tougher line. There was a drought in 823, when he was Governor of Hangchow. He prayed to the Black Dragon of the North in the following words:

We are asking you for a favour, but you depend on us for your divinity. Creatures are not divine on their own account, it is their worshippers that make them so. If within three days there is a real downpour we shall give your holy powers the credit for it, and the rain will certainly be a great blessing to the peasants.[5]

Su Tung-p'o, confronted by a similar problem, worked instead on the spirit's behalf. When there was no response to the usual prayers for rain, he inquired when this spirit had last been co-operative. Never once, he was informed, since the emperor had awarded it the rank of viscount. After some research in the local histories, Su discovered that under the T'ang this particular spirit had been classed as a duke. He prepared a memorial to the emperor, asking that the original rank be restored, and even before the answer came back in the affirmative the rain clouds had appeared.

When Su and his friends gathered together, the two essential ingredients for a good party were both liquid – wine and ink. There is a delightful description of his going to dine alone with another scholar-artist:

> Two long tables were placed facing each other, and on them were piled fine brushes, exquisite ink and 300 sheets of paper, with some food and drink at the side. When Tung-p'o saw this arrangement, he laughed heartily and then sat down. Between each drink they would flatten the paper and write. Two page-boys were kept busy grinding the ink, but they could hardly keep up with the speed of the writers. Towards evening the wine was giving out, and so was the paper. Then each of them took the other's papers and said good-bye. Afterwards they found that they had never done better writing.[6]

On this occasion the order of the day had been calligraphy, but when somebody raised his brush there was no way of knowing for certain what he was about to do with it. Had a poem just occurred to him? Or was he moved to produce some calligraphy, the rhythms of his whole body expressing themselves through the tip of the brush in the almost sacred beauty of Chinese characters? Or was he about to paint a picture? The three activities merged almost imperceptibly. Not only would the same brush serve each purpose, but the poem would be all the more admired for being beautifully written; the calligraphy would make use of precisely those qualities of rhythm and space which are necessary in a painting; and the painting, done in flowing and unalterable sweeps of the brush, would demand the same type of ease and spontaneity as an improvised poem. The different forms were alternative vehicles for the same impulse, a fact recognized in one conventional image in which a 'soundless poem' means a picture:

> *Master Li had a phrase he didn't want to express in words,*
> *So with light ink he sketched out a soundless poem.*[7]

Even the subject-matter was often identical. The following poem, en-

titled *Fisherman*, could be a description of any one of dozens of paintings. It was written by the great Sung scholar and author, Ou-yang Hsiu – who incidentally was something of a patron to Su Tung-p'o, for he was the examiner who first recognized his talents.

> *The wind blows the line out from his fishing pole.*
> *In a straw hat and grass cape the fisherman*
> *Is invisible in the long reeds.*
> *In the fine spring rain it is impossible to see very far*
> *And the mist rising from the water has hidden the hills.*[8]

Paintings of landscapes, flowers, trees and birds became increasingly popular under the Sung and were to remain so in later dynasties, almost to the exclusion of other subjects. Kuo Hsi, one of the leading Sung landscape-painters and a contemporary of Su Tung-p'o, explained this appeal as another aspect of escapism from the cares of official life, a convenient substitute for a more full-scale retreat into Taoism:

It is human nature to resent the hustle and bustle of society, and to wish to see, but not always succeed in seeing, immortals hidden among the clouds. In times of peace, under a good emperor and kind parents, it would be wrong to go off alone and try to find oneself. For there is duty and responsibility which cannot be ignored. . . . . But the dream of a retreat to forests and springs and finding the company of saints in retreat is always there. We are usually excluded from the sights and sounds of nature. Now a good artist has reproduced it for us. One can imagine oneself sitting on rocks in a gully and hearing the

cries of monkeys and birds; while in one's own sitting-room the light of the mountains and the colours of the water dazzle one's eyes. Is it not a joy, a fulfilment of one's dream? That is why paintings of landscape are in such demand.[9]

It may seem fanciful of Kuo Hsi to claim that Chinese painters reproduce any recognizable landscape in their weird groups of towering peaks, but in fact the countryside in certain districts does to an astonishing extent provide the artists with almost equally fantastic models. And so the weary official was able to take down a scroll from the shelf and let his spirit roam in the landscape which literally unfurled, as a Chinese painting does, before his eyes.

The possession of paintings was only one aspect of an increasingly fashionable connoisseurship. During the Sung dynasty many ancient bronzes and jades were found at An-yang. They must have dated, like the recent finds at the same site, from the Shang dynasty, but even if their extreme age was not fully appreciated they stimulated a craze for the collection and study of antiquities. Ou-yang Hsiu, the author of the poem on the fisherman, was a devoted student of ancient inscriptions which he found 'scattered all over the country, in the mountains and around the lakes, on precarious cliffs and inaccessible gorges, in wild forests and abandoned tombs'.[10] He had rubbings made of them and the final result, totalling about 1000 portfolios, was his famous *Collection of Ancient Inscriptions*. Ou-yang was also in the forefront of the move to introduce a simpler style of prose, in place of the extremely artificial forms which were then in vogue. His innovation was known, in a typical Chinese paradox, as the Ancient Style, for it was a return to the more starkly expressive methods of the pre-Han classics. Precisely the same motives were now inspiring scholars to seek a way back to what they believed to be the true spirit of ancient Confucianism, before it had been overlaid by the accretion of centuries. These interests have often led to the Sung being likened to the Renaissance, with its very similar quest for a new lease of life from antiquity. But such attitudes were endemic in China. They were merely applied now with a new intellectual rigour.

Foremost among Sung connoisseurs was the Emperor Hui Tsung, the catalogue of whose collection of art listed 6396 paintings by 231 artists, spanning the nine centuries from the end of the Han to the present time. The emperor was himself a distinguished painter. One of the most beautiful surviving copies of a T'ang painting is his version of *Ladies Making Silk* (colour, pages 146–7). In his own work he liked above all to paint

Fishing in a Mountain Stream *(painting by Hsü Tao-ning), and riverside mountains in Shansi*

birds, in a painstakingly exact style which at its best can be extremely attractive, at its worst somewhat stilted.

But the emperor was not content with his own excellence. He was determined to impose his style on others, and he had the power to do so. He set up a formal academy, in which the artists had to take examinations just like the civil servants. One of the standard tasks at the academy was to make copies of the emperor's own paintings (a situation which has made reliable attribution something of a nightmare for modern scholars). Another was to paint his palace walls, a job in which the artists found themselves liable to constant interruption. The emperor quite often passed by, says an almost contemporary historian, and 'whenever a painting did not correspond to his ideas, he had it plastered over and gave the painter some new advice'.[11]

Almost any academy tends towards the conventional, and in this one, with such a patron, there was no escaping it. Increasingly there became a rift between the careful craftsmanship of the professionals and the ideal of spontaneous self-expression which was being developed by the scholar-artists. Su Tung-p'o was one of the first to describe it. His urge to paint was released, characteristically, by alcohol:

> *Receiving the moisture of wine,*
> *My intestines sprout and fork out,*
> *And from out my liver and lungs*
> *Shoot rocks and bamboos.*
> *Surging through my breast, irresistible,*
> *They find expression on your snow-white wall.*[12]

The scholars were by nature the least likely of people to fulfil this very difficult ideal. It was achieved, instead, by a school of Buddhist painters in the later years of the Sung dynasty. They were of the sect most concerned with spontaneity – Zen, known in China by its original name of Ch'an. One of the best of them, Liang K'ai, was the perfect image of the romantic unruly artist, the extreme opposite end of the spectrum from Hui Tsung's civil servants. He had started in the official academy, where he won great distinction, but when they offered him their highest award, the Golden Girdle, he rudely rejected it and retired to spend the rest of his life, much of it under the influence of drink, in a Ch'an monastery. Here he greeted his students with shouts and roaring and produced, during the brief spells that the mood was upon him, some magnificent paintings. His picture of a Ch'an patriarch cutting bamboo has all the immediacy that

An ideal portrait of Li Po, and the Sixth Patriarch cutting bamboo; both by Liang K'ai

Su Tung-p'o hoped for. The kneeling figure is brilliantly created in broad strokes of the brush almost more familiar in calligraphy (the old man seems a Chinese character in every sense of the word). And his idealized portrait of the great T'ang poet Li Po, achieving great vividness with even greater economy, is rightly one of the most famous of Chinese images.

Painting was only one of the many glories of the Sung dynasty. Almost every period in Chinese history has excelled in the art of pottery, but for classical elegance none can rival the Sung porcelains and celadons, often with glazes of the purest monochrome. (colour, pages 145 and 148.) It is a period of lovely simplicity, between the energy and realism of the T'ang figures and the elaborate ornamentation which was to characterize the equally impressive porcelains of the later dynasties.

In intellectual fields, too, this was a time of unrivalled energy. A huge encyclopedia was completed in 981, gathering together, in a thousand sections, systematic extracts from earlier books. A similar work on architecture, the classic of its kind, appeared in about the year 1100, and another was produced on geography (the rather mole-like labour of compilation was highly attractive to traditional Chinese scholarship). Early in the twelfth century an *Imperial Medical Encyclopedia* was completed, to be followed by monographs on botany and zoology. In about 1086 one of the earliest accounts of the magnetic compass had appeared, and some forty years before that a *Compendium of Military Technology* provided a prescription for gunpowder – at this stage being used only in the form of bombs and fire-balls flung from catapults, or else for fireworks. Out of the mass of detail preserved in the Standard Histories, a single comprehensive account of the history of China was written in this same century by Ssu-ma Kuang, the first such undertaking since Ssu-ma Ch'ien's nearly twelve centuries before; the emperor gave this great work an equally weighty title, *The Comprehensive Mirror for Aid in Government*, which perfectly expresses the Chinese idea of the importance of history. Finally, the entire Confucian canon had by now been printed, as had also the vastly extensive Buddhist and Taoist scriptures.

The development of printing had been crucial to this burst of intellectual activity, and it in its turn had depended on the earlier Chinese discovery of paper, traditionally credited to the eunuch Ts'ai Lun in A.D. 105. Of the four most often quoted Chinese inventions – paper, printing, gunpowder and the compass – paper had been the earliest and was the one which took longest (an amazing ten centuries) to reach Europe.

Within forty years of its supposed invention, it must already have

Celadon wine jug of the Northern Sung period. OVERLEAF *Ladies ironing silk, from a scroll by the T'ang painter Chang Hsüan, copied by the Sung emperor Hui Tsung (detail)*

become a comparatively cheap writing material in China. Some time before 143 a scholar apologizes in a letter to a friend:

> I am sending you the works of Hsü Tzu in ten rolls. Being unable to afford a copy of silk, I provide only a paper copy.[13]

During the following centuries the use of paper spread through East Asia, but it was not till the defeat of the Chinese by the Arabs at the Talas River in 751 that it began its slow and very roundabout journey towards Europe. Certain Chinese prisoners taken to Samarkand were paper-makers and they set up a factory there. A few decades later Harun al-Rashid, of *Arabian Nights* fame, brought several of these craftsmen to Baghdad. In the following century, in about 890, a letter written in Egypt ends with the words 'Excuse the papyrus' – the precise opposite of the earlier Chinese apology, suggesting that paper was still at this stage the latest thing and the height of fashion in Alexandria. From there the techniques of paper-making travelled through the Arab provinces of North Africa and so up into Spain, but it was another three centuries before the first recorded mill was established in Christendom, in 1189, on the French side of the Pyrenees. This was more than 1000 years after it had first become cheap in China, and already the Chinese had anticipated another modern use for it. Arab merchants, travelling east in the ninth century, had responded with horror – as many still would. 'They are not clean', one of them protested; 'they never wash themselves with water when they have defecated, but wipe themselves with Chinese paper.'[14]

Printing developed in a more gradual and even haphazard manner. Many antecedents have been suggested, such as the Chinese use of seals to stamp their marks on paper or silk, or the great demand among the Buddhists for charms and images which were often mass-produced from small blocks. But the most influential single event bore no relationship to the concept of printing. In A.D. 175 a Han emperor ordered that texts of the six main Confucian classics should be carved in stone, to preserve them for posterity in an authenticated version. Once this was done, scholars came to take their own rubbings on paper of the precious documents – in a process very similar to the techniques of brass-rubbing today. It became a tradition for successive dynasties to carve further texts and commentaries, which in their turn were copied. Thus the Confucian classics were spread in a process which was, quite accidentally, akin to that of printing.

Even so, it is from among the Buddhists that the earliest known printed

Celadon tripod vessel made in imitation of an ancient bronze vessel, 12th century

book survives. It is one of the objects brought back by Sir Aurel Stein from the archive at Tun-huang, and is a copy of the *Diamond Sutra*. The text is printed from six large blocks, each of them two and a half feet long by almost a foot broad. The scroll is a worthy and complete ancestor of all subsequent books, for it contains not only a superb woodcut as a frontispiece, but even a dedication and the traditional colophon at the end: 'printed on May 11, 868, by Wang Chieh, for free general distribution, in order in deep reverence to perpetuate the memory of his parents.'[15]

The Confucians, in their turn, can take credit for the world's first large-scale printing project, but it too was almost an accident – the result of economy rather than any wish to see the wider spread of literature. It was also a memorial to how much China achieved even in its periods of apparent chaos, for the project was undertaken and completed in the time of the Five Dynasties, between T'ang and Sung.

An image of Feng Tao, traditionally regarded as the inventor of printing, should have stood on the mantelpiece of the Vicar of Bray, for he contrived to serve as chief minister to no less than four of these five dynasties. In 932 he suggested to the emperor of the second of them, the Later T'ang, that just as the Han and T'ang dynasties had carved a correct version of the classics, so should he. The suggestion was no doubt intended to raise the

prestige of a very shaky little regime, but it was accompanied by a rather lame proviso: 'Our dynasty has too many other things to do and cannot undertake such a task as to have stone inscriptions erected.'[16] Feng Tao followed this up with a startling proposal. In Szechuan he had seen books printed from blocks of wood, and he felt that this compromise, so much cheaper than stone inscriptions, might be acceptable. The emperor agreed. Twenty-one years and three dynasties later Feng Tao was proud to present, to a quite different royal family, his complete edition of the classics and their commentaries in 130 volumes. Within another five years the Sung dynasty had been inaugurated and was able to reap the benefits of this new aid to scholarship and learning.

The Sung whirlpool of intellectual energy was accompanied by a life of increasing luxury for the court and the official classes, and soon the usual economic crises were threatening. In the two earlier periods of comparable lavishness, the Han and the T'ang, some of the wealth had been provided by a successful policy of imperial expansion, bringing in new territories and trade. But where the Han and T'ang had been notably aggressive, the Sung dynasty was different – partly because the frontier provinces had been deliberately weakened to increase imperial control at the centre, and partly due to the very success of the examination system, bringing in a new intellectual élite whose talents were far from military. The profession of soldier had become despised, and was to remain so for many centuries. Wang An-shih, the leading Sung statesman, warned his emperor in 1058 of the dangers:

> Who today is unaware of the fact that the frontier guards and imperial guards cannot be depended upon to keep the peace? But since the educated men of the land regard the carrying of weapons as a disgrace, and since none of them is able to ride, shoot, or has any familiarity with military manœuvres, who is there to take up this responsibility but the hired soldiery?[17]

He also expressed, with great clarity, the dangers of a luxurious way of life in an economy which was neither gaining new territory nor increasing production:

> The deficit of the government nowadays is not due to excessive expenditures alone, but also to the lack of ways to increase incomes. Those who wish to enrich their families merely take from the state; those who wish to enrich the state merely take from the country; and those who wish to enrich the country merely take from natural resources. The case is analagous to that of a family in which no effort is being made for the son to increase his income, but the

demanding father merely takes from him. Though the family hopes to become more wealthy, it never will be, for there are only transactions behind the closed doors of the family, with nothing coming in from outside.[18]

The two problems, military and economic, were closely related. The age-old militia system, in which one of the peasants' obligations was to do occasional military service, had long been replaced by a fully professional army – though professional only in the sense of being paid. The incompetence of those who were willing to be employed as soldiers, combined with the ever-growing pressures from the nomads to the north of this unmartial empire, led to such growth in the sheer size of the army that at one point in the eleventh century it was calculated to be consuming eighty per cent of the government's total expenditure.

Military weakness also caused another drain on the economy which, although insignificant in the sums of money involved, was a portent of dangers to come. In their dealings with the tribes to the north, the Sung emperors had failed to learn from the mirror of history one of the main lessons of the Han dynasty. The Han had been constantly troubled by the Hsiung-nu, just as the Sung now were by the Liao, and they had at first attempted to pacify them with tribute. Naturally the price always rose, while the raids hardly decreased. It had only been when Wu Ti changed to a policy of aggression that the problem had begun to be solved. Yet in 1004 the Sung emperor attempted to buy peace from his wild neighbours on exactly the same basis. The price was an annual payment of 300,000 'units' – a form of currency which allowed payment in any of four commodities, one unit consisting either of a roll of silk or a fixed quantity of grain, copper cash or silver. Forty years later the barbarians' price had almost trebled, and still there was no peace. The quantities, large though they sound, represented less than two per cent of the Sung revenue. But this tribute-in-reverse, little other than protection money, was a humiliating entry in the imperial accounts.

As in other periods, the pressing need for funds led to more and more demands on the tax-paying peasants, while less and less seemed to be contributed by the landowning families and the exempted mandarins – the Chinese equivalents of that class dubbed by Cobbett in England as the tax-eaters. It was to redress this balance that Wang An-shih introduced, between 1069 and 1076, his controversial reforms – controversial not only then, but ever since. The overall intention was to shift the tax burden slightly more on to the shoulders of the richer classes, and it has been much debated whether his measures were socialist in principle or merely an

attempt at a practical solution to the problem, with the evidence tending to suggest the latter. Whatever the motives, the reforms immediately aroused the hostility of the class that stood to lose by them. It seems to have been largely due to official obstruction that they amounted, in practice, to very little.

In 1076 Wang was forced into retirement by the opposition to his policies, and for the next forty years his opponents and his somewhat unscrupulous supporters alternated in power, frustrating each others' measures while the situation steadily deteriorated. There was a succession of peasant uprisings – the invariable warning in Chinese history that the exactions of the ruling classes have at last reached intolerable limits – and during the 1120s the Emperor Hui Tsung laid aside his painting to make a most fateful decision. A new power, calling themselves the Chin, had arisen among the tribes in the north and seemed capable of overwhelming China's barbarian enemies of longer standing, the Liao. Hui Tsung decided to join forces with the Chin for that purpose. The result was all too predictable. The Liao were defeated, but the Chin were not sufficiently civilized to keep their part of the bargain. They continued southwards, seized the imperial capital, Kaifeng, in 1127 and carried off into captivity Hui Tsung, his entire family and much of his court, amounting in all to some 3000 people. They never returned.

One prince escaped, for he was not in Kaifeng when the city fell. The barbarians pressed on towards the Yangtze but in the region south of the Yellow River the Chinese were at last able to hold them. After several uncertain years the new emperor and his court settled at Hangchow. Here, with only half their empire left, the Southern Sung were to enjoy another century of prosperous rule.

The chaos of this retreat from the north is vividly portrayed in the story of one of China's most distinguished lady poets, Li Chiang-chao. Her experiences also give an intriguing glimpse of that obsession with antiquities which was shared by Ou-yang Hsiu, by the Emperor Hui Tsung, and by so many others at this period.

In 1100, when she was nineteen, she married a young student, Chao Ming-cheng. His greatest ambition was to cap the work of Ou-yang Hsiu by compiling a complete account of all the important surviving inscriptions on bronze and stone. She describes their early life together:

> When we were married my husband was twenty-one, he was a student in the National University at Pien-lang. Both our families were poor and we led a simple life since we had to be very careful of our expenditure. But every

month after my husband had received his stipendium he would pawn some clothes and with the 500 cash thus realized stroll to the Hsiang-kuo Temple, and on the market there buy a few copies of old inscriptions together with some fruit. Back home we would together go over those documents, munching fruit all the while, and we felt as happy as if we were living in the Abode of the Immortals.

Two years later my husband received an official appointment in the Provinces. Then our food and clothing were assured, and he could gratify his interest in old documents from near and distant places all over the Empire. In course of time he assembled an extensive collection. . . . When he saw a specimen of the calligraphy or painting by some famous artist of old or later times, or a rare bronze vessel of high antiquity he would again pawn his clothes in order to purchase it.[19]

They would stay up together late at night, inspecting and discussing the pictures and bronzes, 'leaving off only when the candles had burned down'. On other occasions, after their evening meal, they would sit with cups of tea in their library playing a game of quotations, challenging each other to find a given passage in the crowded bookshelves. The winner was allowed to drink his or her tea first, and sometimes, says Li Chiang-chao, she laughed so much that all the tea spilled down her robe and there was nothing left to drink. But the political situation was becoming increasingly alarming:

We heard that the barbarians were attacking the capital. Suddenly we stared at all our treasured belongings, we started to pack them in boxes and baskets, filled with sorrowful foreboding. For we realized that we would probably not be able to keep them much longer.

During the three years after the fall of Kaifeng the couple moved house again and again, as their sophisticated Chinese world shrank steadily southwards. Each time they had to leave behind or sell off part of their collection. Then, in 1129, Chao was ordered to a more than usually dangerous post. He decided to send his wife and what remained of their treasures to somewhere a little safer. They travelled the first part of their two journeys together by boat, till they came to the place where he had to continue on horseback:

Standing there on the shore in his travelling robe his spirit was undaunted as that of a tiger, and his eyes shone. While we were taking leave of each other, I staying in the boat, my heart was suddenly filled with dread. I called out to him: 'What shall I do when I hear that the situation in the city gets worse?'

Waving his hand at me he called out over the water: 'You won't be able to preserve them all. First discard the heavy luggage, then clothes and quilts. Then the books and paintings, and finally the antique bronzes. But the pieces of porcelain you must carry yourself, they should perish or survive together with you!' Then he galloped away along the muddy road.

She never saw him again. He died of an illness, not at the hands of the barbarians. Piece by piece she sold the collection to stay alive as she wandered round the country, sometimes revisiting places where they had been together:

> *In front of our window*
> *Are the banana trees we planted,*
> *Their green shadows fill the yard.*
> *Their green shadows fill the yard,*
> *Their leaves unfold and fold as if*
> *They want to bare their feelings.*
>
> *Sadly reclining on my pillow*
> *Deep in the night I listen to the rain,*
> *Dripping on the leaves.*
> *Dripping on the leaves –*
> *That he can't hear that sound again*
> *Is breaking my heart.*

Thieves took the last few remaining pieces, but she still had his manuscript – all that had been completed of his *magnum opus*. In 1132, when conditions were becoming more stable, she settled at Hangchow and there prepared his work for publication; the *Chin-shih-lu*, or 'Record of Inscriptions on Bronze and Stone', in thirty chapters.

It was in the postscript to this book that she described their life together. When the work was complete, she left Hangchow again. Nothing is known of her later life.

Hangchow had obvious charms as a capital, together with one major strategic advantage – the surrounding countryside of lakes and ricefields was unsuitable to the brilliant feats of horsemanship on which the strength of the northern tribes was based. This beautiful city was to have its greatest days under the Southern Sung, but it was many years before the emperors were willing to acknowledge that it had indeed become their capital. They cherished still the fantasy that they would recover the northern territories. A poem written on the wall of an inn at Hangchow expressed the dichotomy, the beguiling charms of this present place and the longing for that other capital city now in barbarian hands:

Hill beyond green hill, pavilion behind pavilion –
At the West Lake, will the singing and the dancing never cease?
It's the warm wind that lulls them and beguiles them into thinking
That this place is the other one we knew in times of peace.[20]

But their enemies in the north were to fall to a more serious threat than the Chinese could produce. A new power was amassing in the steppes – the Mongols. Incredibly, the Sung emperors repeated their earlier mistake. They sided with the Mongols against the Chin, who were overwhelmed in 1234. The Sung succeeded in holding out against their new neighbours for a few more decades – largely because of other distractions in the vast Mongol empire – but in 1279 they were finally subdued. For the first time in history an alien conqueror was master of all China. He was Kublai Khan.

IT HAD BEEN CHINA'S CONSTANT PROBLEM THAT THE LAND TO THE north was the breeding ground of most of the world's conquering hordes. Indeed the very word horde, or *ordo*, derives from this area. The inhospitable steppes of Mongolia and Siberia were perfectly devised to rear people of unparalleled toughness and then to provide them with the strongest possible motive for moving on to greener pastures elsewhere. In Chinese history the names of many of these tribal groups became painfully familiar, as they pressed south towards the Great Wall and often through it, carving out new territories and even setting up their own minor dynasties. Only three of them impressed themselves on Western minds by striking so far from their original homeland that they entered deep into Europe – the Huns, the Turks and the Mongols. Of these the latter were incomparably the most successful and alarming.

Chapter 6

YÜAN

There is greater disparity between the beginnings and the end of Temujin, who won for himself the title Jenghiz Khan, than can be found in the life of any other human being. His was not the case of a minor potentate successfully extending his territory. Admittedly his father had been the head of a small clan, but he was poisoned when Temujin was only eight, whereupon the clan, lacking an effective chieftain, promptly abandoned the boy and his mother. According to the *Secret History of the Mongols*, an account written within two or three decades of Jenghiz Khan's death, the small family – Temujin himself, his mother, and several other brothers and half-brothers – subsisted at this period on wild plants and small creatures, among them mice. In other words they lacked even the flock of animals which provides a nomad with wealth, food, drink, clothing, fuel, and a soft roof over his head. This may be a slightly romantic account of the depths from which the great man had risen, turning perhaps an occasional mouse into a whole way of life, but one can make the same point in less colourful fashion. So difficult was Temujin's climb to a position of any effective authority, slowly building up an alliance of clans which would accept his leadership, that it was not until he was about forty that he was elected khan of the Mongols, themselves merely one among many tribal groups occupying the steppes. Yet when he died, twenty years later, his rule extended from the Caspian to the northern coast of China.

The physical power of this great empire had been founded on the skills of the Mongol horsemen, standing in their stirrups to fire their heavy bows to devastating effect as they wheeled in battle, or covering unimaginable distances with vital news by the simple device of men galloping in

relay, night and day, between the well-equipped staging posts spread across the steppes and deserts of Central Asia. But the growth of the empire had a psychological basis, too, in a ruthless combination of trust and terror. While building up his own Mongol following, Jenghiz rewarded courage and loyalty. Anyone who had fought well against him and been defeated was offered promotion. Only cowardice and treachery were punished. Later, when he was expanding into alien lands, the conditions were reversed. Towns which put up a brave resistance were brutally and publicly massacred, the inhabitants being herded outside the walls and the Mongol troopers being told to set to with battle-axes (a tally of ears would sometimes be required as proof that each had dispatched his allotted quota). Terror stalked ahead of the horde like an invisible ally. With it went spies to infiltrate the walled cities and to spread the word that immediate surrender might be rewarded with mercy. Often the citizens needed little persuading. The alternative was already notorious.

During the conqueror's lifetime his vast empire had been divided between his four sons. Couriers, capable of travelling up to 200 miles in a day, kept Jenghiz informed of their plans and campaigns. With such a system, and such a father, disunity was out of the question. But in the next generation, when his grandsons had come into the far-flung regions of their inheritance, there was no such natural cohesion.

This was the generation of Kublai Khan. Although his father had been the youngest of the four sons, his was the branch of the family which within twenty-five years of the death of Jenghiz had become the most powerful. In 1351 Kublai's elder brother, Möngke, became the Great Khan, the fourth to hold Jenghiz's proud title. He entrusted the continuing campaign against China to Kublai and sent his next brother, Hulagu, to press further south and west through Iran. By 1258 Hulagu had captured and destroyed Baghdad, and in the following year he took Damascus and reached the Mediterranean. The three brothers formed a mighty pyramid of power, the apex being Möngke in the capital at Karakorum, in the heart of Mongolia, with Kublai on the North China Sea to one side and Hulagu on the Mediterranean to the other. But in this same year, 1259, Möngke died.

Almost immediately signs of disintegration became apparent. In the east Kublai fought yet another brother, younger than himself, for the title of Great Khan – it was the first time that this crucial family decision had been decided by warfare, and it took Kublai four years to establish his claim. At much the same time Hulagu found himself at war in the Caucasus

with a cousin who ruled the Golden Horde in southern Russia. The struggle was partly over territory and partly along religious lines, for the cousin had recently embraced Islam and viewed with outrage the brutal destruction of the caliphate at Baghdad by Hulagu, who still followed the family religion of Shamanism, a cult of medicine men. There was one minor but fascinating result of their war which neither cousin could be aware of. It blocked the route home of two Venetian merchants, Niccolo and Matteo Polo, who were trading near the Caspian. They were advised that their safest course was to continue eastwards. With reluctance they accepted this advice.

Meanwhile Kublai Khan was becoming increasingly Chinese. In 1260 he had begun to use Peking, south of the Great Wall, as his winter capital, and seven years later he started to rebuild on a grandiose scale this city which had been largely destroyed by his grandfather as long ago as 1215. He seemed to be acknowledging that the centre of gravity of his empire had shifted. In 1271 he announced the beginning of a new Chinese dynasty, with himself as the first emperor, and chose for it a Chinese name – Ta Yüan, meaning Great Origin. Jenghiz Khan was given the posthumous title, in traditional Chinese fashion, of T'ai Tsu or Grand Progenitor. Kublai's campaign against the Sung dynasty in the south dragged on for several more years, but at last, in 1276, Hangchow fell to his armies. Three years later the last traces of Sung resistance had been eliminated. The Son of Heaven and the Great Khan were one and the same. Never before had the Chinese empire been so vast – although in truth Kublai's authority as Great Khan over his distant relations was now little more than nominal.

From the start Kublai had shown his intention of governing along Chinese lines. Even when his rule extended no further than a fief given him by his brother in the Wei valley, he had set up at Ch'ang-an a traditional Chinese system of administration. But there was one crucial respect in which he had to depart from the normal pattern. For obvious reasons, as a rank and much resented intruder, he preferred the Chinese civil service to the Chinese civil servants. A few carefully selected scholars were invited to hold office, but the examinations were suspended and were not resumed until 1315, when they were given a built-in bias against Chinese candidates. On the other hand there were not enough Mongols with the ability to fill the higher ranks in the administration. Kublai's solution was to employ foreigners, a considerable supply of whom had been made available by the new stability of Central Asia.

For centuries the Silk Road had been disrupted by the Chinese failure to control the nomads at one end of it, and the clash between Islam and Christianity at the other. Now, with a single power dominating its whole length – in what is often called the Pax Mongolica – it became once more a comparatively safe highway, sufficiently well travelled for an Italian, Francesco Pegolotti, to think it worth compiling a trader's guidebook to the route in about 1340. He gives details of the stopping places, the distances between them, and the duties levied on each type of commodity. His advice is eminently practical. On how to set about the journey: 'In the first place you must let your beard grow long and not shave.' On the cost: 'You may calculate that a merchant with a dragoman, and with two men servants, and with goods to the value of twenty-five thousand golden florins, should spend on his way to Cathay from sixty to eighty *sommi* of silver, and not more if he manage well; and for all the road back again from Cathay to Tana [Azov, on the Black Sea], including the expenses of living and the pay of the servants, and all other charges, the cost will be about five *sommi* per head of pack animals, or something less; and you may reckon the *sommo* to be worth five golden florins.' On comfort: 'If the merchant likes to take a woman with him from Tana, he can do so; if he does not like to take one there is no obligation, only if he does take one he will be kept much more comfortably than if he does not take one.' On danger: 'You may reckon that from Tana to Sara the road is less safe than on any other part of the journey; and yet even when this part of the road is at its worst, if you are some sixty men in the company you will go as safely as if you were in your own house.' On trading conventions at the western end of the trip, at Constantinople: 'Broken almonds in bags; the bag goes as almonds; only if there be more than one sack or cord it must be removed, or deducted, so that the buyer shall not have to take more than one sack and cord as almonds, but for any beyond that there shall be tare allowed; and the cord shall go to the buyer gratis.' Almonds are but one of the commodities he mentions. His lists are enough to make the mouth of any merchant water, then or now: 'Undressed vairs and vair bellies and backs, Slavonian squirrels, martins and fitches, goat skins and ram skins, dates, filberts, walnuts, salted sturgeon tails . . . round pepper, ginger, barked brazil-wood, lac, zedoary, incense, quicksilver, sal ammoniac, copper, amber big middling and small, stript coral . . . raw silk, saffron, clove-stalks and cloves, nutmegs, spike, cardomoms, scammony, pounding pearls, manna, borax, gum Arabic, dragon's blood, sweetmeats, gold wire, dressed silk', and much else besides.[1]

It was along this route that the Polo brothers first reached Kublai's court in the 1260s; along it that he sent them back with a message of friendship for the pope and a request for 100 learned priests (more personnel for the civil service?) and for some oil from the lamp burning over the Holy Sepulchre at Jerusalem; and along it that they returned to him again, in 1275, with a flask of the precious oil and with Niccolo's son Marco, aged about twenty. There were no priests – the Pope had disregarded Kublai's round number and had detailed off for the mission a pair of Dominicans, who made their excuses at the first glimpse of hardship on the road. Marco, not normally given to the personal touch, does on this occasion suggest that his own presence more than made up for Kublai's initial disappointment:

> The great Kaan, when he sees Marc who was a young bachelor of very great and noble aspect, he asks who he is. Sir, says his father Master Nicolau, he is my son and your man, whom as the dearest thing I had in this world I have brought with great peril and ado from such distant lands to present him to thee for thy slave. May he be welcome, says the great Kaan, and it pleases me much; and he held him in great favour and made them write him among the other honoured members of his household, for which reason he was held of great account and value by all those at the court.[2]

Marco graciously returns the compliment in another part of his book, where he gives a glowing account of Kublai's appearance:

> He is of good and fair size, neither too small nor too large, but is of middle size. He is covered with flesh in a beautiful manner, not too fat, nor too lean; he is more than well formed in all parts. He has his face white and partly shining red like the colour of a beautiful rose, which makes him appear very pleasing; and he has the eyes black and beautiful; and the nose very beautiful, well made and well set on the face.[3]

This historic meeting took place at Kublai's summer palace of Shang Tu, north of the Great Wall and some 200 miles from Peking. Marco refers to it as Ciandu. It was his description of its sumptuous pavilions – set within a wall surrounding 'quite sixteen miles of land in which are fountains and rivers and lawns' – that was to inspire, five centuries later, Coleridge's Xanadu.

A more immediate result of Marco's warm welcome from Kublai Khan was that he became one of the foreigners enrolled in the administration. Over the next seventeen years he fulfilled tasks in many different places for his master, and it seems that the notes taken on these expeditions later

formed the basis for his book. He saw China from a somewhat limited viewpoint, for he never learned the Chinese language (Mongolian was sufficient), and he moved everywhere as an agent of those occupying the country by force. The details that caught his eye seem also to have been fairly random. He describes in detail, in one of his most famous sections, how the Chinese dig up and burn a marvellous black stone, which is useless for building with (in other words coal), but he makes no mention of the drinking of tea, which from the third century A.D. had spread slowly from southern China and had long since become a national habit.

A particular refrain occurs so often that one can only suspect it of being Marco's routine reply back home in Italy to that most impossible of questions: 'Tell me, what was China like?' 'The people', Marco would answer wearily, just as he repeats in chapter after chapter, 'are idolaters and subject to the great Kaan, and have money of notes.' It was hardly surprising that Marco, coming from his family of merchants, should have been so struck by the paper money, in common use in China so many centuries before it was first adopted in Europe. The immediate magic of it, to someone familiar only with precious metals as currency, was that it seemed to make it possible for the ruler to get something for nothing. Marco, who refers to the notes as coins, explains the procedure:

> They are made with as much authority and formality as if they were of pure gold or silver, for many officials who are deputed for this write their names on every coin, placing there each one his mark, and when it is all done as it ought to be, the head of them deputed by the lord stains the seal entrusted to him with cinnabar and impresses it upon the coin so that the pattern of the seal dipped in the cinnabar remains printed there, and then that money is authorized. And if anyone were to counterfeit it he would be punished with the last penalty to the third generation. And different marks are printed on them according to their future value. And this money is made in the city of Cambaluc [Peking] by those who are deputed for this by the king, & not by others. And each year he has so great quantity and supply of them made in the city of Cambaluc that he would pay with it for all the treasure of the world, though it costs him nothing.[4]

'Though it costs him nothing' – Marco unwittingly pinpoints the dangerous illusion of paper money, and ultimately the Chinese proved unable to control their invention. It had not been introduced by the Mongols, for the Sung economy was based on paper money which derived from even earlier bills of exchanges. In the last century of the Sung dynasty the value of this money had fallen drastically when people lost confidence

in it (in spite of a new issue which the emperor hoped to make more attractive by printing it on silky paper with a delicate hint of perfume), and the same pattern was to recur during the decline of the Mongol dynasty. The more cautious Ming emperors reduced the proportion of paper money in circulation until, in the early fifteenth century, they abolished it entirely. It was not re-introduced until 1851.

A large part of Marco's book consists of descriptions of different cities and regions of China. Easily his favourite was Hangchow, 'the greatest city which may be found in the world, where so many pleasures may be found that one fancies oneself to be in Paradise'. He hardly knew whether to be more impressed by the number of bridges or the number of prostitutes, though the latter lingered more persistently in the mind. 'The foreigners', he explains, as if speaking of someone else, 'who have once indulged themselves with them stay as it were in an ecstasy, and are so much taken with their sweetness and charms that they can never forget them.'[5]

In commenting on the peacefulness and gentle way of life of the people (it invariably amazed travellers from brawling and swaggering Europe that no one in China carried arms or even kept them at home), he adds that the people show great friendliness to foreigners 'who come to them for the sake of trade', even inviting them to their homes. This would cease to be so in later centuries, when China's spell of xenophobia had set in, and one of the reasons for the change may have been the reaction against the Mongols and their foreign servants. But Marco was one of the first of these, and if his business in Hangchow was mainly trade – and he spent much of his time in China operating on his own account – then he may have benefited from the last of an older Chinese tradition. He does notice that in Hangchow the people object strongly to the sight of the khan's soldiers, 'as it seems to them that by reason of them they have been deprived of their natural kings and lords'. He also remarks with some admiration on the extremely strict curfew imposed on the city – even a light in a house after the stipulated time led to punishment – and he explains that this was a necessary precaution against rebellion. The Mongols were adapting to their own ends a traditional Chinese restriction.

Daytime Hangchow showed less signs of constraint. Only about ten years before Marco's visit it had been the capital of the decadent Southern Sung, and it was still the commercial centre of a very rich district. The main thoroughfare, forty yards wide, ran the full length of the city, and at several points along it there were bustling markets (themselves rigidly

supervised by guards, but then this too had always been the custom). Marco, even though himself a Venetian, was astounded by the luxury of the place. He mentions great carriages moving along the roads with silken curtains, in which a rich man might be taking his family or a party of concubines to one of the parks; he describes painted barges being poled about the lake while their occupants sip wine and admire the great houses, temples and gardens along the banks, or eye the occupants of other boats in this watery promenade; and he is much impressed by small palaces on two islands in the lake, which were fully equipped with furniture, linen and plate, and which could be hired by anyone wanting to give a banquet.

Manuscripts surviving from Hangchow just before the collapse of the Sung go into even greater detail, providing almost a complete consumer's guide to this city of such great wealth (and of equivalently great poverty, but no consumer's guide goes into that). A profit of 1 per cent per day was considered normal among professional shopkeepers, a situation which had led to a proliferation of shops, nearly all of them beyond the means of almost everybody. But for those who were in the market for such things, the best rhinoceros skins were to be found at Ch'ien's, on the way down from the canal to the little Ch'ing-hu lake; for ivory combs Fei's was recommended, and there was a good selection of painted fans at the Coal Bridge; for the finest of all possible turbans, it was well worth paying a visit to K'ang-number-eight's shop in the street of the Worn Cash-coin. Of restaurants too there seems to have been a variety comparable to that in modern capital cities. Boiled pork was particularly good at Wei-the-Big-Knife near the Cat Bridge, as were honey fritters at Chou-number-five, but the apparent simplicity of these *specialités de maison* was not necessarily typical, for the guide also mentions scented shell-fish cooked in rice wine, goose with apricots and pimento soup with mussels.[6] Certain restaurants won fame by limiting themselves to a narrow range of dishes, one for example serving only food that was iced. Culinary ingenuity is one of the most honourable and long-lasting of Chinese traditions. Even today a leading Peking restaurant serves nothing but duck, but does so in fifty-nine different ways.

The traders may have welcomed Marco and resented only actual soldiers, but the scholars and the official classes, whose role he and his like were usurping, would have looked less warmly upon him. So soon after the collapse of their empire, they saw Hangchow through different eyes. If Marco noticed a large and quiet building at the end of the main

The concubine Yang Kuei-fei being assisted to mount her horse, by Chien Hsüan, c. 1280 (detail).
OVERLEAF *Blue and white porcelain vase* LEFT; *and censer of coloured glass, Yüan dynasty*

thoroughfare, he failed to mention it. To a Chinese poet, writing at exactly the same time, it dominated the scene:

On visiting the former Imperial Palace at Hangchow

Like an ancient ruin, the grass grows high: gone are the
*   guards and the gatekeepers.*
Fallen towers and crumbling palaces desolate my soul.
Under the eaves of the long-ago hall fly in and out the swallows
But within: Silence. The chatter of cock and hen parrots
*   is heard no more.*[7]

These lines were written within twenty years of the Sung emperor's departure from the city, so the long grass and the crumbling palaces may well be metaphorical, but they express well the position of the scholars at the time. Many refused to collaborate with the conquerors, and retired into decent obscurity. The painters, as well as the poets, expressed in subtle ways their hostility. Bamboos and plum-blossoms, for long a speciality of the scholar-artists, became more than ever a popular subject. Each plant was seen as a symbol of the scholars in their present predicament. The bamboo bends before the storm but does not break, and the plum-tree puts forth its blossom in the cold weather, like a scholar in retirement who keeps Chinese culture alive in this barbarian winter.

The Mongols had little interest in such esoteric art, but there was one type of Chinese painting which did greatly appeal to them. These were the paintings of horses, a subject with a long tradition in China and one which, although figurative, was still practised with very great skill by some of the scholar-artists. To the difficult question of whether or not to collaborate, the painters of horses gave various answers. Chao Meng-fu, the most distinguished of them all and a descendant of the first Sung emperor, was one of a group of scholars who were summoned to Kublai's court in 1286 and asked to serve. He accepted, later becoming a director of the Hanlin academy and governor of various cities, but his betrayal caused Chinese historians to deny him the very highest reputation among painters.

Altogether more admirable was Ch'ien Hsüan, an older man who 'clenched his teeth and did not join the crowd', preferring to live as a hermit in the south. In a state of almost permanent inebriation he continued to produce paintings of horses which were not only very beautiful but also, in some cases, carried the message of resistance. One of these is his picture of Yang Kuei-fei, perhaps the most famous concubine in Chinese history (colour, page 165). The T'ang emperor Hsüan Tsung became

Carved wood figure of a lohan *or Buddhist saint, Yüan dynasty*

Bamboo leaves, detail from a painting by Li K'an

infatuated with her in his old age, and together they made a favourite of the young general, An Lu-shan, who later betrayed the emperor's trust in his famous rebellion of 755. Ch'ien Hsüan paints the pampered lady being helped onto her horse for a riding party. Further along the scroll the old emperor, already mounted, eyes her thoughtfully. To a Chinese scholar of the time the parallel might already be implicit, between Hsüan Tsung who would later be driven from his capital city by An Lu-shan, himself of barbarian origin, and the Sung emperor who lost Hangchow to the Mongols. The painter makes it even more plain with his inscription: 'Why was it that the august persons here seated on fine horses were obliged to travel on mule-back when flying to distant Shu from the devastated capital?'[8] The answer, presumably, is not a simple one. The barbarity of the invaders in both cases is obvious. But the effete luxury of the lady may, or anyway should, be a major part of Ch'ien Hsüan's comment on the more recent disaster.

170

There was one good result from the unemployment of the intellectuals. Until now a scholar had always expected to derive his income from his career as an official, and in most cases the wage was amply supplemented by the perks of office. To earn money in any direct manner from literature had been considered most ungentlemanly. Now, with the examinations suspended, the situation was different – to the considerable benefit of the drama and the novel, two forms of art which already had a long, lively and popular history from the days of early tumblers and street-corner story-tellers, but which had until now never aspired to literary merit.

More than five centuries before this time the same emperor Hsüan Tsung, so susceptible to the charms of Yang Kuei-fei, had a corresponding love for the delights of the theatre and he established the first dramatic academy in his Pear Garden (until quite recently 'Young Folk of the Pear Garden' remained a polite term for actors). But performances at court were mainly concerned with singing and dancing, or else were simple plays with only two actors. Now, under the Mongols, the unemployed scholars began to write full-scale dramas in which they tackled such serious Confucian topics as the clash between individual passion and filial piety. Their work became the foundation of the Chinese classical theatre, at much the same time as the *noh* was beginning in Japan. The great Chinese novels, the best of which provide richly detailed accounts of everyday life in the scholar classes, date from later dynasties. But in that direction too, educated men now began for the first time to exercise their talents.

Kublai Khan was well able to hold together the China that he had conquered. But would his less forceful successors fare so well? Among those asking themselves this question was the family of wily Venetian merchants, anxious to avoid whatever chaos might then break out. Many times they asked their ageing patron to let them return home, but they were too useful to him and their request was on each occasion refused – no doubt with a present and a shower of compliments on their great merits. At last, in 1392, they had a stroke of luck, for their unparalleled experience as travellers became suddenly of value to the khan. A new seventeen-year-old bride had to be sent to Kublai's great-nephew, the grandson of his brother Hulagu, who was now the Il-khan of Persia. But the land route was blocked – by more squabbles between Mongol cousins – and so the three Venetians were entrusted with taking the lady by sea round the coast of India. Kublai summoned them to a final audience and 'spoke to them many gracious words of the great love which he bore them'. He gave them rubies and other jewels, as well as letters to the pope

and to the kings of Spain and France and even, surprisingly, England. They delivered the lady safely, only to find that the Il-khan had in the meantime died, so she married his son instead. She said farewell to the Polo family with tears in her eyes, and Marco returned to Venice and his place in history.

He did not write his book himself, nor, it seems, have any thought of doing so. But several years later he found himself a prisoner of war (war was endemic between Venice and Genoa) and there he made friends with a fellow-prisoner who was a professional writer of romances. To him he dictated the story of his travels. It was at first the fate of Marco's book too to be treated as a romance, for self-confident Europe was unwilling to take at face value his descriptions of a much more developed civilization in the east, and it was a long time before cartographers were willing to incorporate in their maps the information which he had brought back. Even so Columbus, sailing westward to find China and the Indies, did carry with him a heavily annotated copy of Marco's travels.

Kublai Khan died in 1294, at the age of seventy-nine, and was succeeded by his grandson Timur – 'a valiant man', says Marco, 'full of kindness, wise, and prudent, and has often already behaved very well'. Timur did succeed in maintaining a calm empire until his death in 1307, but after that the dynasty declined. Rivalries between the princes – a family weakness – led to civil war in 1328. The economy was in the grip of inflation, and natural disasters in north China caused further suffering and famine.

A perennial Chinese problem has been the control of the Yellow River, in which vast quantities of water tumble from the mountains into a flat plain. As a European visitor in the next dynasty most aptly put it, 'this Yellow River has no respect at all for Chinese law and order'.[9] One explanation often given for the stability of China over so many centuries, and for her tendency to absolutism in government, is the necessity of strong central control if her waters are to be tamed. In spite of an elaborate system of embankment the Yellow River frequently broke loose, sometimes even shifting the position of its mouth by nearly 300 miles to emerge into the sea either north or south of the Shantung peninsula. In the declining years of the Yüan dynasty a particularly disastrous series of floods forced the emperor to take action. Vast armies of peasants were dragooned into building embankments, and the appalling conditions – however worthwhile the cause – led to a series of rebellions. At the same time the peasants in southern districts, where the crops had not suffered, were once again being subjected to an intolerable burden of taxation. Soon there

Pottery figure of an entertainer, Yüan dynasty

173

was rebellion there too. The resulting chaos was much like that at the end of any dynasty, except that this time there was the added incentive of removing the foreign tyrants.

Of the many groups contending to do so, and hoping to claim for themselves the Mandate of Heaven, it was one headed by a Buddhist monk which emerged as the strongest. Chu Yüan-chang was born a peasant and had been attached by his family to a small temple solely for the two bowls of rice a day which were the salary of an attendant. But even this proved more than the monastery could afford. He found himself on the streets with his begging bowl, and it is thought that he now joined the White Lotus Society, the most famous of the many secret societies which at every period of Chinese history have been the cradle of resistance – inevitably so, when any open dissent would immediately be suppressed. The monk, turned emperor, later denied that he had ever been a member of a secret society, but by then he was on the other side and was engaged in trying to suppress them.

By 1355 Chu had emerged as the leader of one of the rebel bands. In 1356 he captured Nanking, where over the next ten years he consolidated a base for himself, setting up a full-scale administration and constantly warding off other rivals as well as the Mongols. In 1368 he marched north to capture Peking and to announce the beginning of the Ming or 'Brilliant' dynasty.

In choosing for his dynasty an uplifting title, rather than taking the name of a place or district, the new emperor was following a precedent set by the Mongols. He was not above borrowing, too, some of their well-tried techniques of repression. But in principle the key-note of the new dynasty was to be a rejection of everything foreign, a return to the glorious Chinese traditions of the past. The seizing of the throne by a peasant, from the grasp of autocratic barbarians, was in itself a pleasant echo of the founding of that most spectacular of the early dynasties, the Han.

The last of the Mongols were finally driven from the more remote corners of China in 1382. In spite of the powerful personality of Kublai Khan and the influx of foreigners, the years of occupation had made little lasting difference to China. Chinese painting had continued to develop within its own traditions. Porcelain is as visibly Chinese in the Yüan dynasty as in any other. The Chinese arts of government had been adopted by the Mongols, even if they preferred not to let the Chinese apply them. And Confucianism had been made more rather than less attractive

by those ninety years in the wilderness. The Chinese at the end of the fourteenth century were self-confidently themselves again, apparently unscathed.

Nor, in the long run, did China seem to have had much effect on the Mongols. They returned with surprising ease to their harsh way of life on the steppes, almost as if they had never fed on the honey-dew of China or drunk their milk in that particular paradise.

元

Chapter 7

MING
(1368–1644)

明

THE NAME CHOSEN FOR THE FIRST YEAR OF THE MING DYNASTY, AND later extended to cover the whole of the first reign, gave notice of the intentions of the new emperor. It was Hung Wu, meaning Vast Military Power. It seemed to hark consciously back to the last period when China had an expansionist empire, under the T'ang, and in the early part of the dynasty this promise of reviving ancient glories was amply kept. The rulers of Korea, Mongolia, Chinese Turkestan and Vietnam came once again to acknowledge Chinese sovereignty, and Thailand and Burma were now included within this group of vassal states. During the third Ming reign, with its title of Yung Lo or Perpetual Happiness, great armadas of Chinese ships sailed south and west under the command of a eunuch admiral, Cheng Ho, reaching not only Ceylon and India but even the Persian Gulf and the coasts of Africa. Cheng Ho brought back all sorts of pleasant curiosities for the Ming court and enabled a whole new range of distant and presumably indifferent rulers to be entered in the lists as dependencies of China – for any gift arriving at the imperial court was regarded as tribute and its sender as a vassal. This sequence of great maritime expeditions (seven voyages between 1405 and 1433) was unique in the history of the Chinese, who were not normally inclined to venture far by sea, and was also quite exceptional in its scale for any country at this period. The first expedition set off, soon after 1405, with no less than sixty-two vessels carrying some 28,000 men.

At home the emphasis was more on re-establishing past traditions. In 1373, five years after the start of the dynasty, the order went out that every village should revive the ancient Rite of Village Wine Drinking, which had been discontinued under the Mongols. It was a ceremony intended to embody at village level all the Confucian virtues. 'If every rural community does it without exception', wrote an early Ming author, 'then the ancient proprieties will not be difficult to reinstate; even more easily can filial piety then be made to flourish and the people's customs be made more magnanimous.'[1]

The first official to succeed in organizing the rite was the governor of Soochow, and he stage-managed it with such flair that his success won honourable mention in the Standard Histories. As it was meant to be an example to the rest of the province, his ceremony was rather more than a simple village affair. Old men were brought from far afield, and the centrepiece was a person of 105 who had been born under the Sung dynasty, a living link with the true Chinese past. The occasion began with a reading of the law – a short homily or an extract from some Con-

Two Salukis, a painting by the Hsüan Te emperor (reigned 1426–36)

fucian classic on the correct way to behave within society – and then, after a prodigious amount of mutual courtesy, the old men were feasted. A description survives of another such event, with the greybeards 'ranked according to their years, ninety and eighty and seventy, bowing and deferring, greeting and responding ceremoniously all around the circle, offering and returning compliments with deportment, waiting for the reading of the law. There would be a solid wall of observers ringing them about, all of whom would be greatly moved by the scene, their feelings made harmonious thereby.'[2] After the performance in Soochow the governor accompanied the oldest guest as far as the suburbs of the city, where he said farewell to his symbolic veteran with a great show of deference. In the old man's village a Hall of Generations of Longevity was erected to commemorate the event. Confucianism was firmly back in the saddle.

But there was one crucial respect in which the Ming dynasty was profoundly un-Confucian. In place of a benevolent rule, relying heavily on the guidance of learned officials, the Ming emperors for the most part preferred naked despotism. The pattern was set by the founder, Hung

177

Wu (Ming and Ch'ing emperors are known to history by their reign titles rather than their own names – technically he should be referred to as the Hung Wu emperor, but this refinement is frequently dispensed with). In 1380 Hung Wu abolished several senior posts in the administration, concentrating executive power even more than usual in his own imperial hands. At the end of his life he wrote: 'For thirty-one years I have laboured to discharge Heaven's will, tormented by worries and fears, without relaxing for a day.'[3] The effects of this overwork were not always pleasant for his subjects. When a rumour reached the emperor that the governor of Soochow was harbouring rebellious thoughts (that very same governor who only a few years before had won such acclaim for his exceptionally fine Village Wine Drinking) the unfortunate man was executed without further investigation. A month later Hung Wu admitted that he had made a mistake, but it was only the admission that was exceptional. Countless others suffered appalling punishments for the most trivial of offences, and several officials were even put to death on suspicion of having inserted derogatory puns in memorials designed to praise the emperor. The result was increasing caution and conformity on the part of the mandarins. Gone were the free-thinking and free-speaking days of the early Sung.

Now more than ever, official life in China showed a marked similarity to existence in the more traditional of English boarding schools. It was not only the prevalence of examinations. There was the same obsession with rank and privilege, expressed even in the same way – by colours. Yellow was reserved for the emperor, and the button on a mandarin's cap passed through no less than nine different shades as he rose in the hierarchy. There were the same inexplicable taboos, so familiar in school life and so dangerous to transgress. The greatest snare in this line was that a considerable number of words were not allowed to be written or spoken, because they occurred in one of the names of the emperor or of his numerous ancestors. Accidentally to use a word of this type was an extremely serious offence; it could put paid to a promising career, it would certainly mean outright failure in the examinations, and on occasion it had even been punished by death. There was the same school-like proliferation of petty physical rules. Everyone, for example, had to run rather than walk in the presence of the emperor. There were the same regular intervals between bouts of hygiene. Han officials had lived in dormitories near the palace, returning home once every five days for what became known as the 'bath and hair-washing day'. Later there were

no dormitories, but the working week lengthened; only every tenth day was a holiday, and the three periods within each month were referred to as the first, middle and last bath. And there was even the same rather numerical approach to good conduct, for the books known as *Kung-kuo-ko* or Tables of Merits and Demerits provided a scale by which the official could classify his own misbehaviour. One of the most extensive of these books, possibly written under the Yüan but edited in the Ming period, consists of ten different sections, each devoted to a particular type of fault. That on debauchery includes, among many other peccadilloes, the following:

Exciting lustful thoughts in oneself	10
Showing one's nakedness when easing nature in the night	1
Lewd dreams	1
If such a dream occasions a lewd action	5
Singing frivolous songs	2
Studying frivolous songs	20
Not yielding the way to a woman in the street	1
If at the same time one looks at the woman	2
If one looks longingly at her	5
If one conceives lewd thoughts about her	10
Entering one's women's quarters without warning	1
Telling one's women about some love-affair	10
If done with intent to excite lustful thoughts in them	20
Telling smutty stories in order to excite them	20
Exception: If one tells such stories in order	
to develop the women's sense of shame	None[4]

This excessively puritanical attitude had not been true of earlier dynasties and only seems to have gained ground under the Yüan, as also did the seclusion of women – possibly because of the need to protect them from Mongol soldiers. But prudishness was to become typical of the strict Confucian under the Ming and Ch'ing, when the increasing despotism of the rulers served also to heighten this element of life at an old-fashioned school. The first Ming emperor borrowed from the Mongols a final touch to complete the parallel – the cane. Officials who displeased Hung Wu and his successors were beaten, in public and with considerable ceremony. There were even cases of an erring minister being beaten to death.

Not surprisingly, some people preferred to opt out of the system and there were now many families of the scholar class with the wealth to do so. In other societies office has usually been gained through the possession

of land. In the later dynasties of China the pattern was for land to be acquired through the possession of office. Families which had been in the scholar class for a few generations were likely to have an estate, on which they could live at ease, devoting themselves to social life, a little poetry, some painting and a few unpaid but prestigious tasks as leaders of the local community.

An idea of this pleasant though somewhat parasitic existence is given in the standard biographies of Shen Chou, one of the leading scholarly painters of the period:

Shen Chou was born in Ch'ang-chou [in 1427]. His grandfather Ch'eng was offered an official position in the Yung Lo period, but did not accept it. He built himself a studio which he called the West Cottage, and there he received his guests with wine every day. His uncle Chen-chi and his father Heng-chi lived as retired scholars and built themselves a bamboo studio where they used to study, compose poetry, and paint. Even the servants of their household could appreciate literature and calligraphy.

When Shen Chou grew older he read every book he could get hold of. In his poems he imitated Po Chü-i, Su Tung-p'o and Lu Yu, in his calligraphy he followed Huang T'ung-chien, and in all these arts he obtained the admiration of the whole world. But he was most skilled in painting, and has been represented by the critics as the foremost in this art in the Ming period.

The governor wanted to introduce him as a candidate for official service, but Shen Chou consulted the *I Ching* and found there the advice to withdraw. Consequently he decided to stay in retirement. He lived at a beautiful place laid out with watercourses, bamboo groves and pavilions around a palatial residence, and everywhere in the house there were books and antique bronzes. Famous scholars from all over the country came to visit him. His virtuous character and literary talent were, indeed, beacon lights of his day.

He was kind to everybody, but there were few to whom he opened his heart completely. His most intimate friends were Wu K'uan, vice-president of the Board of Civil Office, Tu Mu, president of the Board of War, Wen Lin, governor of Wen-chou, and his son Wen Cheng-ming, the painter, all men of noble conduct, inspired by the spirit of antiquity, pure and upright like gold and jade.[5]

Shen's picture entitled *A Scholar in his Study awaiting a Guest* expresses perfectly the attractions of this way of life.

The book in which Shen found the advice to avoid anything more strenuous – the *I Ching* or *Book of Changes* – is a manual of divination dating originally from early in the Chou dynasty, but with many later additions. It has been enormously consulted throughout Chinese history and is at present enjoying a vogue in the West among those wanting something to add to their horoscope. As with most systems of prophecy the

Shen Shou's painting of A Scholar in his Study Awaiting a Guest

advice tends to be so general ('there will be progress and attainment, but it will be advantageous to be firm and correct') or else so delightfully inconsequential ('the representative of penetration is beneath a couch' . . . 'a young fox wets his tail crossing a stream') that the inquirer can usually find in it good reason to do whatever he chooses. It is hard to believe that Shen Chou required much prompting to follow the pleasant life of his father, uncle and grandfather.

The series of Ming naval expeditions had ended, in the early fifteenth century, as suddenly as it began. Later in the dynasty the traffic was to flow in the other direction, and it brought to China in 1582 one of the most perceptive and intelligent of all the many foreigners who have ever recorded their impressions of the country.

Matteo Ricci had become a Jesuit in 1571, only thirty-one years after the Society of Jesus had been founded 'to labour for the salvation and perfection of one's neighbour'. Already there was a flourishing settlement on the west coast of India, at Goa. Ricci spent four years there, from 1578 to 1582, teaching at the college and completing his own training, before being sent to Macao, where China had recently allowed the Portuguese to establish a trading post. In 1583 he and another Jesuit set up the first mission inside China, but it was another eighteen years before they won permission to present to the emperor, in Peking, the gifts they had brought him from Europe.

During that time a most remarkable transformation had occurred. With astonishing speed Ricci had mastered sufficient Chinese characters to construct a dictionary and grammar for the use of himself and his colleagues. He had studied the classics, had translated five of them into Latin, and had decided that 'of all the pagan sects known to Europe, I know of no people who fell into fewer errors in the early ages of their antiquity than did the Chinese'. He had taken a particular liking to the ancient philosopher K'ung Fu Tzu, who 'preferred to observe silence relative to the future life, rather than put forth erroneous ideas about it', and had invented a Latin name for him – Confucius. He had begun to write his own series of Chinese books, which would eventually include a great many tracts on Christianity, a book of moral paradoxes, a treatise on friendship in the form of a dialogue between himself and a Chinese scholar which became so popular that the Chinese themselves several times reprinted it, and a translation of the first six books of Euclid. He had constructed a great map of the world 'making the Kingdom of China appear right in the centre: this was more in keeping with their ideas and

it gave them a great deal of pleasure and satisfaction.'[6] He had even adopted the silk robes of a mandarin, and went now by the name of Li Ma-t'ou – Li being the nearest family name to Ricci for there is no 'r' in Chinese, and Ma-t'ou for Matteo. A valid question, and one that would later be asked in Rome, was who was converting whom.

But Ricci, unlike so many of the foreigners who would arrive in later centuries, saw that the only way to make progress with the Chinese was to accommodate their ideas instead of trying to disprove them. This was partly a conscious policy towards the practical end of spreading the faith, but it also derived from Ricci's own outstanding quality of open-mindedness. He makes a perfect traveller and reporter, for he rarely falls into the trap of assuming that unfamiliar means inferior, and his powers of observation and of description are both equally sharp. A good example is his very clear account of Chinese printing:

> Their method of making printed books is quite ingenious. The text is written in ink, with a brush made of very fine hair, on a sheet of paper which is inverted and pasted on a wooden tablet. When the paper has become thoroughly dry, its surface is scraped off quickly with great skill, until nothing but a fine tissue bearing the characters remains on the wooden tablet. Then, with a steel graver, the workmen cuts away the surface following the outlines of the characters until these alone stand out in low relief. From such a block a skilled printer can make copies with incredible speed, turning out as many as fifteen hundred copies in a single day. Chinese printers are so skilled in engraving these blocks, that no more time is consumed in making one of them than would be required by one of our printers in setting up a forme of type and making the necessary corrections.[7]

The one area in which the Chinese were eager to learn from Ricci was in matters of science, and in the century or more that the Jesuits remained at court it was this knowledge of Western technology, rather than their religion, which earned them their place. Ricci naturally hoped that the two would go hand in hand, noting in his journal that the Chinese were 'slow to take a salutary spiritual potion, unless it be seasoned with an intellectual flavouring'. In fact the intellectual flavouring that he himself offered was in many respects decidedly stale, for he expounded the heavens of Ptolemy and the elements of Aristotle, both of which were on the verge of being discarded in Europe. Since he was right about so much else, it is rather endearing to find him marvelling, from the sublime heights of his own ignorance, at the abysmal depths of theirs:

They never knew, in fact they had never heard, that the skies are composed of solid substance, that the stars were fixed and not wandering around aimlessly, that there were ten celestial orbs, enveloping one another, and moved by contrary forces. Their primitive science of astronomy knew nothing of eccentric orbits and epicycles.[8]

He was even more brusque with their concept of the elements and with their unscientific basing of it on ancient opinions, although his own theory, deriving from Empedocles and Aristotle, was of almost exactly the same vintage as theirs:

> With no other foundation for their belief than antiquity, Chinese scholars taught that there were five different elements. None of them ever doubted this or thought of questioning it. These elements were: metal, wood, fire, water and earth. . . . Father Matthew paid little or no attention to their devotion to the authority of antiquity [he invariably writes about himself in the third person]. He told them that there were four elements, no more and no less. . . . Father Matthew wrote a commentary on this subject in Chinese, in which he did away with their five elements, as such, and established the four.[9]

It was to be the technical marvels of Western science, rather than its theories, which finally brought the little party of Jesuits to their destination in imperial Peking in 1601. They had been languishing in prison in Tientsin, cast there by a corrupt eunuch who had designs on the presents intended for the emperor, when an imperial edict arrived, as if out of the blue, ordering that the priests should be brought to the palace. They were told later that the emperor had suddenly said, 'Where is that clock, I say, where is that clock that rings of itself; the one the foreigners were bringing here to me, as they said in their petition?'[10]

From then on, the clock that rang by itself continued to smooth their path. The emperor, the pampered and flabby Wan Li, ruled from deep within the palace rarely seeing anyone except his eunuchs, so Ricci never had an audience. His presents were solemnly carried away out of sight by the eunuchs, and after an uneasy period of suspense the same eunuchs reappeared with news of the emperor's approval. Several of the gifts were religious – a crucifix, a statue of the Virgin and various holy relics – but it was the clock that won the fathers the cherished permission to establish a church in Peking. Two eunuchs known to be skilled in mathematics were put in charge of winding it – an appointment which was said to have added considerably to their political power, for the emperor kept the toy always beside him and their task brought them repeatedly

A section of the Great Wall north of Peking, faced in stone under the Ming TOP; *and the main building of the Temple of Heaven at Peking.* OVERLEAF *The guardian figures on the road to the Ming tombs*

into his presence. One day Wan Li's mother asked to see the famous clock. The emperor was so alarmed at the thought of her taking a possible fancy to it that he disconnected the striking mechanism before sending it through to her part of the palace. He had already given her the Blessed Virgin Mary.

The influence of this propitious little machine was acknowledged with typical commonsense by the Jesuit who described the events which followed Ricci's death. During nine years in Peking the learned father, master of the Chinese classics as well as the Western sciences, had become a figure of great fame and prestige, so his mandarin friends advised the Jesuits to petition the emperor for a special burial place, with space for a church and mission house in his memory. It was a bold thought. There was no precedent for such an honour being granted a foreigner. But the proper procedures were gone through, and the fathers stayed at home on the day when they knew that somewhere deep inside the palace the matter was being brought to the emperor's attention.

> Undoubtedly, when the petition was presented to the King, He who holds the hearts of kings in His hand influenced this particular sovereign, by recalling to his memory the gifts he had received from the Fathers, and the presence of the portable clock, which he never left out of his sight.[11]

Undoubtedly He did, for the answer was yes.

The most important accommodation that Ricci made with the ways of China lay in his decision that there was nothing blasphemous in the rites of Confucianism:

> The Literati deny that they belong to a sect and claim that their class or society is rather an academy instituted for the proper government and general good of the kingdom. One might say in truth that the teachings of this academy, save in some few instances, are so far from being contrary to Christian principles, that such an institution could derive great benefit from Christianity and might be developed and perfected by it.[12]

He was delighted to find in the Confucian classics an almost precise statement of the Golden Rule of Saint Matthew – do unto others as you would they should do unto you – and he very much enjoyed pointing out that the principle of filial piety was precisely that of the Fifth Commandment. But the very crux of his decision about Confucianism – and it was on this point that the famous Rites Controversy was later to break out and bring to an effective end the Jesuit work in China – was that there was no element of worship or superstition in the ceremonies to Confucius

The recently restored decoration on the Hall of Annual Prayers at the Temple of Heaven

or to the ancestors. It was merely a case of honouring the dead. On this basis Ricci even allowed himself to attend a ceremony in the Temple of Heaven at Nanking. His own description of the occasion reveals that he was aware of how thin was the ice on which he was skating. The italics are mine:

> The leaders of the literary class observe a solemn day of sacrifice in honour of Confucius, *if sacrifice is the proper word.* . . . On the previous day they invite the Chief of the Magistrates to attend a rehearsal of the orchestra. Father Ricci was invited to this rehearsal and *as there was no question of attending a sacrifice,* he accepted the invitation. . . . Father Matthew was accompanied by the children of the High Magistrate. The priests who composed the orchestra were vested in sumptuous garments, *as if* they were to attend a sacrifice.[13]

Even more disturbing, he had noticed many people who did seem unmistakably to worship at the memorial shrines to great men which were to be found in public places. With his usual shrewdness Ricci arrived at what was undoubtedly the case – that now, more than ever, this was a matter of class:

> The people in general seem to make no distinction between these memorial rites and the worship they pay their deities, as they call upon the deities during the rites. With the educated classes these are ceremonies conducted in recognition of benefits received, but there is little doubt that many of the lower classes confuse the practice with divine worship.[14]

It was a point that had been made almost 2000 years before by Hsün Tzu, in an exceedingly early admission that religion is the opium of the people. Referring to this same sacrificial rite, he said: 'Among Superior Men it is considered to be a human practice; among the common people it is considered to be a serving of the spirits.'[15]

However pure the rites of Confucianism, in other quarters the Jesuit fathers were confronted at every turn by the unmistakable signs of idolatry. The Buddhist and Taoist temples were almost as full of ferocious statues and gory paintings as they were of enthusiastic worshippers, for the popular religions of China were no less varied and colourful than those of India. They always had been, and they would remain so until recent times. Even an early twentieth-century text invokes the help of some 600 named gods and then continues, for good measure:

> in addition to the above, the following gods are hereby invoked: Gods of ten directions; all fairies and sages; all fairy warriors and soldiers; ten extreme

god kings; gods of sun, moon and nine principal stars; three officers and four sages; the stars of five directions; gods guarding four heavenly gates; thirty-six thunder gods guarding the entire heaven; twenty-eight principal stars of the Zodiac; gods for subjugating evil ghosts; god king of flying heaven; great long life Buddha; gods of Tien Kan and Ti Tze; great Sages of Trigrams and Nine Stars; secondary official of five directions; secondary officials of ten directions; gate gods and kitchen gods; godly generals in charge of year, month, day and hour; gods and spirits in charge of four seas, nine rivers, five mountains, four corners; of hills, woods, all rivers and lakes, wells and springs, ditches and creeks, and twelve river sources; all gods; *cheng huangs* and their inferiors; local patron gods; minor local officials; gods of roads and bridges; of trees and lumber; spiritual officers and soldiers under the command of priests; all spirits in charge of protecting the taboos, commands, scriptures, and the right way of religion.[16]

That final desperate 'and the right way of religion' can stand as a poignant image of the problems confronting the Jesuits. The most they could hope for in the Chinese context was that their God should be tacked on to the list of all those others who had made themselves known and accepted rather sooner.

Meanwhile the fathers took a fierce pleasure in destroying any heathen images that came within their power. The building given to them by the emperor after Ricci's death had previously been used as a temple. 'The clay idols were reduced to dust and the wooden ones consigned to the flames', after which 'the picture of Christ, in a gilded frame, was put in place, where idols formerly stood, and the proper worship of the one true God established, in place of idolatry.' There were many ironies in this fervent replacing of one set of images with another, as well as in the friendly embracing of Confucianism, though none would have been apparent to the Jesuits. The Society of Jesus had been formed to fight in Europe against an assault on idolatry and superstition which was remarkably similar to the Jesuits' own assault on the idols of China. Equally, those very qualities which made Confucianism so acceptable were ones which it shared with the Reformation – for the Neo-Confucians had purged their cult of superstitious elements borrowed from Buddhism and Taoism, in a process very similar to Luther's refining of Christianity. The final irony would have been the most painful of all. To a good Confucian it was extremely hard to tell the difference between one foreign religion that came bearing relics and another. When Ricci arrived in Peking, Wan Li's ministers submitted a memorial which deliberately

reminded the emperor of Han Yü's famous strictures on the finger-bone of the Buddha:

> This man [Ricci] has appeared at court twenty years after his arrival in China. And what did he offer to the emperor as tribute? Nothing but strange things which have no resemblance to those rare and precious presents usually offered by the envoys from distant countries. He has brought, for instance, portraits of the Lord of Heaven and of his mother, and also some bones of immortals. As if an immortal who soars up to heaven should be provided with bones! Han Yü of the T'ang period has said that such unclean things can only bring mischief, and therefore ought not to enter into the palace. . . . Now we propose to bestow upon Li Ma-t'ou a cap and a girdle, and to send him back. He ought not to be allowed to live secretly in either of the two capitals, nor to enter into intimacy with our people.[17]

But they had overlooked the clock, and Ricci stayed.

Undoubtedly his greatest single achievement was in the field of language and literature. The written word has played a greater part in Chinese culture than in any other, even to the extent of being more important than the spoken language and acquiring an almost sacred character. It was considered by many people improper to throw away a piece of paper with writing on it (the respectful thing was to burn or bury it), and one of the lists of good and bad conduct proposes five marks of demerit for doing so. One peculiarity of the language lay behind this attitude – the strange fact that it is very much easier to understand Chinese when it is written than when it is spoken. Ricci noted:

> It happens not infrequently that those who are conversing together do not fully and accurately understand one another's ideas even though they enunciate very clearly and concisely. At times they have to repeat what they have said, and more than once, or even to write it. If no writing material is at hand, they will trace the symbol on something with water, or perhaps write it with the finger in the air or even on the palm of the listener's hand.[18]

The reason was the shortage of sounds available to distinguish between the almost exclusively monosyllabic words. The mandarin dialect of Peking used only 412 different monosyllables, with the result – in one quoted example – that a small dictionary, giving a total of no more than 4000 everyday words, was found to contain sixty-nine pronounced *i*. The confusion is slightly modified by the famous four tones of spoken Chinese (level, quickly rising, slowly rising and falling) which are used to distinguish one homophone from another. But these are not distributed

with mathematical fairness, and of those sixty-nine words no less than thirty-eight used the falling tone. Spoken in this fourth tone, *i* could mean *bosom, different, contemplate, wing, city, translate, a hundred thousand, hang* or any of thirty other equally varied possibilities.[19] In practice the Chinese, when speaking, avoid ambiguity by a system of duplication, tacking on another word of the same meaning just as we might distinguish between hang-suspend and hang-execute, or as schoolchildren do between funny-ha-ha and funny-peculiar. But this elaboration was unnecessary with the written language, in which every one of those thirty-eight apparently identical words had its own separate character. One result was that long ago, as early as the Han dynasty, colloquial Chinese began to diverge from the written form until they were almost two separate languages, a fact which greatly reinforced the barrier between the scholar class and the rest. Another result, perhaps even harder to imagine for those with an alphabetic script, is that it is utterly meaningless to read Chinese literature aloud unless one gives the listeners a written text in which to follow. To give an example of the difficulties involved, it would no doubt be possible to compose a brief passage using only words from the list of thirty-eight characters pronounced *i*. It would make perfect sense on the page, but when read out would consist only of an ever-falling repetition of the same sound.

For the same reasons, where other people have prayed or chanted to their spirits, the Chinese have preferred to write them letters. And if Ricci ever saw any of these letters, their matter-of-fact tone would certainly have confirmed his belief that the rituals of Confucianism were concerned with human rather than spiritual relationships. Part of the duty of tending an ancestral shrine was to keep the dead informed of the family's activities. The following is from a letter written by Po Chü-i to his brother, the father of Tortoise, two years after the brother's death. It was presented at the family shrine, in the form of an address to his soul, while performing the sacrifice which marked the end of full mourning:

> Last year in the spring I became head of the Palace Library and received the Order of the Purple Sash, and this spring I was appointed Vice-President of the Board of Punishments. But I feel so utterly desolate without you and have also been in such bad health that I do not care much what becomes of me. In official life at any rate I have definitely lost all interest. . . .
>
> Everyone in the family except Su-su is in good health. Tortoise shows a leaning towards literature and I read the *Book of Odes* and the *Book of History*

with him every day. In two or three years he should, I think, be quite ready to take his examinations. Lo Tzu is getting to be quite a big girl and is turning out better than we expected. I still have no son. Tea-boy, Auntie and the rest are in Cheng-hua; he still has the same job. . . . Yao-lien is on the farm at Fu-li; he is still unmarried. Chai-hsiang is in the salt administration at P'eng-tse. We have good news of both of them. As Bone Helmet, Stone Bamboo and Scented Hairpin have been so long in our service I took the opportunity at the end of your mourning to give them their freedom. We have taken back Shan-niang, and your wife is looking after her and bringing her up. This year I completed the purchase of Yang Lin's farm at Hsia-kuei and have added a hall and courtyard. You will remember that we once discussed this, and you were very anxious it should be done in the event of your death. I have also bought the house on the west of the Hsin-ch'ang Ward.

I have put together your writings and arranged them in order. There are twenty rolls in all. . . . I shall ask His Excellency Mr Ts'ui to write a preface and shall bequeath the book to Tortoise and Lo Tzu to keep along with my own writings. Did you get any benefit from the good works done by the whole family on behalf of your soul last year? Did you come to take the offerings we made at morning and evening on the first and fifteenth days of each month?[20]

When Ricci was finally admitted to the outer courtyards of the Forbidden City, the buildings he saw were in most respects the same as those still surviving today – although he limits his response to the rather perfunctory 'the grace and beauty of its architecture are emphasized by its slender lines'. Peking was a place of some importance as early as the Chou dynasty, and had been a capital city since the twelfth century. The Chin, after driving the Sung emperors south to Hangchow, had laid out with the help of captured Sung architects an imperial palace based on a series of rectangular courtyards similar in style to the present Forbidden City. Jenghiz Khan destroyed this Peking in 1215, but in the 1260s his grandson Kublai began constructing another similar palace a little to the northeast of the Chin ruins. This, within its two great walls, was the Cambaluc at which Marco Polo marvelled:

In the middle of the space which is inside these two walls is the great palace of the great lord, in which he dwells, which is made in such a way as I shall tell you. Know that it is the greatest and most wonderful that ever was seen. The walls of the halls and of the rooms inside are all covered with gold and with silver and blue, and there are portrayed very finely in carved work lions and dragons and beasts and birds . . . and the roof also is made so that nothing else

is seen there but gold and silver and paintings. On each quarter of the palace is a great flight of marble steps which go up from the ground to the top of the said wall of marble, which surrounds the palace, by which steps one goes up into the palace.[21]

A covered way at the Temple of Heaven, leading from the sacrificial slaughter-house and kitchen

Hung Wu, the founder of the Ming dynasty, drove Kublai's successors from Peking but preferred to keep his own capital at Nanking, his secure base further to the south. It was the third Ming emperor, Yung Lo, who moved to Peking and built yet another new complex on the site of Kublai's city. From his reign derive both the layout and the most important ancient monuments of present-day Peking. The masterpiece of the period (the early fifteenth century) is the Temple of Heaven to the south of the city, which also has the distinction of being almost the only Ming building in Peking to have survived in its original structure. It rests on precisely the same type of marble terrace described by Marco Polo in the earlier Peking, and is decorated in the same bright array of gold and

195

silver and blue (the colours have recently been restored: colour, pages 185 and 188). The imperial palace itself, which is the area known also as the Forbidden City, has been so frequently damaged by fire and pillage that in any other context one would have to describe the present buildings as comparatively recent. But the Chinese attitude to architecture introduces a rather different element. Since wood was the chief building material no structure was ever expected to last for long, but as soon as it was decrepit it was usually reconstructed exactly as before. Thus, although very few buildings in China are old in European terms, their appearance is often quite genuinely much earlier than the fabric would indicate.

Another spectacular monument to the Ming dynasty in the region of Peking is the great avenue of stone figures guarding the Spirit Way –

*Lions and camels
lining the Spirit Way
to the Ming tombs*

the road that leads to the secluded valley in which the emperors built
their own tombs. The sculptures include fierce warriors, elephants,
camels and even lions. Ricci says that in about 1570 two Muslims arrived
in China by the overland route with a highly successful present for the
emperor. 'With them, as a present for the King of China, they brought a
lion, an animal about which the Chinese had often heard, but which they
had very seldom seen. They were cordially received by the King and they
were each granted a Magistrature and an income from the royal treasury,
to be made hereditary in their families, provided they took care of the
lion, as long as he lived, and did not return to their own country to start a
war against the Chinese.'[22] It may have been one of the first living lions
the Chinese had seen, but the animal's fanciful relatives in stone had
already, at that time, begun their long and silent vigil.

197

In the European mind the word Ming is almost inseparable from porce-lain. Ricci permits himself no more than a brief paragraph on this marvel of Chinese technology, observing only that 'there is nothing like it in European pottery either from the standpoint of the material itself or its thin and fragile construction', and adding that throughout the world it is 'highly prized by those who appreciate elegance at their banquets rather than pompous display'. His brevity was amply made up for a century later by one of his successors, a Jesuit priest by the name of D'Entrecolles who, like Ricci, took a lively interest in everything Chinese, translating many texts and sending home to France his comments on subjects as diverse as natural history, physics, ethnology, archaeology, astronomy and inoculation for smallpox (many decades before Jenner's discovery of vaccination in the 1790s). But the best known of his writings today are his two letters describing the imperial porcelain factories at Ching Te Chen, which for intricacy of detail are unrivalled even in Chinese sources. He begins his first letter, dated 1712, by maintaining that his real interest in this intriguing city of kilns is purely religious:

> During the visits that I make from time to time to Ching Te Chen, to answer the spiritual needs of my Neophytes there, I have had the opportunity to observe the techniques used in the making of the beautiful porcelain which is so widely admired and is carried to every corner of the world. Although my own curiosity would never have led me to undertake such a study, I have nevertheless considered that a somewhat detailed description of every aspect of this type of work might be of some use in Europe.[23]

This disclaimer may not seem entirely convincing from someone so patently fascinated by what he is about to describe, but he was writing to his religious Superior and he had indeed made many converts among the grossly overworked and underpaid craftsmen. He was informed that the population numbered over a million 'who consume daily over ten thou-sand loads of rice and more than a thousand hogs'. He himself treats the number of people as an exaggeration, but says that it was hardly possible to move for the jostle of porters forcing their way through the narrow streets. He makes the place sound alarmingly like a modern industrial centre:

> The sight with which one is greeted . . . consists of volumes of smoke and flame rising in different places, so as to define all the outlines of the town; approaching at nightfall, the scene reminds one of a burning city in flames, or of a huge furnace with many vent-holes.

Like so much else in imperial China, life here was subject to strict regulations:

> It must be allowed that the policing is admirable; each street has one or more chiefs, according to its length, and each chief has ten subordinates, every one of whom is responsible for ten houses. They must keep order, under pain of the bastinado, which is here administered liberally. The streets have barricades, which are closed at night, and opened by the watchman only to those who have the password.[24]

Ching Te Chen had become such an important centre because two crucial substances were found nearby – china-clay, known also by its Chinese name of kaolin, and china-stone. It is the chemical affinity of these two substances, and their behaviour under a temperature of about 1400 °C., that makes possible the particular mystery of porcelain. The china-stone, which was ground to powder and mixed with the clay, had the property of vitrifying in the heat of the kiln. Left to itself it would melt and run, but if the mixture was right the china-clay held the shape of the pot and the vitrified china-stone gave it the translucent quality of true porcelain. It was a technique which had been perfected in the T'ang dynasty, as early as about 700, but which was not to be discovered in Europe for another thousand years. A few pieces of porcelain found their way to the West during the Middle Ages and were greatly admired. There followed centuries of experiment to try and imitate the process (the superior quality of the Chinese product is charmingly acknowledged in an English couplet of 1685: 'Women, like Cheney, shou'd be kept with care, / One flaw debases her to common ware'[25]), but European potters could only think of mixing ground glass with the clay, which produced a much softer and generally inadequate version of the Chinese original. At last, in what Europe has always regarded as a famous breakthrough, two men working for the Elector of Saxony discovered the secret in 1707. It was the beginning of the porcelain known variously as either Dresden or Meissen, which was on sale for the first time in large quantities at the Leipzig Fair of 1713, the very year after Father D'Entrecolles wrote his description. The immediate usefulness of his letter from the East had been forestalled.

No single porcelain has had such a wide appeal or been so much imitated as the Chinese blue-and-white, the inspiration in Europe of Delft. It was being produced early in the Yüan dynasty and very possibly in the late Sung, but it achieved its perfection under the Ming (colour,

pages 166 and 205). There is a very particular magic connected with the firing of this type of porcelain, for the design vanishes entirely under the glaze, which remains opaque until it is fired. D'Entrecolles gives a splendid description of the process:

> A beautiful blue colour appears on porcelain after having been lost for some time. When the colour is first painted on, it is pale black; when it is dry and the glaze has been put on it, it disappears entirely and the porcelain seems quite white, the colour being buried under the glaze. But the fire makes it appear in all its beauty, almost in the same way as the natural heat of the sun makes the most beautiful butterflies, with all their tints, come out of their eggs.[26]

The Ming potters departed from the classical severity of their Sung predecessors to indulge at times in an almost baroque profusion of decorative fancies, but they were capable of mastering both extremes. There can hardly be a more exquisite simplicity than that of the plain white paper-thin porcelain of the Yung Lo period (colour, page 208).

When Ricci was in Peking, the Ming dynasty was already drifting into its final decline, a state aptly symbolized by the imperial audience which was finally granted him. Like countless others before him, he went through the elaborate preparations – procuring the correct clothes, rehearsing the exact ceremonial – and then at last was led solemnly by the eunuchs to kowtow before an empty throne. This unsatisfactory conclusion came as no surprise to him, for it was common knowledge that for many years hardly anyone had been received in person by Wan Li. Even his ministers rarely saw him. If he did leave the inner quarters of the palace, he was carried in a closed palanquin – one of several identical conveyances in the procession, so that no one should know in which of them he sat. But this withdrawal from the affairs of the world was not the saintly reticence of a Henry VI. It was the self-indulgence of a pampered child who had come to the throne at the age of nine, surrounded almost exclusively by women and eunuchs, and for whom the security and delights of the palace became all that he knew and all that he wished to know. Even within these close confines he succeeded in squandering vast sums of money on presents for his relations or lavish entertainments, among which those for his own marriage were of unprecedented extravagance. When he was twenty-two he began building his tomb near those of his ancestors. Six years later it was finished, and a long line of closed carriages left the Forbidden City to gratify the emperor's latest macabre whim. He wished to give an entertainment in his future home. He entered it again in 1620, this time to stay,

The head of a tortoise, symbol of immortality, outside the tomb of Wan Li

and he lay undisturbed beneath his man-made hill, planted with the traditional pines, until the site was excavated by archaeologists in 1956. Inside there were three lacquer coffins, for two of his wives had been buried beside him. All three skeletons wore splendid black and gold gowns. Of Wan Li there remained, apart from his bones, some wisps of hair and beard. In the tradition of his predecessors, stretching back for so many centuries, he was accompanied in death by models of all the people and implements that might be useful to him in the next world. His tomb is now kept as an underground museum for the class-education of the masses. Like Liu Sheng of the Han dynasty, he was another remarkably apt subject for that purpose.

The obvious people to benefit from Wan Li's singular way of life were the eunuchs. The founder of the dynasty, Hung Wu, almost as if foreseeing its end, had put up in the palace a large metal tablet with the inscription 'Eunuchs must have nothing to do with administration.'[27] He had forbidden them to handle documents, and had decreed that they should remain illiterate. But this tough line, understandable in a man who had seized power for himself, was unlikely to be maintained by later princes who would grow up within the harem, with eunuchs as almost their only childhood friends and advisers. The inevitable affection for them comes out very clearly in letters written to his chief eunuch by one of the greatest and least decadent of China's rulers, K'ang Hsi, the second emperor of the Ch'ing dynasty. When away on his frequent tours of the empire he would send back little tit-bits of gossip or interesting information to what he called 'you people at home' – meaning his womenfolk and the eunuchs. One such letter reads:

> Among the local produce that the Moslems of Hami sent to me along with the [captured] Galdan bandits, only the sun-dried musk-melon had a really beautiful taste. I'm sending some off to you, but as I'm afraid you won't know what to do with it, I'll specifically write it out for you:
>
>> After you have washed it clear in either cold or hot water, steep it in hot water (but only for a short time), and then eat it either cold or hot. It tastes fresh and its juice is like the honeyed juice of a dried peach. Where there are holes, fill them up with little grapes.
>
> Tell the consorts about this. This is a trifling matter, but my heart is truly far away with you – don't laugh at me for this.[28]

K'ang Hsi was fully able to control his eunuchs, however fond he might become of them, but this had not been true of some of the feebler

Ming emperors. Within little more than a century of Hung Wu's edict that eunuchs should be illiterate, a special palace school had been set up for them under the guidance of distinguished members of the Hanlin academy. The numbers living in the palace steadily increased, as did the types of business on which they were employed. During the fifteenth century they were charged with keeping secret files on all official personnel and by the time of Wan Li, when messages could only reach the emperor if carried by themselves, they had their fingers in every pie of state (there were plenty of plums). The evil reached its peak in the 1620s, under a fifteen-year-old emperor who was interested almost exclusively in carpentry and who entrusted the government to a eunuch who had been butler to his mother. This man, Wei Chung-hsien, organized a reign of terror, purging all his enemies among the officials, levying exorbitant new taxes many of which went on erecting temples in his own honour, and maintaining his position with the help of a network of spies and informers throughout the country. Wei was banished by the last Ming emperor, Ch'ung Chen, who came to the throne in 1627, but by now there were too many other of those disturbances so characteristic of the declining years of dynasties. The general disorder, aggravated by the famine which only strong government has been able to keep at bay in China, had led to various local rebellions. Meanwhile the barbarians – in this case the Manchus – were once again pressing down from the north. Early in the dynasty they had lived only in the far eastern corner of the district named after them, Manchuria, but now they were raiding south of the Great Wall and were even able, in 1629 and 1638, to threaten Peking itself.

But it was one of the local Chinese rebels who first succeeded in capturing the capital city, in 1644. Rather than submit to his own personal degradation, the last Ming emperor hanged himself in a pavilion on the private hill which overlooked the Forbidden City. The Ming commander of the region northeast of Peking committed once again the mistake which had been repeated so many times in Chinese history. He enlisted the support of the barbarians to help him solve his immediate problem, the recapture of Peking and the putting down of the Chinese rebels. The Manchus obliged. Then – predictably, and indeed by now with the active assistance of the Ming commander who saw which way the wind was blowing – they seized the Dragon Throne for themselves.

It was a conclusion which the Manchu rulers had for some time had in mind. For many years they had been pursuing a policy of energetic

expansion – Korea, for example, had been invaded and now acknowledged itself to be their vassal state – and in 1636 they had already announced the start of a new Chinese dynasty. Following the Yüan and Ming examples they took a general name – the Ch'ing or 'Pure' dynasty. Eight years later, when they had driven the rebels from Peking, their dynasty made its official appearance in the Chinese annals.

The Ch'ing is recorded in history as an alien dynasty imposed on China, like that of the Mongols, but there was far from the same degree of cultural difference between conquerors and conquered as on the previous occasion. In the sense that barbarism is falling short of the polite ways of China, the Manchus had in most respects long ceased to be barbarians. Their mastery of Chinese traditions appears to excellent effect in an exchange of letters between the Manchu regent (the ruler was still a boy in 1644) and a Chinese general who was defending Yangchow on behalf of the last Ming emperor's cousin, now regarded by his loyal supporters as the rightful Son of Heaven. The Manchu regent, trying to suggest that Heaven has now granted its Mandate to the new dynasty and that surrender would be the wisest course, borrows authority for his arguments from a line in the *Spring and Autumn Annals* (believed at that time to have been written by Confucius himself), quotes in passing from a source of the fourth century A.D., and ends his letter with the words:

> In the *Book of Rites* it is written: 'Only the superior man can fully appreciate good advice.' Therefore I lay bare my inmost heart and respectfully await your decision. Across the Yangtze's flood I turn in spirit to Your Excellency and entreat your early reply. There is still much which remains unsaid.[29]

The Ming general replies with equal scholarly decorum, explaining that his slight delay in answering was 'not because I failed to appreciate your kindness in writing to me, but out of regard for the principle enunciated in the *Spring and Autumn* classic, that a Minister of one State ought not to carry on secret correspondence with the representative of another'. To answer the main point of the Manchu letter, he disputes the regent's thesis at its source:

> The letter which I have had the honour to receive takes me to task for violating the principles laid down by Confucius concerning succession to the throne. I admire the aptness of your allusion, but Confucius was only referring to the deaths of feudal princes who had perished by assassination. . . . The Sage never meant this to apply to a case in which the Sovereign Lord of the whole Empire had committed suicide for the sake of the altar of his gods. In such a case,

Large blue and white Ming vase, mark and period of Hsüan Te. OVERLEAF *Cloisonné water sprinkler* LEFT; *a lacquer plaque* TOP RIGHT *and a lacquer box decorated with camellias; all Ming*

slavish adherence to the letter of the principle in question would show callous indifference to the interests of the Empire as a whole, and would assuredly plunge our ancient state in the horrors of anarchy and civil war.[30]

The general did not surrender, Yangchow was taken, and the most appalling massacre of the inhabitants ensued. But at least the proper civilities had been carried out. The Manchu dynasty, however alien, would yield to none in its care of the Chinese traditions.

明

Paper-thin porcelain Yung Lo wine cup, from the Ching Te Chen kilns

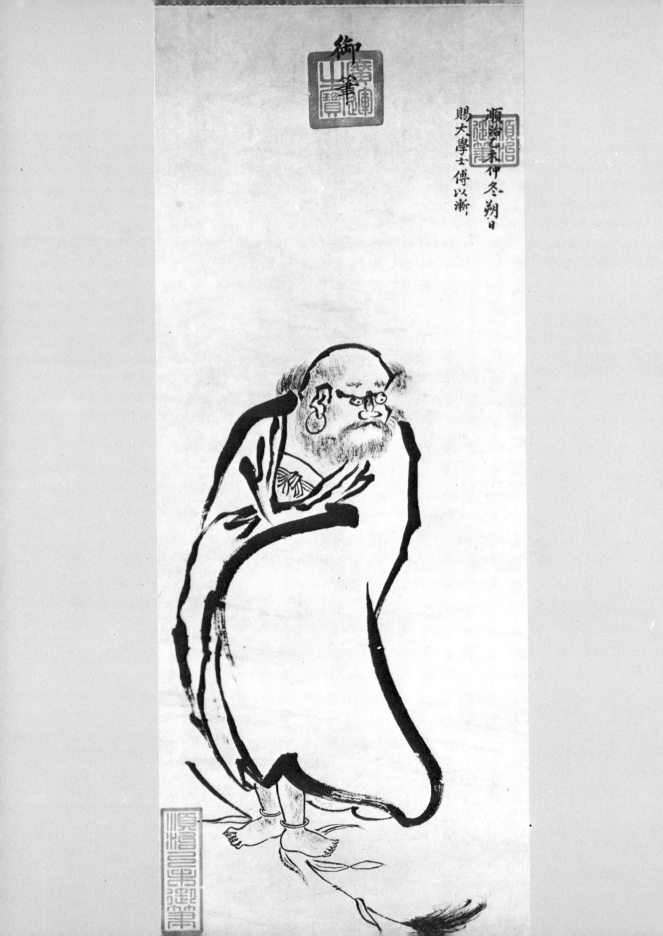

THE BOY-EMPEROR, SHUN CHIH, ONLY SIX WHEN HIS PEOPLE CAPTURED Peking and established him as the Son of Heaven, seemed to personify the unbarbarian nature of these Manchu invaders. He was more interested in the arts than in government, and became a distinguished painter in that freely impressionistic style so much admired by the Chinese scholar-artists. According to the annals he died at the age of only twenty-three, in 1661, although unofficial tradition in China has long maintained that he abdicated in that year to become the abbot of a Buddhist monastery not far from Peking. Whatever the truth, the new Manchu dynasty once again had an infant on the throne in the form of the first emperor's seven-year-old son. But this reign, spanning sixty-one years, was to be very different. For the K'ang Hsi emperor was arguably the most perceptive, civilized and well meaning of all China's rulers.

An example of K'ang Hsi's subtlety was his method of winning the co-operation of the Confucians. Many of these had felt themselves honour-bound, like their predecessors under the Mongols, not to collaborate with the invading dynasty. In 1678 K'ang Hsi ordered that a special effort be made to seek out the most talented people and to recommend them as examination candidates. Of those finally recommended to sit the papers (and a recommendation was tantamount to an order) a few threatened suicide rather than comply, and some did succeed in having their excuses accepted. Many of the 143 who eventually took their places in the examination hall did so in a mood of sullen hostility. But the situation was altered by the discovery of what the emperor had in mind for the fifty who were selected as the top candidates. They were invited to compile the official history of the Ming dynasty. Since their opposition derived from loyalty to the Ming, this was a task which they could hardly decline. Yet it was an official position in a department which brought them into close contact with the palace. Naturally, after a few years, the hard edges of resistance proved almost impossible to maintain and many of the scholars moved later to other more functional posts.

K'ang Hsi was also remarkably shrewd on the topic that was to be the plague and ultimately the downfall of his dynasty – foreigners. From his youth he had greatly enjoyed the company of Jesuits. Their intellectual abilities and philosophical cast of mind chimed well with his, and their scientific skills remained as useful as ever. On several occasions their calculation of the calendar and prediction of eclipses had proved more accurate than any the Chinese or Muslim astronomers could provide, and they had even undertaken to very good effect the casting of cannon –

Bodhidharma Crossing the Yangtze on a Reed, *painting by the first Ch'ing emperor, Shuh Chih*

a service which was much appreciated by the Chinese emperors but which raised a few eyebrows when news of it filtered back to Rome. By 1692 K'ang Hsi felt so warmly towards his Jesuits that he promulgated a famous decree in their favour:

> We have seriously considered this question of the Europeans. . . . They do not excite disturbances in the provinces, they do no harm to anyone . . . and their doctrine has nothing in common with that of the false sects of the empire, nor has it any tendency to excite sedition.
>
> Since, then, we do not hinder either the Lamas of Tartary or the bonzes of China from building temples . . . much less can we forbid these Europeans, who teach only good laws, from having also their churches and preaching their religion publicly in them.[1]

Later events were to alter the emperor's opinion. He was particularly disillusioned by the Rites Controversy, the clash between Rome and the missionaries as to whether the ancestral rites involved a blasphemous worship of the dead. K'ang Hsi supported his Jesuits by writing to inform the pope that Ricci had been correct in seeing the ceremonies merely as an expression of reverence. The pope announced in a subsequent bull that this interpretation of the emperor's was incorrect, a statement which understandably enraged K'ang Hsi when he came to hear of it. The more recently arrived French missionaries agreed with Rome, but then they knew very little about China. K'ang Hsi himself wrote of one of them: 'Maigrot wasn't merely ignorant of Chinese literature, he couldn't even recognize the simplest Chinese characters; yet he chose to discuss the falsity of the Chinese moral system.' These and other similar dissensions within the Christian church led K'ang Hsi to revise his earlier glowing opinion: 'In this Catholic religion, the Society of Peter quarrels with the Jesuits, and among the Jesuits the Portuguese want only their own nationals in their church while the French want only French in theirs. This violates the principles of religion.'[2]

The emperor had also been alarmed to discover in 1703, during a tour of the southern provinces, that there were 'missionaries wandering at will over China'. He resolved that they should henceforth be kept under much stricter control and he identified, even at this early stage, precisely that area of ambiguity between missionary and merchant, religion and trade, which was to cause such trouble 150 years later. 'With so many Westerners coming to China it has been hard to distinguish the real missionaries from other white men pretending to be missionaries', but being in fact mere

'meddlers . . . out for profit, greedy traders, who should not be allowed to live here.' 'I fear', he adds, 'that some time in the future China is going to get into difficulties with these various Western countries. That is my prediction.'[3]

For a great many centuries Arab ships had been calling quite peacefully at China's ports, but the Chinese experience of merchants from Europe was to be painfully different. Almost their first glimpse of Portuguese trading methods was a flotilla of ships which sailed upstream from Macao in 1517, disregarding Chinese instructions to wait at the mouth of the river, and then entered the anchorage at Canton with pennants flying and cannons ablaze. It was later explained that this discharge of artillery was intended as a courtesy – as indeed it probably was, although the ambiguity can only have been deliberate. The confusion was inherent in the very situation of a party of merchants arriving in warships, and it was to remain so throughout the history of European trade in China. The men who left Lisbon, Amsterdam or London on these expeditions were recognized at home as adventurers. It was not surprising that at the other end they seemed almost indistinguishable from pirates, and often their behaviour amply justified one of the Chinese names for them, 'ocean devils'.

The English did not put in an appearance for another 120 years, but their arrival was even less propitious. In 1636 John Weddell sailed from Dover with six ships and a charter from Charles I to trade in China. He too made his way up the Pearl River, contrary to the wishes of the Chinese. By the time he came down again he had captured a fort, had removed from it large numbers of cannon and replaced the Chinese flag with the king's, had burned several junks, had set fire to a small town after commandeering its pigs, and had blown up another fort. After seizing the first fort he sent a note to the local mandarins, assuring them that 'our Desire was to have their Friendship and Free Commerce in their country', but after being given, as he thought, little satisfaction in this respect, and after an unsuccessful attempt by the Chinese to drive him down the river or to destroy his ships, he had resolved to 'doe all the spoile wee could unto the Chinois'.[4]

The Chinese were not against trade in itself, and their method of controlling these unruly Western barbarians was to limit their activities to one port, that of Canton. In 1557 the peninsula of Macao had been leased to the Portuguese. The intention was that all goods from Europe should be landed there, and the Portuguese were given the right to trade into Canton once a year. Anyone wishing to carry merchandise further inland could

only do so on the long-established basis of bearing tribute to the emperor at Peking. For centuries this bringing of tribute, and the awarding of gifts in return by the emperor, had been a convenient fiction both to dignify and to control trade with the nomadic peoples to the north. Vast caravans formed up at the various places of entry through the Great Wall. The merchants, once inside the country, were entertained at Chinese expense and were lodged in Peking in a compound kept exclusively for this purpose. From here they went to the palace to offer their tribute, each pretending to represent some distant ruler who professed himself a vassal of the Chinese. They might, for example, bring horses – a commodity always in short supply in China – and they would receive a gracious gift from the emperor of large quantities of silk. This was genuine trade, an exchange of needed commodities. Sometimes other groups arrived with almost worthless articles and they too received a bounteous reward (if there was tribute in such a case, it was from rather than to the Chinese emperor). But these two relationships – of limited coastal trade or tribute-bearing missions to the centre – were the only ones that the Chinese could conceive of having with foreign peoples. So far they had needed no other.

The empire, historically, had lacked neighbours. It had at various times included within itself the entire habitable subcontinent, and in the bleak territory to the north there lived only nomads. There had been no reason to doubt China's view of herself as a central pool of civilization surrounded by barbarous and vassal races. Now at last, with Europe's development of ocean travel, China did have neighbours and she had them at least a century before she was willing to admit the fact. There was little in their behaviour to suggest that they were not barbarians, but they did strenuously reject the status of vassals. They expected, regardless of the size of China, to exchange ambassadors with her as equal and sovereign states, and they hoped to hawk their wares as freely here as in Europe. The Chinese were frankly amazed.

The most famous embodiment of these two irreconcilable attitudes was the audience given at his summer palace in 1793 by K'ang Hsi's grandson Ch'ien Lung, then in his eighty-third year, to Lord Macartney, the ambassador of George III of England.

The embassy had set sail from Spithead in the *Lion*, a man of war of sixty-four guns, in September 1792. The Secretary to Lord Macartney was Sir George Staunton, who had already served with him in India, and as page to the ambassador there was Sir George's eleven-year-old son. They

were accompanied by two doctors, two artists, a German tutor for young Staunton, and a full complement of attendants, craftsmen, soldiers and musicians. Another ship sailed with them, an Indiaman by the name of the *Hindostan*, in which were more of the retinue and the presents intended for the emperor – scientific instruments, a planetarium, a hot-air balloon, and a great many of the clocks and watches which ever since the days of Ricci had been regarded as the staple gift for the Chinese. When these ships arrived the following July off the mouth of the Pei river, the nearest part of the coast to Peking, it must have seemed to the Chinese self-evident that they came bearing tribute. The contents of both ships were unloaded into some magnificent craft which Macartney refers to as 'yachts', and in these, after much courtesy from the local officials and the usual round of welcoming banquets, the embassy gradually made its way up the river and canal towards Peking. A pretty banner fluttering at the leading mast-head was discovered to say 'The English Ambassador bringing tribute to the Emperor of China', but Macartney, every inch the diplomat, decided to ignore it on the grounds that the meaning of the characters might well not have been explained to him.

From Peking they were to travel further north to the summer palace at Jehol, beyond the Great Wall, where the emperor was residing. Macartney notes in his diary that he covered this part of the journey 'in a neat little English post-chaise which I had provided, and which was drawn by four little Tartar horses not eleven hands high, being, I believe, the first piece of Long-acre manufactory that ever rattled upon the road to Jehol.' Sometimes the two high-ranking mandarins who were accompanying him, Wang and Chou, 'took their turns to come into the post-chaise with me, and were inexpressibly pleased and astonished with its easiness, lightness and rapidity, the ingenuity of the springs, and the various contrivances for raising and lowering the glasses, curtains and jalousies.'[5] Sir George Staunton, having a touch of the gout, was travelling in a palanquin. The party stopped, of course, to inspect the Great Wall. It had never occurred to Wang and Chou that it was as interesting as Macartney found it ('certainly the most stupendous work of human hands') and they urged him back on to the road with so much nervousness that he decided they must suspect him of having strategic designs upon it. For the final entry into Jehol they formed themselves into a spectacular procession. First came a hundred mandarins on horseback, then a detachment of English dragoons, followed by infantrymen with drum and fife and a party of servants and musicians in a livery of rich green and gold, and

finally the ambassador himself with the Stauntons, father and son, 'in a chariot'. Macartney was gratified to hear later that the emperor had viewed their entry from a hill in his garden, and that he had been much pleased by it.

This was a Sunday, 8 September, and the audience was to be held the following Saturday. In the interval Wang and Chou raised once again the delicate problem of the kowtow, the ceremony which during the next century came almost to symbolize the difference between the Chinese and the European view of the world. The word means, in literal Chinese, 'head-knocking'. The full ritual expected of anyone coming into the presence of the emperor consisted of kneeling three times, each occasion being followed by three full-length prostrations in which the forehead must touch the ground. This grovelling, for such it was, was entirely at odds with a European gentleman's idea of his personal dignity, and in political terms it seemed tantamount to admitting that an ambassador's own monarch was the vassal of the Chinese emperor. Already on several occasions Wang and Chou had tried to persuade Macartney that the kowtow would be required of him, and had demonstrated how simple it was to perform. Macartney took the position that he would kowtow to the emperor if someone of his own rank did the same to a portrait of George III. Alternatively, he was more than willing to honour the emperor with the same reverence which he would use towards his own sovereign – in other words to kneel on one knee and kiss his hand. The mere thought of the latter must have profoundly shocked the two mandarins, and on the Wednesday of that first week at Jehol it was conceded that Macartney should merely kneel on one knee and bow his head.

On the great day the ambassador and his aide decked themselves out in the finery which they considered most in keeping with 'oriental customs and ideas'. Macartney wore 'over a rich embroidered velvet, the mantle of the Order of the Bath, with the collar, a diamond badge and a diamond star. Sir George Staunton was dressed in a rich embroidered velvet also, and, being a Doctor of Laws in the University of Oxford, wore the habit of his degree, which is of scarlet silk, full and flowing.' They waited for an hour in a tent prepared for them, and then at last Ch'ien Lung arrived in an open palanquin borne by sixteen men. 'As he passed', writes Macartney, 'we paid him our compliments, by kneeling on one knee, whilst all the Chinese made their usual prostrations.'[6] There is an amusing sidelight on this moment, for young Staunton wrote in his diary for this same day, 'we went down on one knee and Bowed our heads

Down to the ground'[7], but the last three words were later crossed out.
Nevertheless, however low the ambassadorial head may have gone, he
had certainly not kowtowed.

When Ch'ien Lung had mounted his throne, Macartney advanced and
presented him with a gold box, studded with diamonds, which contained
the king's letter. Sir George Staunton followed and gave the emperor 'two
elegant air-guns'. Both received in return pieces of carved jade, in which
they seem to have been rather disappointed ('highly prized by the Chinese,
but to me it does not appear in itself to be of any great value'). There followed a sumptuous five-hour banquet, with continuous wrestling,
tumbling, wire-dancing and play-acting going on in the background.
At one point Ch'ien Lung summoned Macartney to his side to give him
a cup of warm wine and to ask him the age of his king – no doubt a
favourite question on the part of this spry octogenarian, whom Macartney
describes as 'a very fine old gentleman, still healthy and vigorous, not
having the appearance of a man of more than sixty'. This friendliness on
the part of the emperor could only be a hopeful sign, even if there had been
no discussion of King George's wishes, and Macartney ended his day's
entry with the words:

> Thus I have seen 'King Solomon in all his glory'. I use this expression, as the
> scene recalled perfectly to my memory a puppet show of that name which I
> recollect to have seen in my childhood, and which made so strong an impres-
> sion on my mind that I then thought it a true representation of the highest
> pitch of human greatness and felicity.[8]

Almost three weeks later, when still no serious discussions had taken
place, a yellow silk armchair was carried in great state to Macartney's
lodgings. Sitting in it was a letter, the emperor's reply to King George,
and the mandarins made it plain that it was now time for the embassy to
depart. Hastily Macartney put down in writing his requests, most of which
had not been gone into in detail in the king's letter and which so far he had
been unable even to mention to the emperor. Britain hoped to establish
a permanent representative at the Chinese court and asked permission
for English merchants to trade at other ports than Canton, to have a ware-
house in Peking, to use some small unoccupied island as a base comparable
to Portugal's Macao, and to be freed from certain tariffs and duties. No
attention was paid to this new document. Ten days later – sailing down the
river again, accompanied by a special boat with two cows in it because
the Chinese had observed that the English liked milk, unprocurable

One of the many bridges at the Summer Palace, taken from the Marble Boat

normally, with their tea – Macartney professed himself baffled by this nation which could show him such generosity and courtesy and yet disregard entirely the purpose of his visit. He consoled himself with the observation: 'As to the lower orders they are all of a trafficking turn, and it seemed at the sea-ports where we stopped that nothing would be more agreeable to them than to see our ships often in their harbours.'[9] They soon would.

Some maintained that the failure of Macartney's mission had been due to his refusal to kowtow, and the Dutch decided to try the opposite line when they sent two ambassadors to China a few months later. The Dutchmen are calculated to have kowtowed no less than thirty times during the thirty-seven days they were in Peking, being willing to do so, in their eagerness to oblige, in front of a banner with the emperor's name on it and to some dried grapes sent to them from his own hand. They never mastered the gymnastics of prostration with any degree of grace, and when one of them first came to perform it to the emperor himself his wig fell off. The aged Ch'ien Lung burst into laughter. The Dutch left Peking having achieved no more than Macartney, and with considerably less dignity.

The bitter truth was that China had no need of European ambassadors or merchants, a fact which that letter for George III in the yellow armchair expressed with uncompromising clarity:

> As to the request made in your memorial, O King, to send one of your nationals to stay at the Celestial Court to take care of your country's trade with China, this is not in harmony with the state system of our dynasty and will definitely not be permitted. Traditionally people of the European nations who wished to render some service under the Celestial Court have been permitted to come to the capital. But after their arrival they are obliged to wear Chinese court costumes, are placed in a certain residence, and are never allowed to return to their own countries. . . .

> The virtue and prestige of the Celestial Dynasty having spread far and wide, the kings of the myriad nations come by land and sea with all sorts of precious things. Consequently there is nothing we lack, as your principal envoy and others have themselves observed. We have never set much store on strange or ingenious objects, nor do we need any more of your country's manufactures. . . .[10]

The last phrase went to the root of the problem. England's passion for China tea had become such that English merchants now found themselves in the unusual position of buying more abroad than they were selling.

Precious English silver was flowing into China, for this was the only currency that the Chinese would accept. Macartney noted hopefully that the emperor now allowed his court to wear woollen cloth for a short season in between the silk of their summer robes and the fur-lined damasks of winter, as if this might prove the opening that the mills of the West Riding were waiting for. In practice, as he knew and as the Chinese knew, England had found an answer – opium. By the time of Macartney's visit it already represented a quarter of all the goods being sent east from British India, and this in spite of the fact that the sale of the drug had long been illegal in China.

The story of the opium trade is one of the least savoury in the annals of imperialism. Opium was smoked in China throughout the eighteenth century, but the number of addicts had risen only slowly. It was entirely due to the energies of the trading nations, and in particular of Britain, that the problem increased so drastically in the early part of the next century. From about 1815 the quantity of imported opium was doubling almost every five years, and it was not long before the flow of silver into China had been handsomely reversed. As with any illegal traffic, the profits were enormous and a considerable part of them found their way into the pockets of those officials responsible for eliminating the trade – a fact which did much to nullify the frequent imperial edicts banning the import, sale or use of opium.

'Transactions seemed to partake of the nature of the drug; they imparted a soothing frame of mind with three per cent commission on sales, one per cent on returns, and no bad debts!'[11] This was the well-satisfied comment of a young American, William Hunter, who joined the trade in 1837. His account of his own first trip up the coast gives a glimpse of the procedure. The *Rose* anchored in a bay where there were already two other English opium ships and two Chinese 'man-of-war junks', the latter covered in a bright mass of bunting. A boat was immediately rowed across to her from one of these junks. In it was a mandarin, lounging with some elegance in an armchair. He was welcomed aboard with a cheroot and a glass of wine, but he wanted to know why the *Rose* had pulled into this bay when the captain must be aware that it was against the law. It was explained to him that owing to contrary winds and currents they needed to replenish their stocks of wood and water. The mandarin pulled a 'long red document' from his boot and told his secretary to read it aloud to remind him of its contents. It was an imperial edict emphasizing that Canton was the only port at which foreigners could trade, but adding that the Son of

Heaven, whose compassion was boundless, would allow any ship forced in by adverse seas and currents to procure the necessary supplies before continuing her voyage. Once this had been established, a sign was given for all the Chinese except the mandarin's personal secretary to wait for him in the boat. In the privacy of the cabin the dignitary asked how many chests of opium there were on board. There were 200. After more cheroots and wine his price for turning a blind eye was quickly agreed, since he was quite content with the sum received on previous occasions. As soon as he had returned to his junk, Chinese buyers rowed out from the shore to conduct the real business.

The hypocrisy of the Western nations was at least as great as that of the mandarins. The East India Company grew the plant quite openly – vast tracts of Bengal and Bihar were an enchanting sight at the right season of the year, covered in the tall flowering poppies – but outside the safety of its own jurisdiction the Company's ships were prohibited from carrying the cargo or its servants from handling it. Some of the missionaries too, although most of them profoundly disapproved of the trade, were not above using it to the greater glory of God. One of the best known Protestants in China was Karl Friedrich Gützlaff, described by William Hunter, a friend of his, as 'the celebrated Prussian missionary who, for the privilege of distributing the Scriptures and tracts, acted as interpreter for the sale of opium.'[12] Gützlaff accompanied vessels belonging to the most successful of all the smuggling companies, the one set up by that enterprising pair of Scotsmen, Jardine and Matheson. Jardine had frankly explained to him, in requesting his help, that although some considered the trade immoral, it was 'absolutely necessary to give any vessel a reasonable chance of defraying her expenses'. He added that 'the more profitable the expedition, the better we shall be able to place at your disposal a sum that may hereafter be employed in furthering your mission, and for your success in which we feel deeply interested.'[13]

In 1839 the emperor sent to Canton an official of undoubted integrity who became famous in Europe as Commissioner Lin. He was instructed to take whatever steps were necessary to stamp out this noxious trade, and one of his more original notions was an attempt at personal communication between himself and the authorities in those distant countries from which the smugglers came. He considered getting in touch in this way with the Americans, but decided the task would be too inconvenient since they appeared to have twenty-four local headmen instead of a king. And anyway, the English were by far the most important single group.

'They are ruled at present', he explained to the emperor, 'by a young girl. But I am told that it is she who issues commands, and on the whole it seems that it would be best to start by sending instructions to her.'[14]

Commissioner Lin's letter to Queen Victoria is rightly a most famous document. He still, of course, takes the line that he is writing to one of the emperor's vassal states:

> The kings of your honourable country by a tradition handed down from generation to generation have always been noted for their politeness and submissiveness. We have read your successive tributary memorials . . . privately we are delighted with the way in which the honourable rulers of your country deeply understand the grand principles and are grateful for the Celestial grace. For this reason the Celestial Court in soothing those from afar has redoubled its polite and kind treatment. The profit from trade has been enjoyed by them continuously for two hundred years. This is the source from which your country has become known for its wealth.

When he comes to the point, he is no more than realistic about the hypocrisy of the English trade:

> Let us ask, where is your conscience? I have heard that the smoking of opium is very strictly forbidden by your country; that is because the harm caused by opium is clearly understood. Since it is not permitted to do harm to your own country, then even less should you let it be passed on to the harm of other countries – how much less to China! Of all that China exports to foreign countries, there is not a single thing which is not beneficial to people; they are of benefit when eaten, or of benefit when used, or of benefit when resold. . . . Take tea and rhubarb, for example; the foreign countries cannot get along for a single day without them. If China cuts off these benefits with no sympathy for those who are to suffer, then what can the barbarians rely upon to keep themselves alive?

The Chinese were under the impression that without a regular dose of rhubarb Europeans became incurably constipated. Later Lin asks the queen how can she bear to go on 'selling products injurious to others in order to fulfil your insatiable desire', and ends by instructing her:

> After receiving this dispatch will you immediately give us a prompt reply regarding the details and circumstances of your cutting off the opium traffic. Be sure not to put this off.[15]

As far as is known this letter was lost somewhere on its long journey to England (it left Canton on the *Thomas Coutts* on 18 January 1840).

Certainly it never reached the queen, who was then twenty. It is hard to believe that Commissioner Lin's words would not have given her a moment's pause, before her ministers stepped in to explain the economic facts of life.

But Lin was doing more than writing letters. He had forced the English merchants to surrender their stocks of opium and was making preparations to dissolve it and then pour it in the sea (after addressing appropriate memorials to the spirits of the sea informing them of his intentions, regretting the need for this pollution, and suggesting that for their own good they should keep out of the way). Tens of thousands of chests of the drug were disposed of in this manner, and it was the unprecedented thoroughness of Lin's efforts that was to goad the English into fighting, in the Opium War, for what they chose to consider their rights.

The war, broken off intermittently for fruitless negotiations, dragged on until 1842 when the British capture of the important junction between the Grand Canal and the Yangtze frightened the emperor into granting concessions. The result was the notorious Treaty of Nanking, the first of the so-called 'unequal treaties'. The concessions were roughly those which Macartney had asked for half a century earlier. Hong Kong was ceded to Great Britain as a base, five ports were opened to British traders, at each of which a consul could be stationed, and tariffs were to be limited. The only mention of opium was a vague hope that 'smuggling would cease' and the demand that China pay six million dollars of compensation for those illicit cargoes destroyed by Commissioner Lin. There was one further clause, added a year later, which was to open the door to the leap-frogging process by which the Western powers now began to force their way more deeply into China. Britain was to benefit from a favoured-nation clause, which meant that any new concessions later granted to other countries should without further negotiation and at the same time apply to her.

Within a few years the United States and France had exacted for themselves treaties to match Britain's, and in 1856 the British and the French found a pretext for further armed hostilities against China which led eventually in 1860 to their marching on Peking, capturing the city and utterly looting and destroying the emperor's magnificent summer palace a few miles to the northwest. When the dust had cleared, the foreigners were found to have established for themselves the right to travel anywhere in the interior, to sail their ships up the Yangtze, to appoint ambassadors to the imperial court, to set up Christian missions without restriction,

A bronze lion in front of the T'ai Men, in the Imperial Palace at Peking

to import opium legally, and to be paid a large indemnity for the trouble they had been caused.

For the next thirty years there was a gradual increase in the numbers of both merchants and missionaries until at last, in 1895, the floodgates were finally opened wide to foreign encroachment. The occasion was a war between China and Japan over who should control Korea. The utter feebleness of the Manchu dynasty was laid bare in the defeat of their great empire by this small island, which had so recently been as deeply rooted as China in its own feudal past but which had learned more effectively some of the techniques of the foreigners – the modernized Japanese navy, for example, rapidly sank or captured most of China's antiquated junks. The result was an undignified scramble on the part of the Western powers, joined now by Japan, to take up their final positions for what seemed an increasingly attractive probability, the partition of China. Each concession wrung by any one nation from the tottering imperial court was soon capped by the demands of another. Areas of influence were tacitly staked out, earmarked as each country's province when the break-up should occur. The bankers of Britain, France, Germany and Russia fought to provide the lion's share of the loan with which China would meet the large indemnity demanded by victorious Japan.

During the sixteen years that remained of Chinese imperial history, the country was full of foreigners as never before – tourists and even soldiers now, to add to the merchants and missionaries. These people, who had forced their way in by their own modern forms of barbarism, stared with horror at the undoubted barbarities of the ancient Chinese way of life and found in them pleasing evidence of how necessary it was for China to be educated by Europe. Countless letters sailed their slow way home describing the disgraceful habit of foot-binding, and a French doctor wrote up his medical observations after examining some of the eunuchs.

It was indeed fairly remarkable what medieval horrors had survived in China up to the very dawn of the twentieth century. Dr Matignon, who published in 1899 his *Superstition, Crime et Misère en Chine (Souvenirs de biologie sociale)*, revealed that a certain family living near one of the palace gates had the hereditary concession for castration. During this operation, from which about four per cent died within the week from retention of urine, the penis was removed as well as the testicles. The reason was that the slightest surviving trace of masculinity would disqualify the eunuch if noticed in one of the periodical palace inspections – even a slightly suggestive flap of skin had caused such difficulties for one of the eunuchs that

In one of the gardens of the Imperial Palace, Peking. OVERLEAF *The River of Golden Water, which curls its way beneath marble bridges through the first of the great courtyards of the Imperial Palace*

he asked Dr Matignon's advice on the possibility of further surgery. In spite of these horrors there was no shortage of candidates; the disparity between the poverty outside the palace walls and the rich pickings within made sure of that. As a final macabre touch, Dr Matignon added that the family at the gate had a precious collection of relics stored in bottles of alcohol. These had been acquired from patients so innocent of the ways of the world that they had not demanded their own, similarly preserved, at the time of the operation. The bottles were hired out to eunuchs who were unprovided for on other palace parades, at which everyone had to display his remains, or else were sold to the family after a eunuch's death to be included in his coffin, for it was considered essential that no one should go incomplete into the next world.

Foot-binding was more recent in China than the use of eunuchs, but only to the extent that it had existed for one thousand years rather than two or three. It is thought to have started just before the Sung dynasty, in a very modified form, as a fashion among the palace dancers. If this is so there was a sad irony in its origin, for ultimately the fashion would put an end to the dancers' art – imperial China was alone among the nations of the east in no longer having a rich tradition of classical dance. Later the binding became tighter, and the bound foot acquired two connotations which made the abolishing of the fashion almost impossible. In economic terms it was seen at first as a status symbol – a woman able to go through life doing nothing but hobble, and needing to be carried over any but the shortest distances, was clearly not of the labouring classes, nor was she likely to stray far from her proper place as an ornament of her husband's house (eventually the custom spread to poorer sections of the community, obscuring this original aspect). And almost inevitably, over the centuries, these strange distorted limbs came to exercise in the minds of men a fascination which was little short of a national fetish. By virtue of its very secrecy, swathed from sight in the bandages which compressed it, the foot became a symbol of all that was most intimate. Erotic prints of the Sung and Ming periods frequently include women naked in every other respect, sometimes even showing their sexual organs, but in none is there an unbound foot. The nearest is an occasional titillating glimpse of the woman loosening the bandage. A Jesuit writing early in the eighteenth century had correctly identified this aspect of foot-binding: 'In cases of marriage, the parties not being able to see each other, it is customary to send the exact dimensions of the lady's foot to her intended, instead of sending him her portrait, as we do in Europe. In this particular, indeed, their taste is per-

Two peculiarly Chinese horrors: a eunuch and a lady showing her feet (in the cause of reform)

231

A doorway in one of the small private courtyards of the Imperial Palace

verted to such an extraordinary degree, that I knew a physician who lived with a woman with whom he had no other intercourse but that of viewing and fondling her feet.'[16] In the next century Chinese Christians would often admit, in the secrecy of the confessional, to evil thoughts about feet. Lord Macartney wrote of the habit: 'I by no means want to apologize for the Chinese custom of squeezing their women's pettitoes into the shoes of an infant, which I think an infernal distortion.'[17]

An infernal distortion it certainly was. The process began for a little girl at the age of about six. On whatever day had been chosen as propitious, her feet were washed and the nails cut. Then, with a generous sprinkling of alum, the four small toes were turned back under the sole and the whole foot drawn tightly towards the heel, before being bound in its new position with a cloth about two inches wide and ten feet long. After a few days the bandage was replaced and every two weeks the entire bundle was forced into a shoe a tenth of an inch smaller than the previous one. A child who secretly eased the bandage would be beaten if discovered. But if undiscovered, her pain would only be increased by the blood rushing back into the pustulent foot. It took at least two years to achieve the desired length of three inches. The flesh never again rotted as badly as in those first years, but for the rest of her life each little shoe, so carefully fashioned to receive the shrivelled stump, would contain inside it a sachet of perfume – although it was said that even the undisguised stench was one of the pleasures of the true connoisseur.

For centuries there had been campaigns against this grotesque custom. From the start of the Ch'ing dynasty the Manchus tried to abolish it, and they prohibited it within Manchu families. The Manchu women were most indignant at this ruling – such is the power of fashion – and they developed high wedge-soles for their shoes which at first sight, peeping seductively out from beneath skirt or trouser-leg, could almost be mistaken for the desired 'lotus-foot'. Even imperial edicts failed to have any effect on the habit among the Chinese themselves. Only in the late nineteenth century, when dozens of natural-foot societies sprang up, was any progress made. It was a cause to which European and American ladies eagerly devoted their energies, and it was now part of a wider crusade for the emancipation of women and indeed for the modernization of China herself. Suddenly, in the early years of the twentieth century, the age-old custom began to disappear at quite remarkable speed. It had been swept away by precisely those same forces which would bring to an end the Ch'ing dynasty and more than 2000 years of imperial history.

The foreigners were not the only enemy that the Ch'ing emperors had to cope with in the century of their decline. The Manchus had from the start ruled by Chinese methods and with the help of a great many Chinese civil servants, but they had jealously guarded their own identity and had kept control of the country as an occupying force, much as the Mongols had done. Manchus were forbidden to marry Chinese (they numbered less than two per cent of the population, so they would rapidly have been absorbed without this restriction), and no Chinese were allowed to settle in the Manchu homeland – Manchuria was sealed off behind a symbolic frontier, a ditch several hundred miles long lined with willows which was known as the Willow Palisade. Military control was kept exclusively in Manchu hands, and the civil administration was carefully divided in the higher ranks between Manchus and Chinese. Finally, no Manchu was allowed to engage in any form of trade, employment or labour. Every ordinary man had to be a soldier (or 'bannerman', from the Manchu system of companies identified by their coloured banners). At the other extreme of the social scale the imperial relatives – an ever-increasing group – were usually prevented from taking any part in government and so lived as pensioners of the state.

The intelligence and tact of the second Ch'ing emperor, K'ang Hsi, was such that he persuaded the Chinese scholar-classes to accept this state of affairs to an extent that they never had under the Mongols. His own reign of sixty-one years was soon more than matched in length by that of his grandson Ch'ien Lung (on the throne for sixty-three years), and between them they gave the dynasty a long period of stability until nearly the end of the eighteenth century. By then the majority of Manchu families, other than those serving in the civil administration, had done little but draw their pay over a period of some five generations. Their decadence as a ruling and privileged caste coincided ominously with the new threat from Europe.

The first large-scale nineteenth-century uprising against the dynasty, known as the Taiping Revolution, was caused by many separate factors, among them the general anti-Manchu sentiment, the loss of imperial prestige in the Opium War, famine in the south and the influence of a peculiarly garbled form of Christianity. Its leader, Hung Hsiu-chüan, was a village school-teacher who had failed four times in the examinations at Canton when a chance encounter with some Christian pamphlets led him to believe that he was the younger son of Jesus Christ, with a mission to rid China of the Manchus. He proclaimed himself the king of the new

t'ai-p'ing t'ien-kuo, or Heavenly Kingdom of Peace. His own burning sense of his mission, backed up by his promise that all property would be shared, brought great numbers of peasants to join his cause, and a series of victories over inefficient and demoralized Manchu forces had by 1853 yielded Nanking into his hands. In this city he set up his administration, just as had the founder of the Ming dynasty during his campaign to drive out the Mongols. But here the parallel faltered. Although retaining Nanking for eleven years, the Taipings never managed to capture Peking. They tried to take Shanghai instead, but this brought them into conflict with the resident European population and they were defeated by an army of Shanghai irregulars led by 'Chinese' Gordon, the future martyr of Khartoum, who had been seconded from the British army for the purpose. Hung committed suicide (he had long departed from the asceticism imposed on his followers, opting instead for a parody of imperial life, with a court and harem of considerable opulence), and in 1864 the Manchu forces recaptured Nanking. The revolution, seen by many today as the honourable forerunner of those two later revolutions which led to the Republic and to Communism, had cost twenty million lives and achieved nothing. But it was an early demonstration of how little it might take to topple the Ch'ing dynasty.

It is arguable that the life of the dynasty was prolonged by the remarkable empress dowager who presided over its last half-century, although all her actions were such as to make its end more certain. Tz'u Hsi had entered the palace in 1851 as a sixteen-year-old concubine. Her good fortune was that five years later she provided the emperor with his first son. When the child was five his father died, and after several weeks of frantic jockeying for place, Tz'u Hsi, already a dowager empress at the age of twenty-six, entered in 1861 on the first of the periods of regency which would give her an almost unbroken spell of absolute power up to her death in 1908.

Her personal greed and vanity were matched only by the fervour of her opposition to reform – although reform offered the empire its one hope of survival, as that other emperor over the water began to demonstrate with such good effect in Japan in 1868. One example, often quoted, will serve to show her self-interest and short-sightedness. She very much wanted another summer palace to replace the delightful one destroyed by the British and French in 1860, but in the weakened state of the empire such a venture ran the risk of seeming a most unjustified extravagance. A decree of 1888, announcing the plan to build a new palace, recognized this objection:

We are aware that the emperors of our sacred line have in the administration of their government ever paid attention to the wants and sufferings of the people, and that the wanton licence of former dynasties has been conspicuously absent in laying out their pleasure grounds, in the conduct of their hunting expeditions, and in similar recreations. The funds for the work will be drawn from our private savings and will entail no expense or sacrifice on the country.[18]

T'zu Hsi's Shih Fang *or Marble Boat, based on a Mississippi river steamer, at the Summer Palace*

The objection was recognized, but the answer to it was a lie. A large part of the funds recently set aside for the creation of a modern navy were diverted by Tz'u Hsi into her beautiful new lake-side palace. A naval school was established on one part of the lake, as if to honour some half-remembered obligation. Otherwise the only connections with shipping were the steam launch used by the boy-emperor to tow around boatloads of palace ladies, and – the most fanciful of all Tz'u Hsi's follies – the marble pavilion rising from the water in the shape of a Mississippi paddle-steamer. A few years later Japan destroyed the navy which China had failed to modernize.

235

Throughout the nineteenth century there had been popular uprisings in various parts of the empire – that of the Taipings was unusual only in being more extensive than most and in deriving from its strange Christian origins rather than from the traditional secret societies of China. The White Lotus Society, instrumental several centuries earlier in driving out the Mongols and establishing the Ming dynasty, sponsored a great revolt in the north in 1796 in the hope of restoring the Ming. A hundred years later, the most famous of all the Chinese popular uprisings was to be caused by an offshoot of the White Lotus Society – the *I Ho Ch'üan*, sometimes translated as 'Righteous Harmony Fists' but better known to the West as the Boxers.

The aim of the Boxers was to rid China of foreigners. In their early days this included the foreign dynasty on the throne, but the ever-growing presence of the Europeans, behaving more and more as if they already owned China, diverted the hostility more purely towards themselves and their much-hated Chinese converts. One faction at court decided that the Boxers, undisciplined as they were, might be used to advantage, and eventually their attacks on Christians were granted the official favour of Tz'u Hsi herself. Thus a popular uprising escalated into a national one, a final desperate attempt to rid the country of the intruding Europeans. The result was the besieging of the European Legations in their special quarter of Peking, followed by the capture of the city by the forces sent to relieve them. Forty years, almost to the month, after the British and French had last entered Peking as conquerors, the European powers marched in again. Last time only the summer palace out in the countryside had been destroyed, but now the Forbidden City itself was thoroughly looted. Even the wife of the British Minister was observed taking her pick. Tz'u Hsi, just in time, had slipped out of the palace in the blue cloth garments of a peasant woman, riding in a cart with a prince sitting on the shaft. The emperor (by now her sickly nephew, for her son had died) was in a similar wagon behind. The guards at the Summer Palace at first failed to recognize the group, then tea was hurriedly served. After leaving hasty instructions for her treasures to be packed up and taken north of the Great Wall, the empress dowager lurched on into the security of more remote districts. Of the news that followed her, almost the most horrifying was that foreigners had intruded on her private apartments, scrawled *graffiti* on her walls, and even lain down on her bed.

It was sixteen months before she returned. During that time the

Western powers had fixed on another massive indemnity (China was to pay it in instalments up to 1940). However, they had also taken one very tactful decision. They were now of the opinion that the Boxer affair had been an uprising against the Ch'ing dynasty which the Europeans had helped to suppress. This meant that after the sacrifice or removal of some of the more prominent supporters of her own pro-Boxer policy, it was possible for the empress dowager to be welcomed back to her capital city. The foreign community lined the wall to watch her ceremonial entry. She looked up at them, smiled and gave a slight bow.

From the point of view of her policies, she was now a changed woman. There were friendly tea-parties for the ladies of the Legations, with whom she posed for photographs. A Manchu princess, whose father had been China's Minister in Paris, was summoned to court to meet Tz'u Hsi in 1903. She was particularly asked to come in one of her interesting French gowns, and her description of the occasion reveals to what extent Western informality had now replaced the rigid demands of the kowtow:

> Her Majesty stood up when she saw us and shook hands with us. She had a most fascinating smile. . . . While we were talking to her we saw a gentleman standing at a little distance and after a while she said, 'Let me introduce you to the Emperor Kuang Hsü, but you must call him Wan Sway Yeh (Master of 10,000 years) and call me Lao Tsu Tsung (the Great Ancestor).' His Majesty shyly shook hands with us.[19]

To such an extent had the stuffing gone out of the empire.

Tz'u Hsi also began now to introduce some of the reforms which had so long been needed, and which this shy emperor had tried to bring in during a brief period of self-assertion in 1898. His efforts had led to swift retaliation on the part of his aunt, who had not put him on the throne as a three-year-old with this type of independent behaviour in mind. She had him arrested and virtually imprisoned on an island, and six of his advisers were executed. Now, four or five years later, she began to produce several of his policies as her own. The ancient examinations in the Confucian classics were abolished, and steps were taken to provide education in more modern subjects. Many sinecures in the administration were done away with. Confessions extracted by torture were outlawed in the courts. Effective steps were at last taken, with British co-operation now, to control the use of opium. There was even talk of constitutional monarchy, and commissions were sent abroad to study the workings of parliaments.

Educated Chinese wanted these reforms, but they had no need of the

decayed Manchu dynasty to put them into effect – particularly once this ruthless and domineering old lady had passed from the scene. In 1908 her nephew died. She herself was to survive him by only twenty-four hours, but she had already announced her choice of the next emperor. He was to be a two-year-old prince, the third infant under the age of six that she had placed on the dragon throne in her devoted career as a regent.

During the previous few years many of the revolutionary groups and secret societies within China had become allied with the republican movement of Sun Yat-sen, whose hope was to start separate provincial revolutions simultaneously in many different parts of China. Events followed his blueprint almost exactly. An uprising in Szechuan (over the government's railway policy), followed by a rebellion of the soldiers of Wuchang in Hupei, led to revolutionaries seizing important centres all over the country in October 1911. In rapid succession province after province declared themselves independent of the Manchu court, and on 12 February 1912 it was announced from the palace that the child-emperor was abdicating. The edict included the sentence 'The people's wishes are plain', but even now authority was sought, and duly found, in the classics; 'The form of government in China shall be a constitutional Republic, to comfort the longing of all within the empire and to act in harmony with the ancient sages, who regarded the throne as a public heritage.'[20]

Thus ended the world's most remarkable span of imperial history. It was 2133 years since Shih Huang Ti had first unified China. His hope of countless emperors from his own line had been soon frustrated, but the generations of rulers following him on that same imperial throne had been as near to countless as history is likely to come. One loses a normal sense of time in writing or reading of China. Comparison with two of the world's other great empires can serve perhaps to put her dynasties into some sort of perspective. The Roman Empire was founded during the Han dynasty and came to an end in the gap between the Han and the T'ang. The British Empire began early in the Ch'ing dynasty and barely survived it.

During those two millennia the Chinese had developed a consistent and slowly unfolding culture, faithful throughout to its own particular virtues and vices. From the disciples of Confucius in 500 B.C. to those who were still being examined on their understanding of his ideas in A.D. 1900, from the autocracy of Shih Huang Ti to that of Tz'u Hsi, from the pottery of the early tombs to the porcelain turned out by the imperial

A Temple of the Ancestors, near Canton

kilns at Ching Te Chen, from the characters on the oracle-bones to those announcing the last emperor's abdication – in all these respects, and many more like them, the beginnings and the end of Chinese imperial history show closer links over thousands of years than one is accustomed to find elsewhere over hundreds. There has been no story like it in human experience.

清

Detail from a carved and painted lacquer screen, Ch'ing dynasty

I ENDED THE LAST CHAPTER AS IF 1912 WERE THE CONCLUSION OF A long span of Chinese culture and history – partly because that year does bring to an end the subject of this book, the dynasties, but also because the present regime in China seems to imply such a complete break with the country's past. Or is it only with the worst elements of that past?

It may be that to future historians the years between 1912 and 1949 will look much like any other spell of troubled times between two periods of stable rule – or, in the old terminology, between two dynasties. Certainly the first ruler to emerge after 1912 intended this to be the case, for he had all the traditional qualifications of the founder of a new dynasty. He was Yüan Shih-k'ai, a general who was called in by the Manchu court as the only man strong enough to put down the revolution of 1911. Faithful to the old pattern, he used his position to seize power for himself. He advised the imperial family that it would be wise to abdicate (alarming them considerably by his talk of Louis XVI and his relatives), and then, as the commander of the most powerful military forces in the country, he proposed to Sun Yat-sen that if Sun would yield to him the position of President of the Republic, there was no reason why they should not work together for the future of China. Sun, militarily weak and politically over-credulous, agreed to this bargain. Over the next few years Yüan's preparations to establish himself as the new emperor became unmistakable. But his designs, which in the existing climate of opinion would never have stood much chance of success, were brought to an end by his death in 1916.

There followed a period of chaos during which several 'warlords' struggled for dominance, until in 1928 Peking was captured by Chiang Kai-shek, who had emerged as the most powerful figure in Sun Yat-sen's Kuomintang party after Sun's death in 1925. China once more had a government of sorts, although Chiang's twenty years of power can hardly be called a period of stability. He was involved in an almost continuous civil war with the Communists under the leadership of Mao Tse-tung – a struggle interrupted only by the common need to resist the encroaches of Japan – and his administration itself has been aptly described as 'Fascist in every quality except efficiency'.[1]

Stability did return with the final victory of Mao in 1949, and countless modern commentators have since discussed the intriguing question of whether the newly self-confident China represents a complete break with the strong empire of the past, or is a natural development and refinement of it. Obviously the adoption of an international materialist egali-

tarian philosophy represents at one level an utter rejection of all that
ancient China held sacred, but in other respects the contrast is less simple.
Confucianism provided an orthodoxy no less absolute than Marxism,
and to be thoroughly educated in the current orthodoxy remains today,
as it always was, an indispensable qualification for rising in the hierarchy.
Frank and fearless criticism of those who seem to deviate from the correct
way was the positive duty of a good Confucian; during the Sung dynasty
'self-indicting study rooms' were provided, in which the opponents of
Wang An-shih's reforms were encouraged to educate themselves with
further reading until they had corrected their mistaken opinions. The
present Chinese distrust of specialist intellectual solutions, or of decisions
taken by men out of touch with the practical experience of the peasants
and workers, can be seen as prefigured in the ancient Chinese proverb
'For farm work ask the boy servant; for spinning ask the maid.' Even
the same worries are there. Imperial history was full of complaints that
the examinations were becoming too purely literary and were providing
too narrow an intake into the bureaucracy. One of the specific fears leading to the Cultural Revolution was that higher education was again
becoming more easily accessible to a self-perpetuating class of intellectuals than to the rest of the people, and that the old processes of fossiliza-
tion would recur.

Only time will tell how far the parallel holds, or to what extent China's
past tendency to grow rigid can be avoided. Meanwhile it would take an
incorrigible sentimentalist to deny that the balance sheet is so far all on the
side of gain. Individually-minded Westerners may look askance at a
system in which the state controls so many aspects of life, but this is
certainly nothing new in China. The improvement in the lives of ordinary
people speaks for itself. And if the members of the Party are reminiscent
of the Confucians in their orthodoxy, they lack entirely, as all observers
agree, that other notorious characteristic of the mandarin class – the incli-
nation to feather their nests.

Nor do the modern Chinese feel any need to disparage the achievements of their own past. They are as proud of the objects and buildings
reproduced in this book as any Sung or Ming connoisseur would have
been – they merely praise the potter rather than the patron. A small but
intriguing example of this concern with China's heritage occurred during
the siege of Peking in 1949, just before the final Communist victory.
Lin Piao was in charge of the operation, and having selected the best
military vantage point to attempt a breach in the great city wall, he

summoned a leading archaeologist to ask whether there were historical objections to this particular plan. The professor was of the opinion that there were. Lin Piao had chosen one of the few surviving stretches of unrestored Ming architecture, the loss of which would be irreparable. The professor was able to suggest another stretch of wall, equally good from a tactical viewpoint, equally far from the densely inhabited areas of the city, but of no comparable archaeological value. The change of plan was duly made, though in fact the city capitulated before bombardment began.

No other country in the world has had a history, a philosophy and a system of administration which seems to lead so naturally as China's towards the techniques of the Marxist state; and no other country seems so likely to approach the ideals of Communism without needing to reject the best in her own past. It is typical of this hidden cultural continuity that Mao should be a poet (how many artists are there among the Western Heads of State? yet how many there were, of varying degrees of competence, among the emperors of China). The last word can be his. One of his best known poems, *Snow*, expresses with justifiable pride this sense of building on the past:

> *This is the scene in that northern land;*
> *A hundred leagues are sealed with ice,*
> *A thousand leagues of whirling snow.*
> *On either side of the Great Wall*
> *One vastness is all you see.*
> *From end to end of the great river*
> *The rushing torrent is frozen and lost.*
> *The mountains dance like silver snakes,*
> *The highlands roll like waxen elephants,*
> *As if they sought to vie with heaven in their height;*
>   *And on a sunny day*
> *You will see a red dress thrown over the white,*
>   *Enchantingly lovely!*
>
> *Such great beauty like this in all our landscape*
> *Has caused unnumbered heroes to bow in homage.*
> *But alas these heroes! Shih Huang Ti and Han Wu Ti*
> *Were rather lacking in culture;*
> *Rather lacking in literary talent*
> *Were the emperors T'ang Tai Tsung and Sung Tai Tsu;*
>   *And Jenghiz Khan,*

Beloved Son of Heaven for a day,
Only knew how to bend his bow at the golden eagle.
*   Now they are all past and gone:*
To find men truly great and noble-hearted
We must look here in the present.[2]

THE DYNASTIES

SHANG c. 1600–c. 1100 B.C.

From about 1400 B.C. the Shang made their capital at An-yang. Their kingdom spanned the plain of the Yellow River, but it is not known exactly how far it extended. They referred to themselves as the Shang, but the Chou name for them – which therefore appears in many classical sources – was the Yin.

CHOU c. 1100–256 B.C.
Western Chou c. 1100–771 B.C.

Eastern Chou 771–256 B.C.

The Chou originally retained their old capital in the Wei valley, but they were driven from here by barbarians in 771 B.C. They then established themselves at Loyang until they were eliminated by the Ch'in in 256 B.C. The area covered by the Chou vassal states extended from approximately Peking in the north to a little below the Yangtze in the south.

Ch'in 221–206 B.C.

Between 230 and 221 B.C. the Ch'in engulfed their six rival Chou states (Han, Chao, Wei, Ch'u, Yen and Ch'i) to establish the first empire. They too had their capital in the Wei valley. Several states had built walls to protect their frontiers: the Ch'in linked three of these to form the beginnings of the Great Wall.

HAN 206 B.C.–A.D. 220
Western or Former Han 206 B.C.–A.D. 8

Hsin A.D. 8–23

Eastern or Later Han A.D. 23–220

The Han at first made their capital in the Wei valley at Ch'ang-an, close to the sites of the Chou and Ch'in capitals. After the throne had been usurped by Wang Mang and his Hsin ('New') dynasty, the imperial family re-established themselves at Loyang. At its peak the Han empire stretched as far west as the Pamir Mountains, and included North Korea in the north and North Vietnam in the south. The Great Wall now reached all the way to 'Jade Gate' at Tun-huang, and the Silk Road was opened up.

Three Kingdoms 220–265

These were the sections into which three of the Han generals carved up the empire among them.

Six Dynasties 265–589

This so-called Period of Disunion is subdivided into a great many dynasties and kingdoms. The most important were the Wei dynasty in the north, and in the south the six dynasties of Western Chin, Eastern Chin, Liu Sung, Southern Ch'i, Liang and Ch'en.

Sui 589–618

The Sui re-united China, with the capital once more at Ch'ang-an. They built the first Grand Canal, linking the existing waterways from the Yangtze to the Yellow River and then on up the Wei to Ch'ang-an.

T'ANG 618–907

In the first half of the eighth century the T'ang recovered an empire of much the same size as under the Han, but their defeat by the Arabs at the Talas River in 751 led to a loss of the northwest. Their capital was once again at the ancient site of Ch'ang-an, although they also used Loyang as an eastern capital. The dynasty was disrupted by the rebellion in 755 of An Lu-shan, who temporarily captured both capitals.

Five Dynasties and Ten Kingdoms 907–960

The north in this interim period was under a succession of five brief dynasties, established by rival provincial commanders, while the south was divided between ten kingdoms.

SUNG 960–1279
Northern Sung 960–1127

Southern Sung 1127–1279

The Sung made their capital at Kaifeng, but they were driven from it by the Chin in 1127. They established themselves later at Hangchow (called by them Lin-an). The Chin lost Peking to the Mongols in 1215, and were finally conquered by them in 1234. So from 1234 to 1279 the Mongols were the direct neighbours of the Sung. The boundary was roughly half-way between the Yellow and Yangtze Rivers, as it had been with the Chin.

YÜAN 1279–1368

The Mongols took the name Ta Yüan ('Great Origin') for their dynasty; only Wang Mang's brief Hsin or 'New' dynasty had previously used a descriptive name rather than that of a place. Even before finally conquering the Sung, Kublai Khan had begun to make his capital at Peking in the 1260s. It had been the capital of the Chin until taken and destroyed by Jenghiz Khan in 1215. The Mongols built a second Grand Canal, still surviving, to bring grain from the south to this new imperial capital.

MING 1368–1644

The founder of the Ming made his base at Nanking before driving out the Mongols, and he kept this as his capital. The third Ming emperor moved to Peking in 1421 and laid out the present Forbidden City. The boundaries of the Ming empire were comparable to those of the Han and T'ang, but without Chinese Turkestan – the long tongue of land to the north of Tibet which included the Silk Road.

CH'ING 1644–1912

During this final dynasty the empire achieved its greatest expansion, recovering Inner Mongolia and Chinese Turkestan, and including for the first time Tibet, Outer Mongolia and Taiwan. The Manchus established their dynasty by the capture of Peking in 1644. It remained the capital city until the empire came to an end with the abdication of the boy-emperor in 1912. Nanking (meaning southern capital) was used as the capital of the Republic from 1928 till 1949, when the Communists restored Peking (northern capital) to its previous status.

246

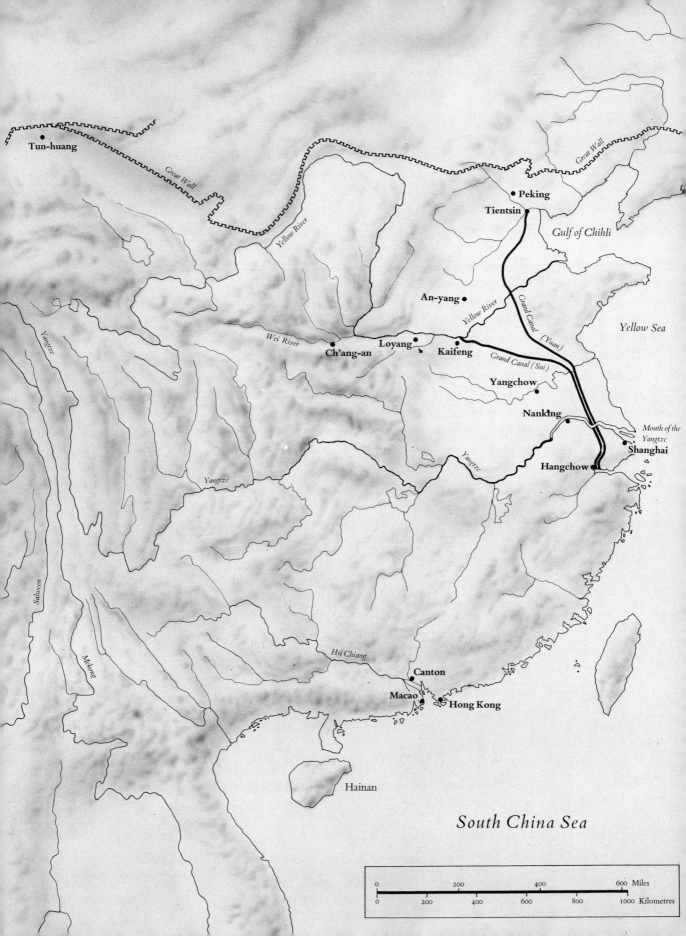

Tun-huang

Great Wall

Yellow River

Great Wall

Peking

Tientsin

Gulf of Chihli

An-yang

Yellow River

Yellow Sea

Wei River

Loyang

Ch'ang-an

Kaifeng

Grand Canal (Yuan)

Grand Canal (Sui)

Yangchow

Nanking

Mouth of the Yangtze

Shanghai

Hangchow

Yangtze

Yangtze

Salween

Mekong

Hsi Chiang

Canton

Macao

Hong Kong

Hainan

South China Sea

0		200		400		600 Miles

0	200	400	600	800	1000 Kilometres

SOURCES OF QUOTATIONS

This is not a select bibliography of the subject, nor is it a full account of all the books that I have found helpful. It is merely a list of those works referred to in the notes as sources of quotations. For a general bibliography, that in *East Asia: The Great Tradition* (by Edwin O. Reischauer and John K. Fairbank, London, 1960) is extremely useful. For a full and descriptive account of available works up to about 1960, C. O. Hucker's *China, A Critical Bibliography* (Tucson, 1962) is invaluable.

Backhouse, E., and Bland, J. O. P., *Annals and Memoirs of the Court of Peking*, London, 1914

Bary, William T. de, *Sources of Chinese Tradition*, 2 vols, New York, 1964

Bauer, Wolfgang, and Franke, Herbert, *The Golden Casket: Chinese Novellas of Two Millennia*, London, 1965

Bingham, Woodbridge, *The Founding of the T'ang Dynasty*, Baltimore, 1941

Bodde, Derk, *China's First Unifier*, Hong Kong, 1967

Bretschneider, E., *Mediaeval Researches from Eastern Asiatic Sources*, 2 vols, London, 1888

Bush, Susan, *The Chinese Literati on Painting (1037–1636)*, Cambridge, Mass., 1971

Bushell, Stephen W., *Description of Chinese Pottery and Porcelain*, Oxford, 1910

Cameron, Nigel, *Barbarians and Mandarins, Thirteen Centuries of Western Travellers in China*, New York, 1970

Carter, Thomas F., *The Invention of Printing in China and its Spread Westwards*, New York, 1925

Ch'en, Kenneth, *Buddhism in China*, Princeton, 1964

Cheng Te-k'un, *Archaeology in China*, 3 vols, Cambridge, 1959–63

Collis, Maurice, *Foreign Mud*, London, 1946

Confucius, (1), *The Analects*, translated by Arthur Waley, London, 1938

Confucius, (2), *The Wisdom of Confucius*, translated by Lin Yutang, London, 1958

Creel, Herrlee Glessner, (1), *The Birth of China*, London, 1936

Creel, H. G., (2), *Confucius, the Man and the Myth*, London, 1951

Creel, H. G., (3), *The Origins of Statecraft in China*, Chicago, 1970

Ennin, *Ennin's Diary: The Record of a Pilgrimage to China in Search of the Law*, translated by Edwin O. Reischauer, New York, 1955

Fairbank, John K., (ed.), *Chinese Thought and Institutions*, Chicago, 1957

Fitzgerald, C. P., *The Birth of Communist China*, Harmondsworth, 1967

Garner, Sir Harry, *Oriental Blue and White*, London, 1970

Gernet, Jacques, *Daily Life in China on the Eve of the Mongol Invasion*, London, 1962

Gulik, R. H. van, *Sexual Life in Ancient China*, Leiden, 1961

Han Fei Tzu, *Basic Writings*, translated by Burton Watson, New York, 1964

Hsü, Francis L. K., *Under the Ancestors' Shadow*, New York, 1948

Hsün Tzu, *Basic Writings*, translated by Burton Watson, 1963

Hunter, W. C., *The 'Fan Kwae' at Canton before Treaty Days*, London, 1882

I-Li, or *Book of Etiquette and Ceremonial*, translated by John Steele, 2 vols, London, 1917

Jenyns, Soame, *Later Chinese Porcelain*, London, 1965

Karlgren, Bernhard, *Sound and Symbol in Chinese* (revised ed.), Hong Kong, 1971

Kracke, E. A., *Civil Service in Early Sung China*, Cambridge, Mass., 1953

Legge, James, *The Chinese Classics*, 5 vols, Hong Kong, 1861–7

Li Po, *The Works of Li Po*, translated by Shigeyoshi Obata, New York, 1922

Lin Yutang, (1), *The Chinese Theory of Art*, London, 1967

Lin Yutang, (2), *The Gay Genius: The Life and Times of Su Tungpo*, London, 1948

Liu, James T. C., (1), *Ou-yang Hsiu*, Stanford, 1967

Liu, J. T. C., (2), *Reform in Sung China*, Cambridge, Mass., 1959

Liu Wu-chi, *An Introduction to Chinese Literature*, Bloomington, 1966

Macartney, Lord, *An Embassy to China: journal*, ed. J. L. Cranmer-Byng, London, 1962

Malone, Carroll B., *History of the Peking Summer Palaces under the Ch'ing Dynasty*, Urbana, 1934

Mao Tse-tung, (1), *Poems*, Peking, 1959

Mao Tse-tung, (2), *Selected Works*, 4 vols, London, 1954–6

Mo Tzu, *Basic Writings*, translated by Burton Watson, New York, 1963

Mote, F. W., *The Poet Kao Ch'i*, Princeton, 1962

Needham, Joseph, *Science and Civilisation in China*, Cambridge, 4 vols (in progress), 1954–71

Pan Ku, *The History of the Former Han Dynasty*, translated by Homer H. Dubs, 3 vols, Baltimore, 1938–55

Pélissier, Roger, *The Awakening of China*, London, 1967

Polo, Marco, *The Description of the World*, ed. A. C. Moule and Paul Pelliot, London, 1938

Reischauer, Edwin O., and Fairbank, John K., *East Asia: The Great Tradition*, London, 1960

Ricci, Matthew, *China in the Sixteenth Century: the Journals of Matthew Ricci*, translated by Louis J. Gallagher, New York, 1953

Ripa, Matteo, *Memoirs*, selected and translated by F. Prandi, London, 1844

Shang, *The Book of Lord Shang*, translated by J. J. L. Duyvendak, London, 1928

Siren, Osvald, *Chinese Painting: Leading Masters and Principles*, 7 vols, London, 1956

Smith, D. Howard, *Confucius*, London, 1973

Spence, Jonathan, *K'ang-Hsi, Emperor of China* (to be published during 1974)

Ssu-ma Ch'ien, *Records of the Grand Historian of China*, translated by Burton Watson, 2 vols, New York, 1962

Stein, Aurel, *Serindia*, 5 vols, Oxford, 1921

Te-ling, Princess, *Two Years in the Forbidden City*, London, 1912

Teng Ssu-yü and Fairbank, John K., *China's Response to the West*, Cambridge, Mass., 1954

Tsien, Tsuen-hsuin, *Written on Bamboo and Silk*, Chicago, 1962

Waley, Arthur, (1), *The Book of Songs*, London, 1937

Waley, A., (2), *Chinese Poems*, London, 1946

Waley, A., (3), *The Life and Times of Po Chü-i*, London, 1949

Waley, A., (4), *The Opium War through Chinese Eyes*, London, 1958

Waley, A., (5), *The Way and its Power*, London, 1934

Waley, A., (6), *Three Ways of Thought in Ancient China*, London, 1939

Watson, Burton, (1), *Early Chinese Literature*, New York, 1962

Watson, B., (2), *Ssu-ma Ch'ien, Grand Historian of China*, New York, 1958

Watson, William, *Ancient Chinese Bronzes*, London, 1962

Yule, Henry, *Cathay and the Way Thither*, 2 vols, London, 1866

AUTHOR'S NOTE

I would like to thank the museums and collectors for allowing photographs of their items to be reproduced, and the following publishers for permission to quote extracts from their books: Allen and Unwin, from three of Arthur Waley's books, *Chinese Poems*, *The Life and Times of Po Chü-i*, and *The Way and its Power*, from *The Golden Casket*, translated by Wolfgang Bauer and Herbert Franke, and from Jacques Gernet's *Daily Life in China*; E. J. Brill, from R. H. van Gulik's *Sexual Life in Ancient China*; Cambridge University Press, from Joseph Needham's *Science and Civilisation in China*; Jonathan Cape, from the typescript of Jonathan Spence's forthcoming *K'ang-Hsi, Emperor of China*; Clarendon Press, from Aurel Stein's *Serindia*; Columbia University Press, from Burton Watson's *Ssu-ma Ch'ien, Grand Historian of China*, from the same author's volumes of translations from Han Fei Tzu, Mo Tzu and Ssu-ma Ch'ien, and from Francis L. K. Hsü's *Under the Ancestors' Shadow*; Dutton, from Shigeyoshi Obata's translations of Li Po; Foreign Languages Press, Peking, from the poems of Mao Tse-tung; Harvard University Press, from *Reform in Sung China* by James T. C. Liu, and from *China's Response to the West* by Teng Ssu-yü and John K. Fairbank; Heinemann, from *Annals and Memoirs of the Court of Peking* by E. Backhouse and J. O. P. Bland, and from Lin Yutang's *The Chinese Theory of Art*; Indiana University Press, from Liu Wu-chi's *Introduction to Chinese Literature*; Lawrence and Wishart, from the *Selected Works* of Mao Tse-tung; Longmans, from J. L. Cranmer-Byng's edition of Lord Macartney's journal; Lund Humphries, from Osvald Sirén's *Chinese Painting*; Michael Joseph, from *The Wisdom of Confucius*, translated by Lin Yutang; Princeton University Press, from F. W. Mote's *The Poet Kao Ch'i*; Probsthain and Co., from *I-Li*, translated by John Steele; Random House, from *China in the Sixteenth Century*, the journals of Matthew Ricci translated by Louis J. Gallagher; Routledge and Kegan Paul, from Marco Polo's *Description of the World*.

B.G.

SHANG

1. Cheng, Vol. II, xxi
2. *Ibid.*, 88
3. Karlgren, 39
4. Watson, B., (1), 14–15
5. Creel (1), 208
6. Watson, W., 101–3
7. Creel (2), opp. title page
8. The O'Neills of Ireland, *Burke's Peerage*, 1970, 2025
9. Legge, Vol. V., Part 1, 310
10. Needham, Vol. 1, 70
11. Cheng, Vol. II, 76
12. *Ibid.*, 231–2

CHOU

1. Creel (1), 215–16
2. Cheng, Vol. III, 294
3. Liu Wu-chi, 19
4. Creel (3), 413
5. Confucius (1), 173–4
6. Smith, 49
7. Confucius (1), 83
8. Confucius (2), 256
9. *Ibid.*, 149
10. *Ibid.*, 146–7
11. Hsün Tzu, 126
12. Watson, B., (2), 24
13. Waley (5), 68–9
14. Mo Tzu, 127
15. *Ibid.*, 125
16. *Ibid.*, 111
17. Needham, Vol. II, 167–8
18. Waley (5), 151
19. *Ibid.*, 171
20. Waley (6), 36
21. Han Fei Tzu, 86
22. Reischauer, 83
23. Han Fei Tzu, 109
24. Shang, 210
25. *Ibid.*, 2
26. Bodde, 21
27. Mo Tzu, 114
28. Bodde, 34, note 1
29. Han Fei Tzu, 111
30. Bodde, 24
31. Han Fei Tzu, 116
32. *Ibid.*, 17–18
33. Bodde, 44

HAN

1. Watson, B., (2), 63–6
2. Mo Tzu, 44
3. Ssu-ma Ch'ien, Vol. I, 206
4. *Ibid.*, 77
5. *Ibid.*, 270
6. *Ibid.*, 323
7. *e.g. ibid.*, 521–2

(Han continued)

8. *Ibid.*, 387
9. Pan Ku, Vol. II, 367–70
10. Ssu-ma Ch'ien, Vol. I, 264
11. Bauer, 48
12. Ssu-ma Ch'ien, Vol. I, 384
13. Confucius (2), 93
14. Hsün Tzu, 92
15. *I-Li*, Vol. II 109
16. *Ibid.*, 136
17. *Ibid.*, 117
18. *Ibid.*, 185
19. Waley (1), 211
20. Ssu-ma Ch'ien, Vol. I, 456–7
21. Waley (2), 86–7
22. *Ibid.*, 43
23. Ssu-ma Ch'ien, Vol. II, 266
24. *Ibid.*, 265
25. *Ibid.*, 264
26. *Ibid.*, 269
27. *Ibid.*, 477
28. *Ibid.*, 493 & 495

T'ANG

1. Ch'en, 171
2. Stein, Vol. II, 809–25
3. Ch'en, 199–200
4. Bingham, 14
5. Bodde, 44
6. Li Po, 290
7. *Ibid.*, 71
8. Liu Wu-chi, 73
9. Waley (3), 58
10. *Ibid.*, 29. I am grateful to Waley's excellent biography of Po Chü-i for all my details of his friendship with Yüan Chen.
11. *Ibid.*, 32
12. *Ibid.*, 34
13. Gernet, 157
14. Waley (3), 177
15. *Ibid.*, 186
16. *Ibid.*, 210
17. *Ibid.*, 212
18. Ennin, 16
19. *Ibid.*, 352
20. *Ibid.*, 355
21. Bary, Vol. I, 373
22. Ennin, 382
23. *Ibid.*, 367–8
24. Gulik, 126
25. *Ibid.*, 145

SUNG

1. Mao (2), Vol. III, 73 & 77
2. Kracke, 127
3. Lin Yutang (2), 108
4. Waley (3), 127–8
5. *Ibid.*, 149

(*Sung continued*)

6. Siren, Vol. II, 29
7. Bush, 25
8. Liu, J. T. C., (1), 132
9. Lin Yutang (1), 71
10. Liu, J. T. C., (1), 101
11. Siren, Vol. II, 77
12. Lin Yutang (1), 92
13. Tsien, 138
14. Gernet, 126
15. Carter, 41
16. *Ibid.*, 50
17. Bary, Vol. I, 417–18
18. Liu, J. T. C., (2), 49
19. Gulik, 240. All my quotations of Li Chiang-chao are from Gulik, 240–2
20. Gernet, 236

YÜAN

1. Yule, Vol. II, 291–306
2. Polo, 85
3. *Ibid.*, 204
4. *Ibid.*, 238–9
5. *Ibid.*, 239
6. Gernet, 85 & 137
7. *Ibid.*, 237
8. Siren, Vol. IV, 31
9. Ricci, 305

MING

1. Mote, 217
2. *Ibid.*, 216
3. Reischauer, 314
4. Gulik, 246–8
5. Siren, Vol. IV, 148–9
6. Ricci, 93, 167 & 337
7. *Ibid.*, 20–1
8. *Ibid.*, 326
9. *Ibid.*, 327
10. *Ibid.*, 364
11. *Ibid.*, 571
12. *Ibid.*, 98
13. *Ibid.*, 335–6
14. *Ibid.*, 71
15. Fairbank, 277
16. Hsu, 139

(*Ming continued*)

17. Bretschneider, Vol. II, 325
18. Ricci, 27
19. Karlgren, 20–1
20. Waley (3), 174–5
21. Polo, 208–9
22. Ricci, 312
23. Bushell, 181
24. Jenyns, 13–14
25. *Oxford English Dictionary*, under *China*, 3b
26. Garner, 5–6
27. Reischauer, 315
28. Spence, Section I. I am extremely grateful to Jonathan Spence for allowing me to see in advance of publication the fascinating items which he has translated from the writings of the K'ang Hsi emperor.
29. Backhouse, 178
30. *Ibid.*, 181

CH'ING

1. Cameron, 248–9
2. Spence, Section VI
3. *Ibid.*
4. Cameron, 210–15
5. Macartney, 106 & 109
6. *Ibid.*, 122–3
7. Cameron, 303
8. Macartney, 123–4
9. *Ibid.*, 153
10. Teng, 19
11. Hunter, 72–3
12. *Ibid.*, 70
13. Collis, 82
14. Waley (4), 58
15. Teng, 24–7
16. Ripa, 58
17. Macartney, 229
18. Malone, 197
19. Te-ling, 19–20
20. Pélissier, 256

POSTSCRIPT

1. Fitzgerald, 106
2. Mao (1), 22–4

SOURCES OF ILLUSTRATIONS

(Italic numbers indicate pages of colour)

SOURCES OF THE OBJECTS

People's Republic of China: Imperial Museum, Peking: 10, 22a, 22b, *27, 28, 32, 38, 56, 65, 66–7, 68, 76–7, 85, 88, 107, 108, 109, 119, 120b, 148, 166, 167,* 173

Great Britain: British Museum (by kind permission of the Trustees): 90, *98,* 129, 150; Sir Harry and Lady Garner Collection, London: *205, 206, 207;* Barlow Collection, University of Sussex: *208;* Victoria and Albert Museum: 94, 117, *168, 240*

France: Musée Cernuschi, Paris: *25, 26, 37,* 86, 87, *110;* Musée Guimet, Paris: 55, *120a, 145*

U.S.A.: Fogg Art Museum, Harvard: 177 (Gift of Charles A. Coolidge); Freer Gallery (courtesy of the Smithsonian Institution, Freer Gallery of Art), Washington, D.C.: *97, 139, 165,* 180–1; Museum of Fine Arts, Boston: 102 (Ross Collection, 31.643), *146–7* (Japanese and Chinese Special Fund, 12.886); Nelson Gallery – Atkins Museum, Kansas City, Missouri, (Nelson Fund): 79, *123a, 140a, 170*

Denmark: National Museum, Copenhagen: 63

Sweden: Museum of Far Eastern Antiquities, Stockholm: *210*

Japan: Tokyo National Museum: *143a, 143b*

Taiwan: Academia Sinica: 14b (Institute of History and Philology; from Special Publications, No. 21, Documents of the Han Dynasty Wooden Slips from Edsin Gol. Pt. I; Plates (1957), compiled by Lao Kan)

SOURCES OF THE PHOTOGRAPHS

Christina Gascoigne: 22a, 22b, *25, 26, 28, 37,* 51, *55, 56, 65, 66–7,* 86, 87, 94, *108, 109, 110,* 117, *120a, 120b, 145, 167, 168,* 173, *185, 186, 187, 188,* 195, *196–7,* 201, *205, 206, 207, 208, 217, 218,* 224, 227, *228–9, 230, 235, 239, 240*

Derrick Witty: 10, *27, 32, 38, 68, 76–7, 85, 88, 107, 119, 148, 166*

Camera Press, London: *123b*

Emil Schulthess, Zurich: *140b*

From *Science and Civilisation in China* by Joseph Needham, by kind permission of Dr Needham and Cambridge University Press: 14a

From *Archaeology in China* by Cheng Te-k'un, Vol. II, Plate VIIb, by kind permission of Dr Cheng and W. Heffer and Sons Ltd, Cambridge: 19

From *Serindia* by Sir Aurel Stein, Vol. II, Plates 196 and 198, by kind permission of The Clarendon Press, Oxford, and the Office of the High Commission of India: 100a, 100b

From *Superstition, Crime et Misère en Chine* by J.-J. Matignon, Paris, 1899, p. 183: 231a

From *Chinese Footbinding* by Howard S. Levy, published by Neville Spearman, London, p. 73: 231b

254

THE TREASURES
AND DYNASTIES
OF CHINA